PON

Sourcebook
and Index

A H I S T O R Y O F U S

Oxford University Press

In these books you will find explorers, farmers, cowboys, heroes, villains, inventors, presidents, poets, pirates, artists, slaves, teachers, revolutionaries, priests, musicians— the girls and boys, men and women, who all became Americans....

A History of Us

BOOK ELEVEN

Sourcebook and Index

Documents that Shaped the American Nation

With introductory notes by
Steven Mintz

Oxford University Press
New York

Oxford University Press

Oxford   New York

Athens Auckland Bangkok Bogotá Buenos Aires Calcutta
Cape Town Chennai Dar es Salaam Delhi Florence Hong Kong Istanbul
Karachi Kuala Lumpur Madrid Melbourne Mexico City Mumbai
Nairobi Paris São Paulo Singapore Taipei Tokyo Toronto Warsaw

and associated companies in
Berlin   Ibadan

Copyright © 1999 by Oxford University Press

First Edition

Published by Oxford University Press, Inc.,
198 Madison Avenue, New York, New York 10016
Oxford is a registered trademark of Oxford University Press

Library of Congress Cataloging-in-Publication Data

Sourcebook and index: documents that shaped the American nation /
with introductory notes by Steven Mintz.

p.   cm.—(A history of US; bk. 11)
Includes bibliographical references and index.
Summary: contains source documents for American history, and the series index.

ISBN 0-19-512773-0 (set hardcover)—ISBN 0-19-512774-9 (set paperback)
ISBN 0-19-512771-4 (book 11 hardcover; alk. paper)—ISBN 0-19-512772-2 (book 11 paperback; alk. paper)

1. United States—History—Sources—Juvenile literature.
[1. United States—History—Sources.]
I. Title. II. Series: Hakim, Joy. *A History of US* (1999); bk. 11.
E178.3.H22 1999 vol. 11   [E173]   973 —dc21   98-40441   CIP   AC

Excerpts from *"I Have a Dream": Address at the March on Washington*
and *"Why We Can't Wait": Letter from Birmingham City Jail*
copyright © 1963 by Martin Luther King, Jr., copyright renewed 1991 by Coretta Scott King.

3 5 7 9 8 6 4 2
Printed in the United States of America on acid-free paper

Contents

Introduction

Toward the end of the summer of 1787, the oldest delegate at the Constitutional Convention was asked what kind of the government the framers had created—a republic or a monarchy. "A republic," Benjamin Franklin replied, "if you can keep it." Our republican system of government requires an educated citizenry. Given our society's extraordinary geographic, religious, and ethnic diversity, it is essential that all Americans grasp the basic principles on which our government institutions rest.

This collection traces the development of the fundamental ideals on which our society is based: free speech and a free press, religious toleration, due process of law, racial equality, and government of the people, by the people, and for the people. Beginning with *Magna Carta*—a charter written in 1215 that limited the power of the English king—and concluding with a speech delivered by President Ronald Reagan at Moscow State University in 1988—celebrating the spread of American ideals of freedom at the end of the Cold War—this sourcebook allows students to analyze the charter documents of American freedom. These include our society's basic constitutional documents, such as the Declaration of Independence and the U.S. Constitution, and their precursors, *Magna Carta* and the English Bill of Rights. Readers can also look up landmark Supreme Court decisions, from *Marbury* v. *Madison,* which established the principle of judicial review, to the Pentagon Papers case, which restricted government's power to censor newspapers prior to publication.

In addition to the many influential Presidential addresses in the book, this volume includes primary sources that illuminate the experience of the diverse groups that make up our society. The voices and experiences of Native Americans, African Americans, immigrants, women, and many other groups are all represented.

How to Use This Book

This book contains excerpts from many of the documents recommended on state frameworks and that support the National History Standards. It is designed to help you learn how to tease out a document's assumptions, uncover its meaning, and assess its historical significance. A typical page layout highlighting the book's features is reproduced below. Although the headnotes to each document provide basic source information, the full citation of an easy-to-locate source for the full documents is listed in the back of the book, along with a glossary and series index for *A History of US.*

For more information section tells you where to look for discussions of the document or topic in *A History of US.*

The headnote provides background to the document and discusses why it is important.

Marginal definitions help you understand words that may be unfamiliar or have unusual meanings. They also identify historical figures mentioned in the documents.

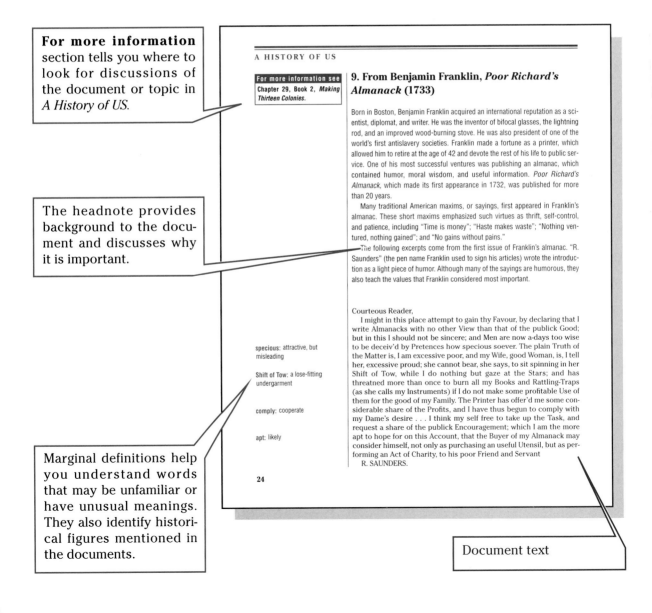

A HISTORY OF US

For more information see
Chapter 29, Book 2, *Making Thirteen Colonies.*

9. From Benjamin Franklin, *Poor Richard's Almanack* (1733)

Born in Boston, Benjamin Franklin acquired an international reputation as a scientist, diplomat, and writer. He was the inventor of bifocal glasses, the lightning rod, and an improved wood-burning stove. He was also president of one of the world's first antislavery societies. Franklin made a fortune as a printer, which allowed him to retire at the age of 42 and devote the rest of his life to public service. One of his most successful ventures was publishing an almanac, which contained humor, moral wisdom, and useful information. *Poor Richard's Almanack,* which made its first appearance in 1732, was published for more than 20 years.

Many traditional American maxims, or sayings, first appeared in Franklin's almanac. These short maxims emphasized such virtues as thrift, self-control, and patience, including "Time is money"; "Haste makes waste"; "Nothing ventured, nothing gained"; and "No gains without pains."

The following excerpts come from the first issue of Franklin's almanac. "R. Saunders" (the pen name Franklin used to sign his articles) wrote the introduction as a light piece of humor. Although many of the sayings are humorous, they also teach the values that Franklin considered most important.

specious: attractive, but misleading

Shift of Tow: a lose-fitting undergarment

comply: cooperate

apt: likely

Courteous Reader,

I might in this place attempt to gain thy Favour, by declaring that I write Almanacks with no other View than that of the publick Good; but in this I should not be sincere; and Men are now a-days too wise to be deceiv'd by Pretences how specious soever. The plain Truth of the Matter is, I am excessive poor, and my Wife, good Woman, is, I tell her, excessive proud; she cannot bear, she says, to sit spinning in her Shift of Tow, while I do nothing but gaze at the Stars; and has threatned more than once to burn all my Books and Rattling-Traps (as she calls my Instruments) if I do not make some profitable Use of them for the good of my Family. The Printer has offer'd me some considerable share of the Profits, and I have thus begun to comply with my Dame's desire . . . I think my self free to take up the Task, and request a share of the publick Encouragement; which I am the more apt to hope for on this Account, that the Buyer of my Almanack may consider himself, not only as purchasing an useful Utensil, but as performing an Act of Charity, to his poor Friend and Servant
R. SAUNDERS.

24

Document text

1. *Magna Carta* (1215)

For more information see Chapter 10, Book 3, *From Colonies to Country.*

Magna Carta ("Great Charter" in Latin) is a 13th-century document on which the United States based much of its law. In 1215, England's powerful barons forced King John to grant a charter, a document that limited the king's ability to tax them and protected the privileges of England's wealthiest landholders. The Great Charter helped establish the principle that no one, not even a king, is above the law. It also argued that individuals hold certain fundamental liberties that no ruler can take away. *Magna Carta* stated that "any freeman" was under the document's protection, and over time this included more of the population than just the barons.

Below is an important "chapter," or section, from *Magna Carta*, one of the four chapters still on the books in England. Note that the Charter is designed to preserve ancient liberties that were threatened by royal tyranny. When the North American colonists rebelled against Britain in 1776, they not only sought to achieve national independence, but to preserve rights that dated back to the 13th century.

No freeman shall be taken or imprisoned or deprived or outlawed or exiled or in any way ruined, nor will we go or send against him, except by lawful judgment of his peers or by the law of the land.

exiled: sent away from one's homeland

This means that the king has to obey "the Law of the Land." He is not above the law. He cannot take land or money from people, or throw them in jail, or throw them out of the country, unless they have broken the law. Along with his power, the king has responsibilities. During the following centuries, Parliament gradually redefined the idea of the "lawful Judgment of [a man's] Peers" to mean "trial by jury." And "the Law of the Land" came to mean "due process of law"—a set of rules for bringing a person accused of a crime to trial. The right to due process was eventually written into the Fifth and the Fourteenth Amendments to the U.S. Constitution.

The same chapter in *Magna Carta* ends this way:

We will sell to no man, we will not deny or defer to any man either Justice or Right.

defer: to hold back for a time

This means that the king cannot deny justice, and he cannot delay it. He cannot sell justice, either: he can't take bribes, and let people who commit crimes buy their way out of trouble. By the early 1600s, this sentence in *Magna Carta* was understood to be the origin of the right of habeas corpus—the right not to be held in jail without being accused of a crime.

Magna Carta was originally intended to apply only to the richest, most important men in England: the barons. Common people are hardly mentioned in the great document at all. But at the last minute, the barons changed the wording of important passages such as the one above to say "no freeman"and "any freeman" instead of "no baron" and "any baron." There were not many freemen in 14th-century England (most people were serfs—peasants bound to the land belonging to a nobleman). But over time, this wording justified extending the rights of *Magna Carta* to all the English people. In the same way, the words "We the People" in the U.S. Constitution have come to apply to all the people, not only to white men, as they did when the Constitution was written.

For more information see
Chapter 29, Book 1, *The First Americans.*

2. Bartolomé de Las Casas, "Of the Island of Hispanola," in *Very Brief Account of the Devastation of the Indies* (1542)

Bartolomé de Las Casas, the first Spanish priest ordained in the New World, is known for his lifelong efforts to protect Indians from Spanish exploitation. His harsh criticism of the exploitation of natives working in the mines and the maltreatment of Indian women earned him the title "Defender of the Indians." In 1542, Las Casas denounced Spanish cruelty toward the Indians in his *Very Brief Account of the Devastation of the Indies.* That same year, Emperor Charles I prohibited the enslavement of Indians, but they continued to be exploited. Because of Las Casas's compassion for the Indians he advised Spain to import African slaves to replace native laborers in New World mines and fields. He later regretted his decision.

In this passage from his book, Las Casas describes the cruel ways that the Spanish conquistadors treated the inhabitants of Hispaniola, the island that now includes Haiti and the Dominican Republic.

malice: a desire to harm others
duplicity: trickery

God has created all these numberless people to be quite the simplest, without malice or duplicity, most obedient, most faithful to their natural Lords, and to the Christians, whom they serve; the most humble, most patient, most peaceful and calm, without strife nor tumults; not wrangling, nor querulous, as free from uproar, hate and desire of revenge as any in the world. . . .

Among these gentle sheep, gifted by their Maker with the above qualities, the Spaniards entered as soon as they knew them, like wolves, tiger and lions which had been starving for many days, and since forty years they have done nothing else; nor do they afflict, torment, and destroy them with strange and new, and divers kinds of cruelty, never before seen, nor heard of, nor read of. . . .

The Christians, with their horses and swords and lances, began to slaughter and practice strange cruelty among them. They penetrated into the country and spared neither children nor the aged, nor pregnant women, nor those in child labour, all of whom they ran through the body and lacerated, as though they were assaulting so many lambs herded in their sheepfold.

They made bets as to who would slit a man in two, or cut off his head at one blow: or they opened up his bowels. They tore the babes from their mothers' breast by the feet, and dashed their heads against the rocks. Others they seized by the shoulders and threw into the rivers, laughing and joking, and when they fell into the water they exclaimed: "boil body of so and so!" They spitted the bodies of other babes, together with their mothers and all who were before them, on their swords.

They made a gallows just high enough for the feet to nearly touch the ground, and by thirteens, in honour and reverence of our Redeemer and the twelve Apostles, they put wood underneath and, with fire, they burned the Indians alive.

They wrapped the bodies of others entirely in dry straw, binding them in it and setting fire to it; and so they burned them. They cut off the hands of all they wished to take alive, made them carry them fastened on to them, and said: "Go and carry letters": that is; take the news to those who have fled to the mountains.

They generally killed the lords and nobles in the following way. They made wooden gridirons of stakes, bound them upon them, and made a slow fire beneath; thus the victims gave up the spirit by degrees, emitting cries of despair in their torture. . . .

3. From an anonymous Aztec chronicler in Fray Bernardino de Sahagun, *General History of Things in New Spain* (1582)

Much of our knowledge about Aztec life before, during, and after the Spanish Conquest is due to the efforts of a Franciscan priest, Bernardino de Sahagun.

---

querulous: likely to complain

afflict: to make suffer
divers: different

Apostles: Jesus's first followers

emitting: letting out

For more information see
Chapters 21–24, Book 1, *The First Americans*.

Sahagun arrived in the New World in 1529 and soon became fluent in the Aztec language, Nahuatl. Recognizing that knowledge of Aztec history was rapidly disappearing, Sahagun began to gather information about Aztec life from surviving Aztec nobles and from students at a church school.

The product of Sahagun's labors was a 12-volume *General History of the Things of New Spain*. Among other subjects, Sahagun's history provides graphic firsthand accounts of the sufferings of the inhabitants of Tenochtitlán, the Aztec capital that became Mexico City, from smallpox and the cruelty of the Spanish conquistadors. In 1577, the Spanish king, Philip II, prohibited further research on Indian history and religion. Many of Sahagun's works were confiscated and were not made public again for nearly 300 years. After reading the account of the Spanish conquest of Tenochtitlán, try to explain why a small number of conquistadors were able to capture this mighty city.

[In 1519, at the town of Cholula,] there arose from the Spaniards a cry summoning all the noblemen, lords, war leaders, warriors, and common folk; and when they had crowded into the temple courtyard, then the Spaniards and their allies blocked the entrances and every exit. There followed a butchery of stabbing, beating, killing of the unsuspecting Cholulans armed with no bows and arrows, protected by no shields . . . with no warning, they were treacherously, deceitfully slain. . . .

[As Cortés and his army approached Tenochtitlán, the people of the city] rose in tumult, alarmed as if by an earthquake, as if there were a constant reeling of the face of the earth.

Shocked, terrified, Moctezuma himself wept in the distress he felt for his city. Everyone was in terror; everyone was astounded, afflicted. Many huddled in groups, wept in foreboding for their own fates and those of their friends. Others, dejected, hung their heads. Some groups exchanged tearful greetings; others tried mutual encouragement. Fathers would run their hands over their small boys' hair and, smoothing it, say, "Woe, my beloved sons! How can what we fear be happening in your time?" Mothers, too: "My beloved sons, how can you live through what is in store for you?" . . .

The iron of [the Spaniards'] lances . . . glistened from afar; the shimmer of their swords was as of a sinuous water course. Their iron breast and back pieces, their helmets clanked. Some came completely encased in iron—as if turned to iron. . . . And ahead of them . . . ran their dogs, panting, with foam continually dripping from their muzzles. . . .

sinuous: winding; comes from the Latin sinus, meaning curve

Moctezuma's own property was then brought out . . . precious things like necklaces with pendants, arm bands tufted with quetzal feathers, golden arm bands, bracelets, golden anklets with shells, rulers' turquoise diadems, turquoise nose rods; no end of treasure. They took all, seized everything for themselves . . . as if it were theirs. . . .

quetzal: brilliant Central American birds with green and red plumage and flowing tail feathers
diadems: headbands or crowns of royalty

[In 1520, the Spanish occupied Tenochtitlán, took Moctezuma hostage, and finally strangled him. Then] they charged the crowd with their iron lances and hacked us with their iron swords. They slashed the backs of some . . . . They hacked at the shoulders of others, splitting their bodies open . . . . The blood of the young warriors ran like water; it gathered in pools . . . . And the Spaniards began to hunt them out of the administrative buildings, dragging out and killing anyone they could find . . . even starting to take those buildings to pieces as they searched.

[The Aztecs, led by Moctezuma's brother, Cuitlehuac, counterattacked, and trapped the Spanish in Moctezuma's palace. One night two months later, Cortés and his army tried to escape. But they were so burdened with loot that two-thirds of them died trying to cross the aqueducts leading out of the city.]

aqueducts: manmade channels for water

That night, at midnight, the enemy came out, crowded together, the Spaniards in the lead, the Tlaxcallans following . . . . Screened by a fine drizzle, a fine sprinkle of rain, they were able undetected to cross the canals . . . just as they were crossing, a woman drawing water saw them. "Mexicans! Come, all of you . . . . They are already leaving! They are already secretly getting out!" Then a watcher at the top of the temple . . . also shouted, and his cries pervaded the entire city. . . .

pervaded: spread throughout

The canal was filled, crammed with them. Those who came along behind walked over . . . on corpses. . . . It was as if a mountain of men had been laid down; they had pressed against one another, smothered one another. . . .

[Then] at about the time that the Spaniards had fled from Mexico . . . there came a great sickness, a pestilence, the smallpox. It . . . spread over the people with great destruction of men. It caused great misery. . . . The brave Mexican warriors were indeed weakened by it. It was after all this had happened that the Spaniards came back.

[By the time the Spanish returned in 1521, Cuitlehuac had died of smallpox. He was succeeded by Cuauhtémoc. Tenochtitlán held out against the Spanish seige for 75 days. Finally the Spanish took the city, destroying it and killing hundreds of thousands of Aztec citizens. Many of them were already sick and starving. Cuauhttémoc was forced to surrender, and later executed.] Fighting continued, both sides took captives, on both sides there were deaths . . . great became the suffering of the common folk. There was hunger. Many died of famine. . . . The people ate anything—lizards, barn swallows, corn leaves, saltgrass. . . . Never had such suffering been seen. . . . The enemy pressed about us like a wall . . . they herded us. . . . The brave warriors were still hopelessly resisting . . . .

Finally the battle just quietly ended. Silence reigned. Nothing happened. The enemy left. All was quiet, and nothing more took place. Night fell, and the next day nothing happened, either. No one spoke aloud; the people were crushed. . . . So ended the war.

For more information see

Chapter 13, Book 2, *Making Thirteen Colonies.*

4. *The Mayflower Compact* (1620)

The Mayflower Compact is one of the documents that helped establish the principle of self-government in America. In September 1620, a group of people (later called Pilgrims) set sail from Plymouth, England, to start a settlement in the New World. They left because they thought that the Church of England and their country had become corrupt. The Pilgrims knew that they would need some type of government when they left their ship, the Mayflower. While still on board, they gathered together and drafted a compact, or agreement, that formed the basis for their community in the New World.

This document was one of the first charters of government to clearly state that legitimate political authority flows from the people. It begins with a prayer; the signers then agreed to consult each other about matters affecting the community and to abide by majority rule. The compact calls for "just and equal laws . . . for ye [the] general good of ye [the] Colonie, unto which we promise all due submission and obedience."

sovereign: a ruler with unmatched power

In the name of God Amen. We whose names are underwritten, the loyal subjects of our dread sovereign Lord King James by the grace of God, of Great Britain, France, and Ireland king, defender of the faith, etceteras.

Having undertaken, for the glory of God, and advancements of the Christian faith and honor of our king & country, a voyage to plant the first colony in the Northern parts of Virginia, do by these presents solemnly & mutually in the presence of God, and one of another, covenant & combine our selves together into a civil body politick; for our better ordering, & preservation & furtherance of the ends aforesaid; and by virtue hear of to enact, constitute, and frame such just & equal laws, ordinances, acts, constitutions, and offices, from time to

covenant: here, to promise formally

time, as shall be thought most meet and convenient for the general good of the Colony: unto which we promise all due submission and obedience.

In witness whereof we have hereunder subscribed our names at Cape Cod the eleventh of November, in the year the reign of our sovereign Lord King James of England, France, and Ireland the eighteenth and of Scotland the fifty fourth, Anno Dominie, 1620.

[signatures]

Anno Dominie: Latin for "year of our lord," meaning a year of the Christian era

5. *Massachusetts School Laws* (1642 and 1647)

For more information see
Chapter 16, Book 1, *The First Americans.*

From the early days of settlement, Americans attached special importance to education. Convinced that salvation and social order were impossible without knowledge and understanding of the Bible and the colony's laws, in 1642 Massachusetts required parents or guardians to teach every child "to read and understand the principles of religion and the capital lawes of the country." Five years later, Massachusetts abandoned the idea that families should have sole responsibility for educating children.

In 1647, the state required every town with 50 or more families to appoint a schoolmaster "to teach all . . . children . . . to write and read." The law also stated that every town with a hundred or more families was "to set up a grammar school" to prepare youth "so far as they may be fitted, for the university." This law did not, however, require parents to send their children to school. Nor did it require towns to build decent schoolhouses. Some schools actually met in primitive hospitals.

Learning in 17th-century New England schools was very unpleasant. Students sat on uncomfortable plank seats without backs. During the cold winter months, heat from a smoky fireplace left pupils with "blue noses, chattering jaws, and aching toes." With just two or three small windows, most light for reading came from the fireplace.

Massachusetts School Law of 1642

This court, taking into consideration the great neglect of many parents and masters in training up their children in learning and labor, and other employments which may be profitable to the commonwealth, do hereupon order and decree, that in every town the

commonwealth: nation or state governed by the people

prudential: requiring good judgment
redress: solution

jurisdiction: area over which an authority has power
masters: experts in a working trade

magistrate: court official
apprentices: students of a working trade
suffered: allowed
occasion: provide an opportunity for
wanton: out of control
hemp: a plant with thick fibers
flax: a plant whose stems are used in weaving cloth

chosen men appointed for managing the prudential affairs of the same shall henceforth stand charged with the care of the redress of this evil, so as they shall be sufficiently punished by fines for the neglect thereof, upon presentment of the grand jury, or other information or complaint in any court within this jurisdiction; and for this end they, or the greater number of them, shall have power to take account from time to time of all parents and masters, and of their children, concerning their calling and employment of their children, especially of their ability to read and understand the principles of religion and the capital laws of this country, and to impose fines upon such as shall refuse to render such accounts to them when they shall be required; and they shall have power, with consent of any court or the magistrate, to put forth apprentices the children of such as they shall [find] not to be able and fit to employ and bring them up. They shall [under]take . . . that boys and girls be not suffered to converse together, so as may occasion any wanton, dishonest, or immodest behavior; and for their better performance of this trust committed to them, they may divide the town amongst them, appointing to every of the said townsmen a certain number of families to have special oversight of. They are also to provide that a sufficient quantity of materials, [such] as hemp, flax, etc., may be raised in their several towns and tools and implements provided for working out the same; and for their assistance in this so needful and beneficial employment, if they meet with any difficulty or opposition which they cannot well master by their own power, they may have recourse to some of the magistrates, who shall take such course for their help and encouragement as the occasion shall require according to justice; and the said townsmen, at the next court in those limits, after the end of their year, shall give a brief account in writing of their proceedings herein, provided that they have been so required by some court or magistrate a month at least before; and this order to continue for two years, and till the court shall take further order.

Massachusetts School Law of 1647

It being one chief project of the old deluder, Satan, to keep men from the knowledge of the Scriptures, as in former times by keeping them in an unknown tongue, so in these latter times by persuading from the use of tongues, that so at least the true sense and meaning of the original might be clouded by false glosses of saint-seeming deceivers, that learning may not be buried in the grave of our fathers in the church and commonwealth, the Lord assisting our endeavors:

It is therefore ordered, that every township in this jurisdiction, after the Lord has increased the[ir] number to 50 householders, shall

Satan: the devil

glosses: shine

householders: a house and all its inhabitants

then forthwith appoint one within their town to teach all such children as shall resort to him to write and read, whose wages shall be paid either by the parents or masters of such children, or by the inhabitants in general, by way of supply, as the major part of those that order the prudentials the town shall appoint; provided, those that send their children be not oppressed by paying much more th[an] they can have them taught for in other towns; and it is further ordered, that where any town shall increase to the number of 100 families or householders, they shall set up a grammar school, the master thereof being able to instruct youth so far as they shall be fitted for the university, provided, that if any town neglect the performance hereof above one year, that every such town shall pay 5 pounds to the next school till they shall perform this order.

prudentials: business and administrative affairs

6. From Roger Williams, *Letter to Providence* (1655)

For more information see
Chapters 17, 20, and 21, Book 2, *Making Thirteen Colonies*.

Best remembered as the man who founded Rhode Island, Roger Williams was also the founder of America's first Baptist church and one of the strongest supporters of the separation of church and state. Williams, who named his second child "Freeborn," was fiercely committed to religious and intellectual liberty. More than a century before the First Amendment to the Constitution was drafted, Williams argued for freedom of speech. Williams also advocated equal rights for Native Americans, arguing that the colonists had no claim to Indian land unless they purchased it.

Because of his beliefs that individuals should be free to worship as they pleased and that secular authorities had no right to interfere in people's religious practices, he was driven out of Salem, Massachusetts, in 1636, "in a bitter winter season, not knowing what bread or bed did mean." Along with twelve followers, Williams sailed up Narragansett Bay and founded Providence, Rhode Island, as a place where government would have no power over spiritual matters. Rhode Island's reputation for religious freedom quickly attracted people whose beliefs were not tolerated elsewhere, including Quakers and Jews.

In this letter, Roger Williams argues that no members of a community—not Protestants, Catholics (whom he refers to as "papists," meaning followers of the Pope), Jews, or Muslims (whom he calls "Turks")—should be forced to worship in a single way, so long as all are willing to respect the "common peace."

weal: good fortune

papists: Catholics

compelled: forced

sobriety: not drinking alcohol

mutiny: rebel

That ever I should speak or write a title, that tends to such an infinite liberty of conscience, is a mistake, and which I have ever disclaimed and abhorred. To prevent such mistakes, I shall at present only propose this case: There goes many a ship to sea, with many hundred souls in one ship, whose weal and woe is common, and is a true picture of a commonwealth, or a human combination or society. It hath fallen out sometimes, that both papists and protestants, Jews and Turks, may be embarked in one ship; upon which supposal I affirm, that all the liberty of conscience, that ever I pleaded for, turns upon these two hinges—that none of the papists, protestants, Jews, or Turks, be forced to come to the ship's prayers or worship, nor compelled from their own particular prayers or worship, if they practice any. I further add, that I never denied, that notwithstanding this liberty, the commander of this ship ought to command the ship's course, yea, and also command that justice, peace and sobriety, be kept and practiced, both among the seamen and all the passengers. If any of the seamen refuse to perform their services, or passengers to pay their freight; if any refuse to help, in person or purse, towards the common charges or defence; if any refuse to obey the common laws and orders of the ship, concerning their common peace or preservation; if any shall mutiny and rise up against their commanders and officers; if any should preach or write that there ought to be no commanders or officers, because all are equal in Christ, therefore no masters nor officers, no laws nor orders, nor corrections nor punishments;—I say, I never denied, but in such cases, whatever is pretended, the commander or commanders may judge, resist, compel and punish such transgressors, according to their deserts and merits. This if seriously and honestly minded, may, if it so please the Father of lights, let in some light to such as willingly shut not their eyes.

I remain studious of your common peace and liberty.

For more information see
Book 2, *Making Thirteen Colonies.*

7. *Resolution of the Germantown Quakers* (1688)

In 1688, Dutch-speaking Quakers who had settled in Germantown, Pennsylvania, signed the New World's first antislavery petition. These Quakers, whose European ancestors had been tortured and persecuted for their religious beliefs, saw a striking similarity between their ancestors' sufferings and the sufferings of slaves. The Germantown Quakers were descendants of Mennonites, a Protestant religious group founded in Switzerland in 1525. The Mennonites emphasized a simple style of life and believed that the Bible forbade them from going to war, swearing oaths, or holding public office.

The Germantown Quakers argued that slavery violated God's law. They charged that Africans had been seized illegally from their homelands, shipped across the Atlantic against their will, and sold away from their families. In 1688, the Germantown Quakers stood alone in their protests against slavery. They passed their petition on to Quaker meetings elsewhere in Pennsylvania, only to see their protest against slavery ignored. Indeed, the Germantown petition was forgotten until it was rediscovered by historians a century and a half later. In the following resolution, the Germantown Quakers say that if it is wrong for North African pirates (whom they call "Turks," because some were Muslims) to enslave Christians, then it is equally wrong for Christians to take Africans as slaves.

This is to the monthly meeting held at Richard Worrell's:

These are the reasons why we are against the traffic of men-body, as followeth: Is there any that would be done or handled at this manner? viz., to be sold or made a slave for all the time of his life? How fearful and faint-hearted are many at sea, when they see a strange vessel, being afraid it should be a Turk, and they should be taken, and sold for slaves into Turkey. Now, what is *this* better done, than Turks do? Yea, rather it is worse for them, which say they are Christians; for we hear that the most part of such negers are brought hither against their will and consent, and that many of them are stolen. Now, though they are black, we cannot conceive there is more liberty to have them slaves, as it is to have other white ones. There is a saying, that we should do to all men like as we will be done ourselves; making no difference of what generation, descent, or colour they are. And those who steal or rob men, and those who buy or purchase them, are they not all alike? Here is liberty of conscience, which is right and reasonable: here ought to be likewise liberty of the body, except of evil-doers, which is another case. But to bring men hither, or to rob and sell them against their will, we stand against. In Europe there are many oppressed for conscience-sake; and here there are those oppressed which are of a black colour. And we who know that men must not commit adultery—some do commit adultery in others, separating wives from their husbands, and giving them to others; and some sell the children of these poor creatures to other men. Ah! do consider well this thing, you who do it, if you would be done at this manner—and if it is done according to Christianity! You surpass Holland and Germany in this thing. This makes an ill report in all those countries of Europe, where they hear

negers: African slaves

adultery: sexual relations between a married person and someone other than his or her spouse

profess: declare openly

of [it], that the Quakers do here handel men as they handel there the cattle. And for that reason some have no mind or inclination to come hither. And who shall maintain this your cause, or plead for it? Truly, we cannot do so, except you shall inform us better hereof, viz.; that Christians have liberty to practice these things. Pray, what thing in the world can be done worse towards us, than if men should rob or steal us away, and sell us for slaves to strange countries; separating husbands from their wives and children. Being now this is not done in the manner we would be done at; therefore, we contradict, and are against this traffic of men-body. And we who profess that it is not lawful to steal, must, likewise, avoid to purchase such things as are stolen, but rather help to stop this robbing and stealing, if possible. And such men ought to be delivered out of the hands of the robbers, and set free as in Europe. Then is Pennsylvania to have a good report, instead, it hath now a bad one, for this sake, in other countries; Especially whereas the Europeans are desirous to know in what manner *the Quakers* do rule in *their* province; and most of them do look upon us with an envious eye. But if this is done well, what shall we say is done evil?

Now consider well this thing, if it is good or bad. And in case you find it to be good to handel these blacks in that manner, we desire and require you hereby lovingly, that you may inform us herein, which at this time never was done, viz., that Christians have such a liberty to do so. To the end we shall be satisfied on this point, and satisfy likewise our good friends and acquaintances in our native country, to whom it is a terror, or fearful thing, that men should be handelled so in Pennsylvania. . . .

For more information see

Chapter 37, Book 2, *Making Thirteen Colonies.*

8. From *The English Bill of Rights* (1689)

The English Bill of Rights, a model for the U.S. Bill of Rights, set strict limits on the powers of the English king. It prohibited him from suspending laws enacted by Parliament. It also declared that Parliament alone had the right to tax the people.

The English Bill of Rights established many of the principles that were later incorporated into the U.S. Bill of Rights. It listed certain rights that were the "true, ancient, and indubitable rights and liberties of the people." It guaranteed the right of the people to bring complaints before the king. It forbade the king from raising an army in peacetime without Parliament's consent. It guaranteed the people's right to bear arms. And it prohibited courts from requiring excessive bail in criminal cases or imposing cruel and unusual punishments.

And . . . the lords spiritual and temporal, and commons, . . . being now assembled in a full and free representative of this nation, . . . do . . . (as their ancestors in like cases have usually done) for the vindicating and asserting their ancient rights and liberties, declare:

spiritual: religious
temporal: non-religious
commons: of the common people
vindicating: proving the value of
asserting: strongly stating

That the pretended power of suspending of laws, or the execution of laws, by regal authority, without consent of parliament, is illegal.

regal: having to do with a king or queen

That the pretended power of dispensing with laws, or the executions of laws, by regal authority, as it hath been assumed and exercised of late, is illegal.

That the commission for erecting the late court of commissioners for ecclesiastical causes, and all other commissions and courts of like nature are illegal and pernicious.

ecclesiastical: church
pernicious: having a bad effect
levying: collecting
prerogative: an exclusive right

That levying money for or to the use of the crown, by pretence of prerogative, without grant of parliament, for longer time, or in other manner than the same is or shall be granted, is illegal.

That it is the right of the subjects to petition the King, and all commitments and prosecutions for such petitioning are illegal.

That the raising or keeping a standing army within the kingdom in time of peace, unless it be with consent of parliament, is against law.

That the subjects which are protestants, may have arms for their defence suitable to their conditions, and as allowed by law.

That election of members of parliament ought to be free.

That the freedom of speech, and debates or proceedings in parliament, ought not to be impeached or questioned in any court or place out of parliament.

impeached: charged with misconduct
bail: money held in exchange for the temporary release of a prisoner before trial
impanelled: enrolled
freeholders: landowners who can vote

That excessive bail ought not to be required, nor excessive fines imposed; nor cruel and unusual punishments inflicted.

That jurors ought to be duly impanelled and returned, and jurors which pass upon men in trials of high treason ought to be freeholders.

That all grants and promises of fines and forfeitures of particular persons before conviction, are illegal and void.

And that for redress of all grievances, and for the amending, strengthening and preserving of the laws, parliaments ought to be held frequently.

And they do claim, demand, and insist upon all and singular the premisses, as their undoubted rights and liberties; and that no declarations, judgments, doings, or proceedings, to the prejudice of the people in any of the said premisses, ought in any wise to be drawn hereafter into consequence or example; to which demand of their rights they are particularly encouraged by the declaration of this highness the prince of Orange, as being the only means for obtaining a full redress and remedy therein.

wise: way

prince of Orange: William III, King of England (1689-1702)

For more information see

Chapter 29, Book 2, *Making Thirteen Colonies.*

9. From Benjamin Franklin, *Poor Richard's Almanack* (1733)

Born in Boston, Benjamin Franklin acquired an international reputation as a scientist, diplomat, and writer. He was the inventor of bifocal glasses, the lightning rod, and an improved wood-burning stove. He was also president of one of the world's first antislavery societies. Franklin made a fortune as a printer, which allowed him to retire at the age of 42 and devote the rest of his life to public service. One of his most successful ventures was publishing an almanac, which contained humor, moral wisdom, and useful information. *Poor Richard's Almanack,* which made its first appearance in 1732, was published for more than 20 years.

Many traditional American maxims, or sayings, first appeared in Franklin's almanac. These short maxims emphasized such virtues as thrift, self-control, and patience, including "Time is money"; "Haste makes waste"; "Nothing ventured, nothing gained"; and "No gains without pains."

The following excerpts come from the first issue of Franklin's almanac. "R. Saunders" (the pen name Franklin used to sign his articles) wrote the introduction as a light piece of humor. Although many of the sayings are humorous, they also teach the values that Franklin considered most important.

Courteous Reader,

I might in this place attempt to gain thy Favour, by declaring that I write Almanacks with no other View than that of the publick Good; but in this I should not be sincere; and Men are now a-days too wise to be deceiv'd by Pretences how specious soever. The plain Truth of the Matter is, I am excessive poor, and my Wife, good Woman, is, I tell her, excessive proud; she cannot bear, she says, to sit spinning in her Shift of Tow, while I do nothing but gaze at the Stars; and has threatned more than once to burn all my Books and Rattling-Traps (as she calls my Instruments) if I do not make some profitable Use of them for the good of my Family. The Printer has offer'd me some considerable share of the Profits, and I have thus begun to comply with my Dame's desire . . . I think my self free to take up the Task, and request a share of the publick Encouragement; which I am the more apt to hope for on this Account, that the Buyer of my Almanack may consider himself, not only as purchasing an useful Utensil, but as performing an Act of Charity, to his poor Friend and Servant
R. SAUNDERS.

specious: attractive, but misleading

Shift of Tow: a lose-fitting undergarment

comply: cooperate

apt: likely

Visits should be short, like a winters day,
Lest you're too troublesome hasten away.

A house without woman and firelight, is like a body without soul or sprite.

Kings & Bears often worry their keepers.

Light purse, heavy heart.

He's a fool that makes his doctor his heir.

Hunger never saw bad bread.

Beware of meat twice boiled, & an old foe reconciled.

Great talkers, little doers.

A rich rogue is like a fat hog, who never does good til as dead as a log.

Eat to live, and not live to eat.

March windy, and April rainy,
makes May the pleasantest month of any.

Beware of the young doctor and the old barber.

He has changed his one eyed horse for a blind one.

The poor have little, beggars none, the rich too much, enough not one.

After three days men grow weary, of a wench, a guest, and weather rainy.

To lengthen thy life, lessen thy meals.

He that lies down with dogs, shall rise up with fleas.

Distrust & caution are the parents of security.

Tongue double, brings trouble.

Take counsel in wine, but resolve afterwards in water.

He that drinks fast, pays slow.

Great famine when wolves eat wolves.

A good wife lost is God's gift lost.

A taught horse, and a woman to teach, and teachers practising what they preach.

He is ill clothed, who is bare of virtue.

The heart of a fool is in his mouth, but the mouth of a wise man is in his heart.

Men and Melons are hard to know.

He's the best physician that knows the worthlessness of the most medicines.

There is no little enemy.

Keep your mouth wet, feet dry.

Where bread is wanting, all's to be sold.

There is neither honour nor gain got in dealing with a villain.

Snowy winter, a plentiful harvest.

Nothing more like a fool than a drunken man.

God works wonders now and then;
Behold! a lawyer, an honest man!

He that lives carnally, won't live eternally.

Innocence is its own defence.

Time eateth all things, could old poets say;
The times are chang'd, our times drink all away.

For more information see
Chapter 11, Book 3, *From Colonies to Country.*

10. *Resolutions of the Stamp Act Congress* (1765)

In 1765, the British Parliament adopted the Stamp Act, which required official documents—such as marriage licenses and legal papers—as well as pamphlets and newspapers, to have an official stamp placed on them. The stamps were expensive and money was short, so purchasing the stamps was very difficult.

Colonists opposed the Stamp Act not only because it caused economic hardship, but because it violated a fundamental principle of English liberties: that no taxes should be imposed on a people "but with their own consent, given personally, or by their representatives." Since the colonies were not represented in Parliament, the British had no right to tax them. Representatives from nine of the thirteen colonies met at City Hall in New York to decide how to respond to the Stamp Act, and the following resolutions were sent to England in protest. After the colonists had rioted and boycotted British goods for a year, Parliament withdrew the Stamp Act.

The members of this Congress, sincerely devoted with the warmest sentiments of affection and duty to His Majesty's person and Government, inviolably attached to the present happy establishment of the Protestant succession, and with minds deeply impressed by a sense of the present and impending misfortunes of the British colonies on this continent: having considered as maturely as time will permit the circumstances of the said colonies esteem it our indispensable duty to make the following declarations of our humble opinion respecting the most essential rights and liberties of the colonists, and of the grievances under which they labour, by reason of several late Acts of Parliament.

I. That His Majesty's subjects in these colonies owe the same aliegiance to the Crown of Great Britain that is owing from his subjects born within the realm, and all due subordination to that august body the Parliament of Great Britain.

II. That His Majesty's liege subjects in these colonies are intitled to all the inherent rights and liberties of his natural born subjects within the kingdom of Great Britain.

liege: loyal

III. That it is inseparably essential to the freedom of a people and the undoubted right of Englishmen, that no taxes be imposed on them but with their own consent, given personally or by their representatives.

IV. That the people of these colonies are not, and from their local circumstances cannot be, represented in the House of Commons in Great Britain.

V. That the only representatives of the people of these colonies are persons chosen therein by themselves and that no taxes ever have been, or can be constitutionally imposed on them, but by their legislatures.

VI. That all supplies to the Crown being free gifts of the people it is unreasonable and inconsistent with the principles and spirit of the British Constitution, for the people of Great Britain to grant to His Majesty the property of the colonists.

VII. That trial by jury is the inherent and invaluable right of every British subject in these colonies.

VIII. That the late Act of Parliament, entitled *An Act for granting and applying certain stamp duties, and other duties, in the British colonies and plantations in America, etc.*, by imposing taxes on the inhabitants of these colonies; and the said Act, and several other Acts, by extending the jurisdiction of the courts of Admiralty beyond its ancient limits, have a manifest tendency to subvert the rights and liberties of the colonists.

jurisdiction: area over which an authority has power
courts of Admiralty: British courts in large port towns where judges made decisions without a jury

IX. That the duties imposed by several late Acts of Parliament, from the peculiar circumstances of these colonies, will be extremely

Burthensome: heavy
specie: coined money

manufactures: man-made goods

intercourse: interaction

procure: get

For more information see

Chapter 12, Book 3, *From Colonies to Country.*

burthensome and grievous; and from the scarcity of specie, the payment of them absolutely impracticable.

X. That as the profits of the trade of these colonies ultimately center in Great Britain, to pay for the manufactures which they are obliged to take from thence, they eventually contribute very largely to all supplies granted there to the Crown.

XI. That the restrictions imposed by several late Acts of Parliament on the trade of these colonies will render them unable to purchase the manufactures of Great Britain.

XII. That the increase, prosperity, and happiness of these colonies depend on the full and free enjoyments of their rights and liberties, and an intercourse with Great Britain mutually affectionate and advantageous.

XIII. That it is the right of the British subjects in these colonies to petition the King or either House of Parliament.

Lastly, That it is the indispensable duty of these colonies to the best of sovereigns, to the mother country, and to themselves, to endeavour by a loyal and dutiful address to His Majesty, and humble applications to both Houses of Parliament, to procure the repeal of the Act for granting and applying certain stamp duties, of all clauses of any other Acts of Parliament, whereby the jurisdiction of the Admiralty is extended as aforesaid, and of the other late Acts for the restriction of American commerce.

11. From Patrick Henry, *"Give Me Liberty or Give Me Death!": Speech to the Virginia Convention* (1775)

Patrick Henry's fiery speeches helped ignite the American struggle for independence. Before entering politics, Henry worked as a shop clerk, innkeeper, tobacco grower, and lawyer. He first gained fame for his strong and vocal protest against the Stamp Act of 1765, in which Parliament heavily taxed the colonists. Arguing that only the Virginia Assembly could legally tax Virginians, he warned King George III not to violate the liberties guaranteed by the colony's charter. In a speech that frightened many delegates because it referred to the violent downfall of earlier rulers, Henry declared that "Caesar had his Brutus [Brutus was one of Caesar's assassins]—Charles the First, his Cromwell [Oliver Cromwell led Parliament's armed forces to victory over Charles I during the English Civil War]—and George the Third—may profit by their example."

In 1775, Henry delivered his resounding phrase—"Give me liberty or give me death!"—in a speech before the Virginia Provincial Convention. In this speech, Henry argued passionately in favor of arming a citizens' militia. Henry's now famous "Liberty or Death" remark has become a slogan for America's determination and freedom, and his speech to the Virginia Convention marked the peak of his political career.

I have but one lamp by which my feet are guided; and that is the lamp of experience. I know of no way of judging the future but by the past. And judging by the past, I wish to know what there has been in the conduct of the British ministry for the last ten years, to justify those hopes with which gentlemen have been pleased to solace themselves and the House? Is it that insidious smile with which our petition has lately been received? Trust it not, sir: it will prove a snare to your feet. Suffer not yourselves to be betrayed by a kiss . . . .

solace: comfort

Sir, we have done everything that could be done to avert the storm which is now coming on. We have petitioned; we have remonstrated, we have supplicated; we have prostrated ourselves before the throne, and have implored its interposition to arrest the tyrannical hands of the ministry and Parliament. Our petitions have been slighted; our remonstrances have produced additional violence and insult; our supplications have been disregarded; and we have been spurned, with contempt, from the foot of the throne. In vain, after these things, may we indulge the fond hope of peace and reconciliation? There is no longer any room for hope. If we wish to be free—if we mean to preserve inviolate those inestimable privileges for which we have been so long contending—if we mean not basely to abandon the noble struggle in which we have been so long engaged, and which we have pledged ourselves never to abandon until the glorious object of our contest shall be obtained, we must fight! I repeat sir, we must fight! An appeal to arms and to the God of Hosts is all that is left us! . . .

avert: avoid
remonstrated: protested
supplicated: pleaded
prostrated: humbled

It is in vain, sir, to extenuate the matter. Gentlemen may cry, "Peace, Peace!"—but there is no peace. The war is actually begun! The next gale that sweeps from the north will bring to our ears the clash of resounding arms! Our brethren are already in the field! Why stand we here idle? What is it that gentlemen wish? What would they have? Is life so dear, or peace so sweet, as to be purchased at the price of chains and slavery? Forbid it, Almighty God! I know not what course others may take; but as for me, give me liberty, or give me death!

extenuate: lengthen

For more information see

Book 3, *From Colonies to Country.*

12. *Memorial of the Presbytery of Hanover* (1776)

Before the American Revolution, only one colony, Rhode Island, permitted complete religious freedom. Nine of the 13 colonies had an official church. In many colonies, citizens were required to take religious tests before they could vote or hold public office. During the 1740s and 1750s, a growing number of colonists—especially Baptists, Presbyterians, and Methodists—began to demand complete religious freedom and an end to tax support for an established, or state-supported church.

During the Revolution, demands for religious freedom grew more insistent. This "memorial," or petition, to Virginia's General Assembly, presented by Presbyterians from the village of Hanover, asks the group to stop supporting the established Anglican Church with tax money and to permit the free practice of religion.

Presbytery: a court made up of church ministers and elders
dissenters: those who do not belong to the Church of England
glebes: land given to church officials

zealous: devoted to a goal or ideal
invidious: likely to harm

concur: cooperate
propriety: social correctness
tenets: religious principles
Mahomed: Muhammad, the prophet of Islam
Alcoran: variation of Quran, the sacred text of Islam

To the Honorable the General Assembly of Virginia:

The Memorial of the Presbytery of Hanover humbly represents:

[. . .] It is well known, that in the frontier counties, which are justly supposed to contain a fifth part of the inhabitants of Virginia, the dissenters have borne the heavy burdens of purchasing glebes, building churches, and supporting the established clergy, where there are very few Episcopalians, either to assist in bearing the expense, or to reap the advantage; and that throughout the other parts of the country, there are also many thousands of zealous friends and defenders of our State, who, besides the invidious, and disadvantageous restrictions to which they have been subjected, annually pay large taxes to support an establishment, from which their consciences and principles oblige them to dissent: all which are confessedly so many violations of their natural rights; and in their consequences, a restraint upon freedom of inquiry, and private judgment.

In this enlightened age, and in a land where all, of every denomination are united in the most strenuous efforts to be free, we hope and expect that our representatives will cheerfully concur in removing every species of religious, as well as civil bondage. Certain it is, that every argument for civil liberty, gains additional strength when applied to liberty in the concerns of religion; and there is no argument in favour of establishing the Christian religion, but what may be pleaded, with equal propriety, for establishing the tenets of Mahomed by those who believe the Alcoran: or if this be not true, it is at least impossible for the magistrate to adjudge the right of preference among the various sects that profess the Christian faith, without erecting a chair of infallibility, which would lead us back to the church of Rome.

sects: divisions within a larger group

infallibility: freedom from all error

13. From Thomas Paine, *Common Sense* (1776)

For more information see

Chapter 12, Book 3, *From Colonies to Country.*

John Adams called Thomas Paine "the first man of the Revolution." Paine, the author of *Common Sense, The Rights of Man,* and *The Age of Reason,* was probably the most widely read political writer of the 18th century. An active participant in the American and French Revolutions, Paine was also an early supporter of antislavery, women's rights, animal protection, and free public education. Born in England in 1737, he was a ship's hand, schoolteacher, and tax collector before he became involved with groups secretly opposed to Britain's king. At the age of 37, he left England, carrying letters of introduction from Benjamin Franklin.

In January 1776, shortly after he arrived in the colonies, he published the pamphlet *Common Sense.* It called for an end to monarchy and argued that governmental authority derives from the people. Paine's pamphlet sold 150,000 copies and converted thousands of colonists to the cause of revolution and social justice. "Where liberty is, there is my country," Benjamin Franklin supposedly said to Paine. "Where liberty is not, there is my country," Paine replied.

Introduction

Perhaps the sentiments contained in the following pages, are not *yet* sufficiently fashionable to procure them general Favor; a long Habit of not thinking a Thing *wrong*, gives it a superficial appearance of being *right*, and raises at first a formidable outcry in defence of Custom. But the Tumult soon subsides. Time makes more Converts than Reason.

As a long and violent abuse of power is generally the means of calling the right of it in question, (and in matters too which might never have been thought of, had not the sufferers been aggravated into the inquiry,) and as the King of England hath undertaken in his *own right*, to support the Parliament in what he calls *Theirs*, and as the good People of this Country are grievously oppressed by the

formidable: impressive

Usurpation: taking over

extirpating: wiping out

censure: criticism

divest: rid
prepossession: already established opinions
suffer: allow

ineffectual: unable to perform well

posterity: future generations

Combination, they have an undoubted privilege to enquire into the Pretensions of both, and equally to reject the Usurpation of *either. . . .*

The cause of America is in a great measure the cause of all mankind. Many circumstances have, and will arise, which are not local, but universal, and through which the principles of all lovers of mankind are affected, and in the event of which their affections are interested. The laying a country desolate with fire and sword, declaring war against the natural rights of all mankind, and extirpating the defenders thereof from the face of the earth, is the concern of every man to whom nature hath given the power of feeling; of which class, regardless of party censure, is.

THE AUTHOR.

Thoughts on the Present State of American Affairs

In the following pages I offer nothing more than simple facts, plain arguments, and common sense: and have no other preliminaries to settle with the reader, than that he will divest himself of prejudice and prepossession, and suffer his reason and his feelings to determine for themselves: that he will put on, or rather that he will not put off, the true character of a man, and generously enlarge his views beyond the present day.

Volumes have been written on the subject of the struggle between England and America. Men of all ranks have embarked in the controversy, from different motives, and with various designs; but all have been ineffectual, and the period of debate is closed. Arms as the last resource decide the contest; the appeal was the choice of the King, and the Continent has accepted the challenge. . . .

The Sun never shined on a cause of greater worth. 'Tis not the affair of a City, a County, a Province, or a Kingdom; but of a Continent—of at least one eighth part of the habitable Globe. 'Tis not the concern of a day, a year, or an age; posterity are virtually involved in the contest, and will be more or less affected even to the end of time, by the proceedings now. Now is the seed-time of Continental union, faith and honour. The least fracture now will be like a name engraved with the point of a pin on the tender rind of a young oak; the wound would enlarge with the tree, and posterity read it in full grown characters.

By referring the matter from argument to arms, a new æra for politics is struck—a new method of thinking hath arisen. All plans, proposals, &c. prior to the nineteenth of April, i.e. to the commencement of hostilities, are like the almanacks of the last year; which tho' proper then, are superceded and useless now. Whatever was advanced by the advocates on either side of the question then, terminated in one and the same point, *viz.* a union with Great Britain; the only difference between the parties was the method of effecting it; the one proposing force, the other friendship; but it hath so far happened that the first hath failed, and the second hath withdrawn her influence. . . .

I have heard it asserted by some, that as America has flourished under her former connection with Great-Britain, the same connection is necessary towards her future happiness, and will always have the same effect. Nothing can be more fallacious than this kind of argument. We may as well assert that because a child has thrived upon milk, that it is never to have meat, or that the first twenty years of our lives is to become a precedent for the next twenty. But even this is admitting more than is true; for I answer roundly, that America would have flourished as much, and probably much more, had no European power taken any notice of her. The commerce by which she hath enriched herself are the necessaries of life, and will always have a market while eating is the custom of Europe.

fallacious: false

precedent: pattern

But she has protected us, say some. That she hath engrossed us is true, and defended the Continent at our expense as well as her own, is admitted; and she would have defended Turkey from the same motive, *viz.* for the sake of trade and dominion.

dominion: control

Alas! we have been long led away by ancient prejudices and made large sacrifices to superstition. We have boasted the protection of Great Britain, without considering, that her motive was *interest* not *attachment*; and that she did not protect us from *our enemies* on *our account*; but from *her enemies* on *her own account*, from those who had no quarrel with us on any *other account*, and who will always be our enemies on the *same account*. Let Britain waive her pretensions to the Continent, or the Continent throw off the dependence, and we should be at peace with France and Spain, were they at war with Britain. The miseries of Hanover's last war ought to warn us against connections.

waive: give up

"Hanover's last war": French and Indian War

It hath lately been asserted in parliament, that the Colonies have no relation to each other but through the Parent Country, *i.e.* that Pennsylvania and the Jerseys, and so on for the rest, are sister Colonies by the way of England; this is certainly a very roundabout way of proving relationship, but it is the nearest and only true way of proving enmity (or enemyship, if I may so call it.) France and Spain never were, nor perhaps ever will be, our enemies as *Americans*, but as our being the *subjects of Great Britain*. . . .

In this extensive quarter of the globe, we forget the narrow limits of three hundred and sixty miles (the extent of England) and carry our friendship on a larger scale, we claim brotherhood with every European Christian, and triumph in the generosity of the sentiment. . . .

Not one third of the inhabitants, even of this province are of English descent. Wherefore, I reprobate the phrase of Parent or Mother Country applied to England only, as being false, selfish narrow and ungenerous.

But, admitting that we were all of English descent, what does it amount to? Nothing. Britain, being now an open enemy, extinguishes every other name and title: and to say that reconciliation is our duty, is truly farcical. The first king of England, of the present line (William the Conqueror) was a Frenchman, and half the peers of England are descendants from the same country; wherefore, by the same method of reasoning, England ought to be governed by France.

Much hath been said of the united strength of Britain and the Colonies, that in conjunction they might bid defiance to the world: But this is mere presumption; the fate of war is uncertain, neither do the expressions mean any thing; for this continent would never suffer itself to be drained of inhabitants, to support the British arms in either Asia, Africa, or Europe.

Besides, what have we to do with setting the world at defiance? Our plan is commerce, and that, well attended to, will secure us the peace and friendship of all Europe; because it is the interest of all Europe to have America a free port. Her trade will always be a protection, and her barrenness of gold and silver secure her from invaders.

I challenge the warmest advocate for reconciliation to show a single advantage that this continent can reap by being connected with Great Britain. I repeat the challenge; not a single advantage is derived. Our corn will fetch its price in any market in Europe, and our imported goods must be paid for by them where we will.

But the injuries and disadvantages which we sustain by that connection, are without number; and our duty to mankind at large, as well as to ourselves, instruct us to renounce the alliance: because, any submission to, or dependance on, Great Britain, tends directly to involve this Continent in European wars and quarrels, and set us at variance with nations who would otherwise seek our friendship, and against whom we have neither anger nor complaint. As Europe is our market for trade, we ought to form no partial connection with any part of it. It is the true interest of America to steer clear of European contentions, which she never can do, while, by her dependance on Britain, she is made the makeweight in the scale of British politics.

Europe is too thickly planted with Kingdoms to be long at peace, and whenever a war breaks out between England and any foreign

farcical: crazy

conjunction: state of being joined
bid defiance to: rebel against
presumption: lack of modesty and understanding

barrenness: lack

advocate: supporter

contentions: competitions
makeweight: counter balance

power, the trade of America goes to ruin, *because of her connection with Britain*. The next war may not turn out like the last, and should it not, the advocates for reconciliation now will be wishing for separation then, because neutrality in that case would be a safer convoy than a man of war. Everything that is right or reasonable pleads for separation. The blood of the slain, the weeping voice of nature cries. 'Tɪs ᴛɪᴍᴇ ᴛᴏ ᴘᴀʀᴛ. Even the distance at which the Almighty hath placed England and America is a strong and natural proof that the authority of the one over the other, was never the design of Heaven. The time likewise at which the Continent was discovered, adds weight to the argument, and the manner in which it was peopled, encreases the force of it. The Reformation was preceded by the discovery of America: As if the Almighty graciously meant to open a sanctuary to the persecuted in future years, when home should afford neither friendship nor safety.

The authority of Great Britain over this continent, is a form of government, which sooner or later must have an end: And a serious mind can draw no true pleasure by looking forward, under the painful and positive conviction that what he calls "the present constitution" is merely temporary. As parents, we can have no joy, knowing that this government is not sufficiently lasting to ensure anything which we may bequeath to posterity: And by a plain method of argument, as we are running the next generation into debt, we ought to do the work of it, otherwise we use them meanly and pitifully. In order to discover the line of our duty rightly, we should take our children in our hand, and fix our station a few years farther into life; that eminence will present a prospect which a few present fears and prejudices conceal from our sight. . . .

Men of passive tempers look somewhat lightly over the offences of Great Britain, and, still hoping for the best, are apt to call out, *Come, come, we shall be friends again for all this*. But examine the passions and feelings of mankind: bring the doctrine of reconciliation to the touchstone of nature, and then tell me whether you can hereafter love, honour, and faithfully serve the power that hath carried fire and sword into your land? If you cannot do all these, then are you only deceiving yourselves, and by your delay bringing ruin upon posterity. Your future connection with Britain, whom you can neither love nor honour, will be forced and unnatural, and being formed only on the plan of present convenience, will in a little time fall into a relapse more wretched than the first. But if you say, you can still pass the violations over, then I ask, hath your house been burnt? Hath your property been destroyed before your face? Are your wife and children destitute of a bed to lie on, or bread to live on? Have you lost a parent or a child by their hands, and yourself the ruined and

reconciliation: a peaceful return to the way things were
neutrality: not taking one side or another
convoy: protector

Reformation: 16th-century Protestant movement against the Catholic Church
sanctuary: safe place

bequeath: give as an inheritance
posterity: future generations

eminence: prominence

passive: inactive

relapse: return to being weak

destitute of: without

sycophant: person who praises others dishonestly

precariousness: uncertainty

disquietudes: uncomfortable states

deluge: flood

wretched survivor? If you have not, then you are not a judge of those who have. But if you have, and can still shake hands with the murderers, then are you unworthy the name of husband, father, friend, or lover, and whatever may be your rank or title in life, you have the heart of a coward, and the spirit of a sycophant. . . .

A government of our own is our natural right: and when a man seriously reflects on the precariousness of human affairs, he will become convinced, that it is infinitely wiser and safer, to form a constitution of our own in a cool deliberate manner, while we have it in our power, than to trust such an interesting event to time and chance. If we omit it now, some Massanello may hereafter arise, who, laying hold of popular disquietudes, may collect together the desperate and the discontented, and by assuming to themselves the powers of government, finally sweep away the liberties of the Continent like a deluge. Should the government of America return again into the hands of Britain, the tottering situation of things will be a temptation for some desperate adventurer to try his fortune; and in such a case, what relief can Britain give? Ere she could hear the news, the fatal business might be done; and ourselves suffering like the wretched Britons under the oppression of the Conqueror. Ye that oppose independence now, ye know not what ye do: ye are opening a door to eternal tyranny, by keeping vacant the seat of government. There are thousands and tens of thousands, who would think it glorious to expel from the Continent, that barbarous and hellish power, which hath stirred up the Indians and the Negroes to destroy us; the cruelty hath a double guilt, it is dealing brutally by us, and treacherously by them.

To talk of friendship with those in whom our reason forbids us to have faith, and our affections wounded thro' a thousand pores instruct us to detest, is madness and folly. Every day wears out the little remains of kindred between us and them; and can there be any reason to hope, that as the relationship expires, the affection will encrease, or that we shall agree better when we have ten times more and greater concerns to quarrel over than ever?

Ye that tell us of harmony and reconciliation, can ye restore to us the time that is past? Can ye give to prostitution its former innocence? neither can ye reconcile Britain and America. The last cord now is broken, the people of England are presenting addresses against us. There are injuries which nature cannot forgive; she would cease to be nature if she did. As well can the lover forgive the ravisher of his mistress, as the Continent forgive the murders of Britain. The Almighty hath implanted in us these unextinguishable feelings for good and wise purposes. They are the Guardians of his Image in

ravisher: man who forces himself physically on women

our hearts. They distinguish us from the herd of common animals. The social compact would dissolve, and justice be extirpated from the earth, or have only a casual existence were we callous to the touches of affection. The robber and the murderer would often escape unpunished, did not the injuries which our tempers sustain, provoke us into justice.

    O! ye that love mankind! Ye that dare oppose not only the tyranny but the tyrant, stand forth! Every spot of the old world is overrun with oppression. Freedom hath been hunted round the Globe. Asia and Africa have long expelled her. Europe regards her like a stranger, and England hath given her warning to depart. O! receive the fugitive, and prepare in time an asylum for mankind.

compact: agreement
extirpated: destroyed completely
callous: insensitive

fugitive: runaway

14. Thomas Jefferson, *The Declaration of Independence* (1776)

Over a year passed between the outbreak of fighting at the battles of Lexington and Concord and the decision to issue the Declaration of Independence. Although New England, Virginia, and South Carolina were ready to declare independence in 1775, other colonies still hoped to settle their disagreements with Britain peacefully. During the spring of 1776, many colonies and communities adopted resolutions supporting independence. These resolutions encouraged the Continental Congress to appoint a five-member committee to draft a formal declaration.

    Thomas Jefferson wrote the initial draft of the declaration. Other members of the committee, and then Congress as a whole, edited it. The declaration listed the complaints that justified a break with Britain. The most radical idea in the document was that "all men are created equal, that they are endowed by their Creator with certain inalienable Rights, that among these are Life, Liberty, and the pursuit of Happiness." One of the most important themes in American history is the effort to realize the ideals of liberty and equality included in the Declaration.

    In a famous paragraph that was deleted from the final text, Jefferson condemned the king of England for having "waged cruel war against human nature itself, violating its most sacred rights of life and liberty" by maintaining the practice in which "MEN should be bought and sold." This paragraph suggests that Jefferson meant to include slaves when he wrote, "All men are created equal."

impel: force

unalienable: cannot be separated from

Prudence: common sense

Usurpations: acts of theft
evinces: shows
Despotism: unchecked power

Sufferance: difficult experience

Assent: agreement

Accommodation: meeting the needs
relinquish: give up
formidable: impressive

When in the Course of human Events, it becomes necessary for one People to dissolve the Political Bands which have connected them with another, and to assume among the Powers of the Earth, the separate and equal Station to which the Laws of Nature and of Nature's God entitle them, a decent Respect to the Opinions of Mankind requires that they should declare the causes which impel them to the Separation.

We hold these Truths to be self-evident, that all Men are created equal, that they are endowed by their Creator with certain unalienable Rights, that among these are Life, Liberty, and the Pursuit of Happiness—That to secure these Rights, Governments are instituted among Men, deriving their just Powers from the Consent of the Governed, that whenever any Form of Government becomes destructive of these Ends, it is the Right of the People to alter or to abolish it, and to institute new Government, laying its Foundation on such Principles, and organizing its Powers in such Form, as to them shall seem most likely to effect their Safety and Happiness. Prudence, indeed, will dictate that Governments along established should not be changed for light and transient Causes; and accordingly all Experience hath shewn, that Mankind are more disposed to suffer, while Evils are sufferable, than to right themselves by abolishing the Forms to which they are accustomed. But when a long Train of Abuses and Usurpations, pursuing invariably the same Object, evinces a Design to reduce them under absolute Despotism, it is their Right, it is their Duty, to throw off such Government, and to provide new Guards for their future Security. Such has been the patient Sufferance of these Colonies; and such is now the Necessity which constrains them to alter their former Systems of Government. The History of the present King of Great-Britain is a History of repeated Injuries and Usurpations, all having in direct Object the Establishment of an absolute Tyranny over these States. To prove this, let Facts be submitted to a candid World.

He has refused his Assent to Laws, the most wholesome and necessary for the public Good.

He has forbidden his Government to pass Laws of immediate and pressing Importance, unless suspended in their Operation till his Assent should be obtained; and when so suspended, he has utterly neglected to attend to them.

He has refused to pass other Laws for the Accommodation of larger Districts of People, unless those People would relinquish the Right of Representation in the Legislature, a Right inestimable to them, and formidable to Tyrants only.

He has called together Legislative Bodies at Places unusual, uncomfortable, and distant from the Depository of their public

Records, for the sole Purpose of fatiguing them into Compliance with his Measures.

He has dissolved Representative Houses repeatedly, for opposing with manly Firmness his Invasions on the Rights of the People.

He has refused for a long Time, after such Dissolutions, to cause others to be elected; whereby the Legislative Powers, incapable of Annihilation, have returned to the People at large for their exercise; the State remaining in the meantime exposed to all the Dangers of Invasion from without, and Convulsions within.

He has endeavored to prevent the Population of these States; for that Purpose obstructing the Laws for Naturalization of Foreigners; refusing to pass others to encourage their Migrations hither, and raising the Conditions of new Appropriations of Lands.

He has obstructed the Administration of Justice, by refusing his Assent to Laws for establishing Judiciary Powers.

He has made Judges dependent on his Will alone, for the Tenure of their Offices, and the Amount and Payment of their Salaries.

He has erected a Multitude of new Offices, and sent hither Swarms of Offices to harass our People, and eat out their Substance.

He has kept among us, in Times of Peace, Standing Armies, without the consent of our Legislatures.

He has affected to render the Military independent of and superior to the Civil Power.

He has combined with others to subject us to a Jurisdiction foreign to our Constitution, and unacknowledged by our Laws; giving his Assent to their Acts of pretended Legislation:

For quartering large Bodies of Armed Troops among us:

For protecting them, by a mock Trial, from Punishment for any Murders which they should commit on the Inhabitants of these States:

For cutting off our Trade with all Parts of the World:

For imposing Taxes on us without our Consent:

For depriving us, in many Cases, of the Benefits of Trial by Jury:

For transporting us beyond Seas to be tried for pretended Offences:

For abolishing the free System of English Laws in a neighbouring Province, establishing therein an arbitrary Government, and enlarging its Boundaries, so as to render it at once an Example and fit Instrument for introducing the same absolute Rule into these Colonies:

For taking away our Charters, abolishing our most valuable Laws, and altering fundamentally the Forms of our Governments:

For suspending our own Legislatures, and declaring themselves invested with Power to legislate for us in all Cases whatsoever.

Compliance: obedience

dissolved: broken up

Annihilation: wiping out an enemy
Convulsions: rebellions or other social disruptions
Naturalization: granting of citizenship
Appropriations: transfers

Tenure: stability

Jurisdiction: area over which an authority has power

a neighboring Province: Canada

absolute: strict

39

abdicated: given up

Mercenaries: people who fight not for a cause, but for money
Perfidy: violation of one's faith

Insurrections: rebellions

Redress: solution

unwarrantable: cannot be justified
Emigration: departure from a country
Magnanimity: generosity, kindness
disavow: publicly condemn
Consanguinity: blood ties, connectedness
acquiesce: give in

Rectitude: rightness

absolved: freed

levy: collect

He has abdicated Government here, by declaring us out of his Protection and waging War against us.

He has plundered our Seas, ravaged our Coasts, burnt our Towns, and destroyed the Lives of our People.

He is, at this Time, transporting large Armies of foreign Mercenaries to compleat the works of Death, Desolation, and Tyranny, already begun with circumstances of Cruelty and Perfidy, scarcely paralleled in the most barbarous Ages, and totally unworthy of the Head of a civilized Nation.

He has constrained our fellow Citizens taken Captive on the high Seas to bear Arms against their Country, to become the Executioners of their Friends and Brethren, or to fall themselves by their Hands.

He has excited domestic Insurrections amongst us, and has endeavoured to bring on the Inhabitants of our Frontiers, the merciless Indian Savages, whose known Rule of Warfare, is an undistinguished Destruction, of all Ages, Sexes and Conditions.

In every stage of these Oppressions we have Petitioned for Redress in the most humble Terms: Our repeated Petitions have been answered only by repeated Injury. A Prince, whose Character is thus marked by every act which may define a Tyrant, is unfit to be the Ruler of a Free People.

Nor have we been wanting in Attentions to our British Brethren. We have warned them from Time to Time of Attempts by their Legislature to extend an unwarrantable Jurisdiction over us. We have reminded them of the Circumstances of our Emigration and Settlement here. We have appealed to their native Justice and Magnanimity, and we have conjured them by the Ties of our common Kindred to disavow these Usurpations, which would inevitably interrupt our Connections and Correspondence. They too have been deaf to the Voice of Justice and of Consanguinity. We must, therefore, acquiesce in the Necessity, which denounces our Separation, and hold them, as we hold the rest of Mankind, Enemies in War, in Peace, Friends.

We, therefore, the Representatives of the UNITED STATES OF AMERICA, in GENERAL CONGRESS Assembled, appealing to the Supreme Judge of the World for the Rectitude of our Intentions, do, in the Name, and by the Authority of the good People of these Colonies, solemnly Publish and Declare, That these United Colonies are, and by Right ought to be, FREE AND INDEPENDENT STATES; that they are absolved from all Allegiance to the British Crown, and that all political Connection between them and the State of Great-Britain, is and ought to be totally dissolved; and that as FREE AND INDEPENDENT STATES, they have full Power to levy War, conclude Peace, contract Alliances, establish Commerce, and to do all other Acts and Things which INDEPENDENT STATES may of right do. And for the support of this Declaration, with a firm Reliance on the Protection of divine Providence, we mutually pledge to each other our Lives, our Fortunes, and our sacred Honor.

Signed by ORDER and in BEHALF of this CONGRESS,

JOHN HANCOCK, PRESIDENT.

15. From Abigail Adams, *Letter to John Adams* (1776)

For more information see Chapter 22, Book 3, *From Colonies to Country.*

The Revolutionary era marked a turning point in the history of American women. Many women managed family farms and businesses while their husbands were away on military duty. This experience led a growing number of women to question their subordinate position to men. During the war, Abigail Adams, the wife of John Adams, the nation's future second President, was often left alone to raise four children and manage the family farm and finances. While her lawyer husband was serving in the Continental Congress, Abigail Adams housed and fed ill soldiers and homeless refugees from British-occupied Boston. She also sewed winter coats for American soldiers, using wool from her sheep.

In her letters to her husband, Abigail Adams argued that young women needed to be better educated. In 1776, she urged her husband to "Remember the Ladies" in framing laws for the new Republic. Otherwise, she wrote, "we are determined to foment a rebellion, and will not hold ourselves bound by any laws in which we have no voice or representation." John Adams responded to his wife's letter in a joking manner, replying, "We have been told that our struggle has loosened the bands of government every where . . . but your letter was the first intimation that another tribe more numerous and powerful than all the rest were grown discontented." Despite his playful tone, John Adams clearly recognized that the Revolution had thrown into question all forms of inequality and undermined many forms of subordination, including that of women.

Braintree, March 31, 1776

I wish you would ever write me a Letter half as long as I write you; and tell me if you may where your Fleet are gone? What sort of

Gentery: gentry, people of high birth
vassals: workers with no property of their own

Defence Virginia can make against our common Enemy? Whether it is so situated as to make an able Defence? Are not the Gentery Lords and the common people vassals, are they not like the uncivilized Natives Brittain represents us to be? I hope their Riffel Men who have shewen themselves very savage and even Blood thirsty; are not a specimen of the Generality of the people. . . .

I have sometimes been ready to think that the passion for Liberty cannot be Eaqually Strong in the Breasts of those who have been accustomed to deprive their fellow Creatures of theirs. Of this I am certain that it is not founded upon that generous and christian princical of doing to others as we would that others should do unto us. . . .

I long to hear that you have declared an independancy—and by the way in the new Code of Laws which I suppose it will be necessary for you to make I desire you would Remember the Ladies, and be more generous and favourable to them than your ancestors. Do not put such unlimited power into the hands of the Husbands. Remember all Men would be tyrants if they could. If perticuliar care and attention is not paid to the Laidies we are determined to foment a Rebelion, and will not hold ourselves bound by any Laws in which we have no voice, or Representation.

foment: start

That your Sex are Naturally Tyrannical is a Truth so thoroughly established as to admit of no dispute, but such of you as wish to be happy willingly give up the harsh title of Master for the more tender and endearing one of Friend. Why then, not put it out of the power of the vicious and the Lawless to use us with cruelty and indignity with impunity. Men of Sense in all Ages abhor those customs which treat us only as the vassals of your Sex. Regard us then as Beings placed by providence under your protection and in immitation of the Supreem Being make use of that power only for our happiness.

impunity: freedom from punishment
providence: divine direction

For more information see

Chapter 32, Book 3, *From Colonies to Country.*

16. *Articles of Confederation* (1778)

Articles of Confederation served as the United States' first constitution. Written in 1776 and ratified in 1781, it provided the nation's framework of government from 1781 to 1789 and was a victory for those who wanted to protect the power of the states. Under the Articles of Confederation, each state retained its "sovereignty, freedom, and independence." Each state was given one vote in Congress, regardless of its population, and nine of the 13 states had to approve legislation.

The *Articles* created a loose confederation among thirteen independent states, each with its own militia, currency, and interests. The central government was composed of a one-chamber Congress, elected by state representatives. (Note that there was no President or Supreme Court under this arrangement.) Because of a fear that Congress would place the national interest over their state's interests, the Articles required members of Congress to be elected every year, and stated that no representative could serve more than three years out of any six.

The *Articles* granted Congress limited powers. It could conduct foreign affairs, negotiate with Indian nations, and establish a national postal system. But Congress was denied the power to tax or to draft citizens into the army. Nor could it regulate foreign or interstate trade. In 1784, George Washington described the Confederation government as "a half-starved, limping government, that appears to be always moving upon crutches, and tottering at every step." These weaknesses convinced the founders of the nation to establish the more flexible and powerful federal government that is detailed in the U.S. Constitution.

To all to whom these Presents shall come, we the undersigned Delegates of the States affixed to our Names send greeting. Whereas the Delegates of the United States of America in Congress assembled did on the fifteenth day of November in the Year of our Lord One Thousand Seven Hundred and Seventy seven, and in the Second Year of the Independence of America agree to certain articles of Confederation and perpetual Union between the States of Newhampshire, Massachusetts-bay, Rhodeisland and Providence Plantations, Connecticut, New York, New Jersey, Pennsylvania, Delaware, Maryland, Virginia, North-Carolina, South-Carolina and Georgia in the Words following, viz. "Articles of Confederation and perpetual Union between the states of Newhampshire, Massachusetts-bay, Rhodeisland and Providence Plantations, Connecticut, New York, New Jersey, Pennsylvania, Delaware, Maryland, Virginia, North-Carolina, South-Carolina and Georgia.

perpetual: lasting forever

Art. I. The Stile of this confederacy shall be "The United States of America."

Stile: name

Art. II. Each state retains its sovereignty, freedom and independence, and every Power, Jurisdiction and right, which is not by this confederation expressly delegated to the United States, in Congress assembled.

sovereignty: the right of self-rule
Jurisdiction: area over which an authority has power

Intercourse: interaction
vagabonds: tramps, bums

ingress and regress: the right to go in and out

treason: crime against the state
felony: serious crime
misdemeanor: an offense that is not serious

magistrates: court officials

emolument: payment

Art. III. The said states hereby severally enter into a firm league of friendship with each other, for their common defence, the security of their Liberties, and their mutual and general welfare, binding themselves to assist each other, against all force offered to, or attacks made upon them, or any of them, on account of religion, sovereignty, trade, or any other pretence whatever.

Art. IV. The better to secure and perpetuate mutual friendship and intercourse among the people of the different states in this union, the free inhabitants of each of these states, paupers, vagabonds and fugitives from Justice excepted, shall be entitled to all privileges and immunities of free citizens in the several states; and the people of each state shall have free ingress and regress to and from any other state, and shall enjoy therein all the privileges of trade and commerce, subject to the same duties, impositions and restrictions as the inhabitants thereof respectively, provided that such restriction shall not extend so far as to prevent the removal of property imported into any state, to any other state of which the Owner is an inhabitant; provided also that no imposition, duties or restriction shall be laid by any state, on the property of the united states, or either of them.

If any Person guilty of, or charged with treason, felony, or other high misdemeanor in any state, shall flee from Justice, and be found in any of the united states, he shall upon demand of the Governor or executive power, of the state from which he fled, be delivered up and removed to the state having jurisdiction of his offence.

Full faith and credit shall be given in each of these states to the records, acts and judicial proceedings of the courts and magistrates of every other state.

Art. V. For the more convenient management of the general interests of the united states, delegates shall be annually appointed in such manner as the legislature of each state shall direct, to meet in Congress on the first Monday in November, in every year, with a power reserved to each state, to recal its delegates, or any of them, at any time within the year, and to send others in their stead, for the remainder of the Year.

No state shall be represented in Congress by less than two, nor by more than seven Members; and no person shall be capable of being a delegate for more than three years in any term of six years; nor shall any person, being a delegate, be capable of holding any office under the united states, for which he, or another for his benefit receives any salary, fees or emolument of any kind.

Each state shall maintain its own delegates in a meeting of the states, and while they act as members of the committee of the states.

In determining questions in the united states, in Congress assembled, each state shall have one vote.

Freedom of speech and debate in Congress shall not be impeached or questioned in any Court, or place out of Congress, and the members of congress shall be protected in their persons from arrests and imprisonments, during the time of their going to and from, and attendance on congress, except for treason, felony, or breach of the peace.

impeached: charged with misconduct

breach: disruption

Art. VI. No state without the Consent of the united states in congress assembled, shall send any embassy to, or receive any embassy from, or enter into any conference, agreement, or alliance or treaty with any King, prince or state; nor shall any person holding any office of profit or trust under the united states, or any of them, accept of any present, emolument, office or title of any kind whatever from any king, prince or foreign state; nor shall the united states in congress assembled, or any of them, grant any title of nobility.

No two or more states shall enter into any treaty, confederation or alliance whatever between them, without the consent of the united states in congress assembled, specifying accurately the purposes for which the same is to be entered into, and how long it shall continue.

No state shall lay any imposts or duties, which may interfere with any stipulations in treaties, entered into by the united states in congress assembled, with any king, prince or state, in pursuance of any treaties already proposed by congress, to the courts of France and Spain.

imposts or duties: kinds of taxes
stipulations: conditions

No vessels of war shall be kept up in time of peace by any state, except such number only, as shall be deemed necessary by the united states in congress assembled, for the defence of such state, or its trade; nor shall any body of forces be kept up by any state, in time of peace, except such number only, as in the judgment of the united states, in congress assembled, shall be deemed requisite to garrison the forts necessary for the defence of such state; but every state shall always keep up a well regulated and disciplined militia, sufficiently armed and accoutred, and shall provide and constantly have ready for use, in public stores, a due number of field pieces and tents, and a proper quantity of arms, ammunition and camp equipage.

requisite: required
garrison: defend with troops

accoutred: dressed in uniform

equipage: equipment

No state shall engage in any war without the consent of the united states in congress assembled, unless such state be actually invaded by enemies, or shall have received certain advice of a resolution being formed by some nation of Indians to invade such state, and the danger is so imminent as not to admit of a delay, till the united states in congress assembled can be consulted: nor shall any state grant

imminent: close by

letters of marque and reprisal: permission granting a citizen to seize goods or citizens of another nation

commissions to any ships or vessels of war, nor letters of marque or reprisal, except it be after a declaration of war by the united states in congress assembled, and then only against the kingdom or state and the subjects thereof, against which war has been so declared, and under such regulations as shall be established by the united states in congress assembled, unless such state be infested by pirates, in which case vessels of war may be fitted out for that occasion, and kept so long as the danger shall continue, or until the united states in congress assembled shall determine otherwise.

Art. VII. When land-forces are raised by any state for the common defence, all officers of or under the rank of colonel, shall be appointed by the legislature of each state respectively by whom such forces shall be raised, or in such manner as such state shall direct, and all vacancies shall be filled up by the state which first made the appointment.

defrayed: paid

Art. VIII. All charges of war, and all other expences that shall be incurred for the common defence or general welfare, and allowed by the united states in congress assembled, shall be defrayed out of a common treasury, which shall be supplied by the several states, in proportion to the value of all land within each state, granted to or surveyed for any Person, as such land and the buildings and improvements thereon shall be estimated according to such mode as the united states in congress assembled, shall from time to time direct and appoint. The taxes for paying that proportion shall be laid

levied: collected

and levied by the authority and direction of the legislatures of the several states within the time agreed upon by the united states in congress assembled.

Art. IX. The united states in congress assembled, shall have the sole and exclusive right and power of determining on peace and war, except in the cases mentioned in the sixth article—of sending and receiving ambassadors—entering into treaties and alliances, provided that no treaty of commerce shall be made whereby the legislative power of the respective states shall be restrained from imposing such imposts and duties on foreigners, as their own people are subjected to, or from prohibiting the exportation or importation of any

commodities: materials

species of goods or commodities whatsoever—of establishing rules for deciding in all cases, what captures on land or water shall be legal, and in what manner prizes taken by land or naval forces in the service of the united states shall be divided or appropriated.—of granting letters of marque and reprisal in times of peace—appointing courts for the trial of piracies and felonies committed on the high seas and establishing courts for receiving and determining finally appeals in all cases of captures, provided that no member of congress shall be appointed a judge of any of the said courts.

The united states in congress assembled shall also be the last resort on appeal in all disputes and differences now subsisting or that hereafter may arise between two or more states concerning boundary, jurisdiction or any other cause whatever; which authority shall always be exercised in the manner following. Whenever the legislative or executive authority or lawful agent of any state in controversy with another shall present a petition to congress, stating the matter in question and praying for a hearing, notice thereof shall be given by order of congress to the legislative or executive authority of the other state in controversy, and a day assigned for the appearance of the parties by their lawful agents, who shall then be directed to appoint by joint consent, commissioners or judges to constitute a court for hearing and determining the matter in question: but if they cannot agree, congress shall name three persons out of each of the united states, and from the list of such persons each party shall alternately strike out one, the petitioners beginning, until the number shall be reduced to thirteen; and from that number not less than seven, nor more than nine names as congress shall direct, shall in the presence of congress be drawn out by lot, and the persons whose names shall be commissioners or judges, to hear and finally determine the controversy, so always as a major part of the judges who shall hear the cause shall agree in the determination: and if either party shall neglect to attend at the day appointed, without shewing reasons, which congress shall judge sufficient, or being present shall refuse to strike, the congress shall proceed to nominate three persons out of each state, and the secretary of congress shall strike in behalf of such party absent or refusing; and the judgment and sentence of the court to be appointed, in the manner before prescribed, shall be final and conclusive; and if any of the parties shall refuse to submit to the authority of such court, or to appear to defend their claim or cause, the court shall nevertheless proceed to pronounce sentence, or judgment, which shall in like manner be final and decisive, the judgment or sentence and other proceedings being in either case transmitted to congress, and lodged among the acts of congress for the security of the parties concerned: provided that every commissioner, before he sits in judgment, shall take an oath to be administered by one of the judges of the supreme or superior court of the state, where the cause shall be tried, "well and truly to hear and determine the matter in question, according to the best of his judgment, without favour, affection or hope of reward:" provided also that no state shall be deprived of territory for the benefit of the united states.

All controversies concerning the private right of soil claimed under different grants of two or more states, whose jurisdictions as

antecedent to: before

alloy: mix

emit: put in circulation
bills: paper money
credit: account

requisitions: demands
quota: assigned amount

they may respect such lands, and the states which passed such grants are adjusted, the said grants or either of them being at the same time claimed to have originated antecedent to such settlement of jurisdiction, shall on the petition of either party to the congress of the united states, be finally determined as near as may be in the same manner as is before prescribed for deciding disputes respecting territorial jurisdiction between different states.

The united states in congress assembled shall also have the sole and exclusive right and power of regulating the alloy and value of coin struck by their own authority, or by that of the respective states—fixing the standard of weights and measures throughout the united states—regulating the trade and managing all affairs with the Indians, not members of any of the states, provided that the legislative right of any state within its own limits be not infringed or violated—establishing and regulating post-offices from one state to another, throughout all the united states, and exacting such postage on the papers passing thro' the same as may be requisite to defray the expences of the said office—appointing all officers of the land forces, in the service of the united states, excepting regimental officers.—appointing all the officers of the naval forces, and commissioning all officers whatever in the service of the united states—making rules for the government and regulation of the said land and naval forces, and directing their operations.

The united states in congress assembled shall have authority to appoint a committee, to sit in the recess of congress, to be denominated "A Committee of the States," and to consist of one delegate from each state; and to appoint such other committees and civil officers as may be necessary for managing the general affairs of the united states under their direction—to appoint one of their number to preside, provided that no person be allowed to serve in the office of president more than one year in any term of three years: to ascertain the necessary sums of Money to be raised for the service of the united states, and to appropriate and apply the same for defraying the public expences—to borrow money, or emit bills on the credit of the united states, transmitting every half year to the respective states an account of the sums of money so borrowed or emitted.—to build and equip a navy—to agree upon the number of land forces, and to make requisitions from each state for its quota, in proportion to the number of white inhabitants in such state; which requisition shall be binding, and thereupon the legislature of each state shall appoint the regimental officers, raise the men and cloath, arm and equip them in a soldier like manner, at the expence of the united states, and the officers and men so cloathed, armed and equipped shall march to the place appointed, and within the time agreed on by the united states in congress assembled: But if the united states in congress assembled shall, on consideration of circumstances judge proper that any state should not raise men, or should raise a smaller number than its quota, and that any other state should raise a greater number of men than the quota thereof, such extra number shall be raised, officered, cloathed, armed and equipped in the same manner as the quota of such state, unless the legislature of such state shall judge that such extra number cannot be safely spared out of the same, in which case they shall raise officer, cloath, arm and equip as many of such extra number as they judge can be safely spared. And the officers and men so cloathed, armed and equipped, shall march to the place appointed, and within the time agreed on by the united states in congress assembled.

The united states in congress assembled shall never engage in a war, nor grant letters of marque and reprisal in time of peace, nor enter into any treaties or alliances, nor coin money, nor regulate the value thereof, nor ascertain the sums and expences necessary for the defence and welfare of the united states, or any of them, nor emit bills, nor borrow money on the credit of the united states, nor appropriate money, nor agree upon the number of vessels of war, to be built or purchased, or the number of land or sea forces to be raised, nor appoint a commander in chief of the army or navy, unless nine states assent to the same: nor shall a question on any other point, except for adjourning from day to day be determined, unless by the votes of a majority of the united states in congress assembled.

assent: agreement

The congress of the united states shall have power to adjourn to any time within the year, and to any place within the united states, so that no period of adjournment be for a longer duration than the space of six Months, and shall publish the Journal of their proceedings monthly, except such parts thereof relating to treaties, alliances or military operations as in their judgment require secresy; and the yeas and nays of the delegates of each state on any question shall be entered on the Journal, when it is desired by any delegate; and the delegates of a state, or any of them, at his or their request shall be furnished with a transcript of the said Journal, except such parts as are above excepted, to lay before the legislatures of the several states.

adjourn: stop for a while

yeas and nays: votes for and against

Art. X. The committee of the states, or any nine of them, shall be authorised to execute, in the recess of congress, such of the powers of congress as the united states in congress assembled, by the consent of nine states, shall from time to time think expedient to vest them with; provided that no power be delegated to the said

expedient: fitting well with a purpose

acceding to: becoming part of

committee, for the exercise of which, by the articles of confederation, the voice of nine states in the congress of the united states assembled is requisite.

Art. XI. Canada acceding to this confederation, and joining in the measures of the united states, shall be admitted into, and entitled to all the advantages of this union: but no other colony shall be admitted into the same, unless such admission be agreed to by nine states.

Art. XII. All bills of credit emitted, monies borrowed and debts contracted by, or under the authority of congress, before the assembling of the united states, in pursuance of the present confederation, shall be deemed and considered as a charge against the united states, for payment and satisfaction whereof the said united states, and the public faith are hereby solemnly pledged.

Art. XIII. Every state shall abide by the determinations of the united states in congress assembled, on all questions which by this confederation are submitted to them. And the Articles of this confederation shall be inviolably observed by every state, and the union shall be perpetual; nor shall any alteration at any time hereafter be made in any of them; unless such alteration be agreed to in a congress of the united states, and be afterwards confirmed by the legislatures of every state.

Great Governor of the World: God

AND WHEREAS it hath pleased the Great Governor of the World to incline the hearts of the legislatures we respectively represent in congress, to approve of, and to authorize us to ratify the said articles of confederation and perpetual union. KNOW YE that we the undersigned delegates, by virtue of the power and authority to us given for that purpose, do by these presents, in the name and in behalf of our respective constituents, fully and entirely ratify and confirm each and every of the said articles of confederation and perpetual union, and all and singular the matters and things therein contained: And we do further solemnly plight and engage the faith of our respective constituents, that they shall abide by the determinations of the united states in congress assembled, on all questions, which by the said confederation are submitted to them. And that the articles thereof shall be inviolably observed by the states we respectively represent, and that the union shall be perpetual. In Witness whereof we have hereunto set our hands in Congress. Done at Philadelphia in the state of Pennsylvania the ninth Day of July in the Year of our Lord one Thousand seven Hundred and Seventy-eight, and in the third year of the independence of America.

17. From Thomas Jefferson, *Notes on the State of Virginia* (1785)

For more information see
Chapter 34, Book 3, *From Colonies to Country.*

Although Thomas Jefferson was one of the most influential of the Founding Fathers, he published only one book, *Notes on Virginia.* He wrote it for an audience of French statesmen and intellectuals, and published the volume anonymously in France in 1785. His goal was not only to provide information about his native Virginia, but to show that the state's planters shared the ideals of the Enlightenment, a movement that valued reason over traditional social, political, and religious beliefs.

In the following selection, Jefferson supports the Enlightenment's arguments in favor of religious freedom and people's right to question and choose their own religious beliefs. He declares that freedom of conscience is a natural right and that competition among religious sects will bring people closer to moral truth.

The error seems not sufficiently eradicated, that the operations of the mind, as well as the acts of the body, are subject to the coercion of the laws. But our rulers can have no authority over such natural rights, only as we have submitted to them. The rights of conscience we never submitted, we could not submit. We are answerable for them to our God. The legitimate powers of government extend to such acts only as are injurious to others. But it does me no injury for my neighbor to say there are twenty gods, or no God. It neither picks my pocket nor breaks my leg. If it be said, his testimony in a court of justice cannot be relied on, reject it then, and be the stigma on him. Constraint may make him worse by making him a hypocrite, but it will never make him a truer man. It may fix him obstinately in his errors, but will not cure them. Reason and free inquiry are the only effectual agents against error. Give a loose to them, they will support the true religion by bringing every false one to their tribunal, to the test of their investigation. They are the natural enemies of error, and of error only. Had not the Roman government permitted free inquiry, Christianity could never have been introduced. Had not free inquiry been indulged at the era of the reformation, the corruptions of Christianity could not have been purged away. If it be restrained now, the present corruptions will be protected, and new ones encouraged. Was the government to prescribe to us our medicine and diet, our bodies would be in such keeping as our souls are now. . . .

eradicated: destroyed
coercion: forceful action

stigma: mark of pain or shame
constraint: holding back

inquiry: questioning
effectual: powerful

censor morum: person who
watches over morals

hypocrites: liars
roguery: devilry

For more information see
Chapter 8, Book 2, *Making Thirteen Colonies.*

Difference of opinion is advantageous in religion. The several sects perform the office of a *censor morum* over such other. Is uniformity attainable? Millions of innocent men, women, and children, since the introduction of Christianity, have been burnt, tortured, fined, imprisoned; yet we have not advanced one inch towards uniformity. What has been the effect of coercion? To make one half the world fools, and the other half hypocrites. To support roguery and error all over the earth.

18. From J. Hector St. John de Crevecoeur, *"What is an American?": Letters from an American Farmer,* Letter III (1782)

In 1782, a French immigrant tried to explain to Europeans what it was like to be American. An American, wrote Michel-Guillaume Jean de Crevecoeur (under the pen name of J. Hector St. John), was a new man, a member of a new, composite race made up of many nationalities and ethnic backgrounds. Unlike Europeans, Americans were free of oppressive taxes and tyrannical kings. They had easy access to farmland and enjoyed a rough equality.

According to Crevecoeur, the typical American was a hardworking farmer, who lived free from the luxuries that corrupted Europeans. Crevecoeur arrived in America in 1755 along with the French army during the French and Indian War. He traveled through the American colonies as a surveyor after the war, and later settled on a farm in New York. Crevecoeur's portrait of Americans as a "new race of men" won him acclaim in Europe and the United States.

Crevecoeur's *Letters from an American Farmer* offers the classic answer to the question, "What is an American?" But some critics found Crevecoeur's description overly idealized. As one critic wrote in 1818, he had "exceedingly exaggerated the excellencies of the United States, by representing them as the abode of more than all the perfection of innocence, happiness, plenty, learning, and wisdom, that can be allotted to human beings to enjoy."

I wish I could be acquainted with the feelings and thoughts which must agitate the heart and present themselves to the mind of an enlightened Englishman, when he first lands on this continent. He must greatly rejoice that he lived at a time to see this fair country discovered and settled; he must necessarily feel a share of national pride, when he views the chain of settlements which embellishes these extended shores. When he says to himself, this is the work of my countrymen, who, when convulsed by factions, afflicted by a variety of miseries and wants, restless and impatient, took refuge here. They brought along with them their national genius, to which they principally owe what liberty they enjoy, and what substance they possess. Here he sees the industry of his native country displayed in a new manner, and traces in their works the embrios of all the arts, sciences, and ingenuity which flourish in Europe. Here he beholds fair cities, substantial villages, extensive fields, an immense country filled with decent houses, good roads, orchards, meadows, and bridges, where an hundred year ago all was wild, woody and uncultivated! What a train of pleasing ideas this fair spectacle must suggest; it is a prospect which must inspire a good citizen with the most heartfelt pleasure. The difficulty consists in the manner of viewing so extensive a scene. He is arrived on a new continent; a modern society offers itself to his contemplation, different from what he had hitherto seen. It is not composed, as in Europe, of great lords who possess every thing and of a herd of people who have nothing. Here are no aristocratical families, no courts, no kings, no bishops, no ecclesiastical dominion, no invisible power giving to a few a very visible one; no great manufacturers employing thousands, no great refinements of luxury. The rich and the poor are not so far removed from each other as they are in Europe. Some few towns excepted, we are all tillers of the earth, from Nova Scotia to West Florida. We are a people of cultivators, scattered over an immense territory communicating with each other by means of good roads and navigable rivers, united by the silken bands of mild government, all respecting the laws, without dreading their power, because they are equitable. We are all animated with the spirit of an industry which is unfettered and unrestrained, because each person works for himself. If he travels through our rural districts he views not the hostile castle, and the haughty mansion, contrasted with the clay-built hut and miserable cabbin, where cattle and men help to keep each other warm, and dwell in meanness, smoke, and indigence. A pleasing uniformity of decent competence appears throughout our habitations. The meanest of our log-houses is a dry and comfortable habitation. Lawyer or merchant are the fairest titles our towns afford; that of a farmer is the only appellation of the rural inhabitants of our country. It must take some time ere he can reconcile himself to our dictionary, which is but short in words of dignity, and names of honour. (There, on a Sunday, he sees a congregation of respectable farmers and their wives, all clad in neat homespun, well mounted, or riding in their own humble waggons. There is not among them an esquire, saving the

embellishes: decorates

convulsed: shaken
afflicted: made to suffer

substance: things

embrios: embryos, beginnings

ecclesiastical dominion: church authority

cultivators: people who grow things

indigence: poverty

fairest: most important
appellation: identification
ere: before

esquire: gentleman

transitory: temporary
replenished: filled

promiscuous: rapidly reproducing

variegated: many colored

ancient college: Harvard
University
hemisphere: Western
hemisphere, here North and
South America
prevalent: commonly found

asylum: safe place

penury: poverty

procured: got

regenerate: give new life
vegitative mould: rotting plants
used as fertilizer

unlettered magistrate. There he sees a parson as simple as his flock, a farmer who does not riot on the labour of others. We have no princes, for whom we toil, starve, and bleed: we are the most perfect society now existing in the world. Here man is free; as he ought to be; nor is this pleasing equality so transitory as many others are. Many ages will not see the shores of our great lakes replenished with inland nations, nor the unknown bounds of North America entirely peopled. Who can tell how far it extends? Who can tell the millions of men whom it will feed and contain? For no European foot has as yet travelled half the extent of this mighty continent!

The next wish of this traveller will be to know whence came all these people? They are mixture of English, Scotch, Irish, French, Dutch, Germans, and Swedes. From this promiscuous breed, that race now called Americans have arisen. The eastern provinces must indeed be excepted, as being the unmixed descendants of Englishmen. I have heard many wish that they had been more intermixed also: for my part, I am no wisher, and think it much better as it has happened. They exhibit a most conspicuous figure in this great and variegated picture; they too enter for a great share in the pleasing perspective displayed in these thirteen provinces. I know it is fashionable to reflect on them, but I respect them for what they have done; for the accuracy and wisdom with which they have settled their territory; for the decency of their manners; for their early love of letters; their ancient college, the first in this hemisphere; for their industry; which to me who am but a farmer, is the criterion of everything. There never was a people, situated as they are, who with so ungrateful a soil have done more in so short a time. Do you think that the monarchical ingredients which are more prevalent in other governments, have purged them from all foul stains? Their histories assert the contrary.

In this great American asylum, the poor of Europe have by some means met together, and in consequence of various causes; to what purpose should they ask one another what countrymen they are? Alas, two thirds of them had no country. Can a wretch who wanders about, who works and starves, whose life is a continual scene of sore affliction or pinching penury; can that man call England or any other kingdom his country? A country that had no bread for him, whose fields procured him no harvest, who met with nothing but the frowns of the rich, the severity of the laws, with jails and punishments; who owned not a single foot of the extensive surface of this planet? No! urged by a variety of motives, here they came. Every thing has tended to regenerate them; new laws, a new mode of living, a new social system; here they are become men: in Europe they were as so many useless plants, wanting vegitative mould, and refreshing showers; they withered, and were mowed down by want, hunger, and war; but now by the power of transplantation, like all other plants they have taken root and flourished! Formerly they were not numbered in any civil lists of their country, except in those of the poor; here they rank as citizens.

By what invisible power has this surprising metamorphosis been performed? By that of the laws and that of their industry. The laws, the indulgent laws, protect them as they arrive, stamping on them the symbol of adoption; they receive ample rewards for their labours; these accumulated rewards procure them lands; those lands confer on them the title of freemen, and to that title every benefit is affixed which men can possibly require. This is the great operation daily performed by our laws. From whence proceed these laws? From our government. Whence the government? It is derived from the original genius and strong desire of the people ratified and confirmed by the crown. This is the great chain which links us all. . . . What attachment can a poor European emigrant have for a country where he had nothing? The knowledge of the language, the love of a few kindred as poor as himself, were the only cords that tied him: his country is now that which gives him land, bread, protection, and consequence: *Ubi panis ibi patria,* is the motto of all emigrants. What then is the American, this new man? He is either an European, or the descendant of an European, hence that strange mixture of blood, which you will find in no other country. I could point out to you a family whose grandfather was an Englishman, whose wife was Dutch, whose son married a French woman, and whose present four sons have now four wives of different nations. He is an American, who leaving behind him all his ancient prejudices and manners, receives new ones from the new mode of life he has embraced, the new government he obeys, and the new rank he holds. He becomes an American by being received in the broad lap of our great Alma Mater. Here individuals of all nations are melted into a new race of men, whose labours and posterity will one day cause great changes in the world. Americans are the western pilgrims, who are carrying along with them that great mass of arts, sciences, vigour, and industry which began long since in the east; they will finish the great circle. The Americans were once scattered all over Europe; here they are incorporated into one of the finest systems of population which has ever appeared, and which will hereafter become distinct by the power of the different climates they inhabit. The American ought therefore to love this country much better than that wherein either he or his forefathers were born. Here the rewards of his industry follow with equal steps the progress of his labour; his labour is founded on the basis of nature, self-interest; can it want a stronger allurement? Wives and

metamorphosis: development

indulgent: generous

procure: get

emigrant: foreigner

Ubi panis ibi patria: "Where ever there is bread, there is my fatherland."

Alma Mater: institution of learning
posterity: future generations

allurement: attraction

despotic: exercising unchecked power

servile: slavish
penury: poverty
ample subsistence: more than enough to live on

For more information see
Page 201, Book 3, *From Colonies to Country.*

children, who before in vain demanded of him a morsel of bread, now, fat and frolicsome, gladly help their father to clear those fields whence exuberant crops are to arise to feed and to clothe them all; without any part being claimed, either by a despotic prince, a rich abbot, or a mighty lord. I lord religion demands but little of him; a small voluntary salary to the minister, and gratitude to God; can he refuse these? The American is a new man, who acts upon new principles; he must therefore entertain new ideas, and form new opinions. From involuntary idleness, servile dependence, penury, and useless labour, he has passed to toils of a very different nature, rewarded by ample subsistence.—This is an American.

19. From Thomas Jefferson, *The Virginia Statute for Religious Freedom* (1786)

On his gravestone, Thomas Jefferson listed the three accomplishments for which he most wanted to be remembered: drafting the Declaration of Independence, founding the University of Virginia, and writing the Virginia Statute for Religious Freedom. Enacted in 1786, the Statute for Religious Freedom prohibited government interference or support for religion and became an inspiration for Article VI and the First Amendment to the United States Constitution.

Jefferson originally drafted the statute in 1777, during the American Revolution. Patrick Henry and many of Virginia's larger religious denominations, fearing that churches would decline without tax support, opposed the statute. Jefferson argued that religious liberty was one of the reasons Americans waged the Revolution, and that the right to freedom of conscience extended to non-Christians and even to nonbelievers. Jefferson felt that religion would flourish if left alone. "It is error alone which needs the support of government," he wrote. "Truth can stand by itself."

During the years following the Revolution, every state ended tax support for established, or state-supported, churches. Religious denominations had to compete for followers without government support. There can be no doubt that the "American system" of voluntary support for religion proved to be enormously successful. Between 1800 and 1840, the proportion of Americans who attended church doubled. Older denominations thrived—including Baptist, Methodist, and Catholic churches—while a host of new denominations arose, including the Church of Christ, the Mormons, and new African-American churches.

Whereas, Almighty God has created the mind free; that all attempts to influence it by temporal punishment, or burthens, or by civil incapacitations, tend only to beget habits of hypocrisy and meanness, and are a departure from the plan of the Holy Author of our religion, who, being Lord both of body and mind, yet chose not to propagate it by coercions on either, as was in his Almighty power to do; that the impious presumption of legislators and rulers, civil as well as ecclesiastical, who, being themselves but fallible and uninspired men, have assumed dominion over the faith of others, setting up their own opinions and modes of thinking as the only true and infallible and as such endeavoring to impose them on others, have established and maintained false religions over the greatest part of the world, and through all time; that to compel a man to furnish contributions of money for the propagation of opinions which he disbelieves, is sinful and tyrannical, and even the forcing him to support this or that teacher of his own religious persuasion, is depriving him of the comfortable liberty of giving his contributions to the particular pastor whose morals he would make his pattern, and whose powers he feels most persuasive to righteousness, and is withdrawing from the ministry those temporary rewards which, proceeding from an approbation of their personal conduct, are an additional incitement to earnest and unremitting labors, for the instruction of mankind; that our civil rights have no dependence on our religious opinions any more than our opinions in physics or geometry; that therefore the proscribing any citizen as unworthy of the public confidence by laying upon him an incapacity of being called to offices of trust and emolument, unless he profess or renounce this or that religious opinion, is depriving him injuriously of those privileges and advantages to which, in common with his fellow citizens, he has a natural right; that it tends only to corrupt the principles of that religion it is meant to encourage, by bribing, with a monopoly of worldly honors and emoluments, those who will externally profess and conform to it; that though indeed, those are criminal who do not withstand such temptation, yet, neither are those innocent who lay the bait in their way; that to suffer the civil magistrate to intrude his powers into the field of opinion, and to restrain the profession or propagation of principles on supposition of their ill tendency, is a dangerous fallacy, which at once destroys all religious liberty, because he, being of

temporal: taking place in this world
civil incapacitations: public problems
beget: create
hypocrisy: dishonesty
propagate: increase
coercions: acts intended to force a particular outcome
impious: lacking in faith
presumption: lack of modesty and understanding
ecclesiastical: of the church
fallible: likely to make errors

approbation: approval
incitement to: cause of
unremitting: unending

proscribing: sentencing

emolument: payment for employment

profession: belief
propagation: reproduction
fallacy: false belief

antagonist: opponent
interposition: action

course judge of that tendency, will make his opinions the rules of judgment, and approve or condemn the sentiments of others only as they shall square with or differ from his own; that it is time enough for the rightful purposes of civil government, for its officers to interfere, when principles break out into overt acts against peace and good order; and finally, that truth is great and will prevail, if left to herself; that she is the proper and sufficient antagonist to error, and has nothing to fear from the conflict, unless by human interposition disarmed of her natural weapons, free argument and debate; errors ceasing to be dangerous when it is permitted freely to contradict them:

Be it enacted by the General Assembly, that no man shall be compelled to frequent or support any religious worship, place or ministry whatsoever, nor shall he otherwise suffer on account of his religious opinions or belief; but that all men shall be free to profess, and by argument to maintain, their opinions in matters of religion, and that the same shall in no wise diminish, enlarge or affect their civil capacities.

wise: way
civil capacities: social and public limits

And though we well know that this Assembly, elected by the people for the ordinary purposes of legislation only, have no power to restrain the acts of succeeding assemblies constituted with powers equal to our own, and that, therefore, to declare this act to be irrevocable would be of no effect in law; yet we are free to declare, and do declare, that the rights hereby asserted are of the natural rights of mankind; and that if any act shall be hereafter passed to repeal the present, or to narrow its operation, such act will be an infringement of natural right.

irrevocable: cannot be undone

20. *The Constitution of the United States (1787)*

The Articles of Confederation failed to establish an effective national government. Britain and Spain refused to recognize the new nation's boundaries. Seven years of war had left the country $79 million in debt. The currency was almost worthless and foreign credit was unavailable. The states fought fiercely over fishing and oyster-harvesting rights. Shays's Rebellion, an uprising of Massachusetts farmers and debtors, made many people fear mob violence.

The delegates who designed a new constitution in Philadelphia during the summer of 1787 believed that the country needed a strong government with broad powers to collect taxes, pay the nation's bills, regulate trade, and defend the country from foreign enemies. The country needed a strong, energetic President to conduct foreign policy, negotiate treaties, and ensure that acts of Congress were properly executed. And it needed a national court system to resolve conflicts between the states and citizens of different states.

But Americans feared a centralized government. The people had fought a revolution to protect their liberties from a large, distant government and many worried that the new government would limit the powers of the states. They also feared that a strong President might be even more powerful than a king. To address these concerns, the delegates designed a republican system of government with limited and carefully defined powers. The Constitution created a federal system, dividing authority between the states and the central government. To assure checks and balances, it established a two-house legislature, and three separate branches of government (legislative, executive, and judicial).

Unlike *Magna Carta* or the English Bill of Rights, the Constitution was intended to represent the interests of "We the People." Originally, the Constitution's framers did not include a bill of rights. They believed that individual rights were safeguarded by state constitutions and limitations on the power of the central government. But popular pressure for a Bill of Rights proved irresistible, and the first Congress crafted a series of carefully worded amendments that reaffirmed freedoms Americans already enjoyed—including religion, press, speech, assembly, and petition.

WE, the PEOPLE of the UNITED STATES, in order to form a more perfect union, establish justice, ensure domestic tranquility, provide for the common defence, promote the general welfare, and secure the blessings of liberty to ourselves and our posterity, do ordain and establish this Constitution for the United States of America.

posterity: future generations

ARTICLE I.
Sect. 1. All legislative powers, herein granted, shall be vested in a Congress of the United States, which shall consist of a Senate and House of Representatives.

Sect. 2. The House of Representatives shall be composed of Members chosen every second year by all the people of the several States, and the Electors in each State shall have the qualifications requisite for Electors of the most numerous branch of the State Legislature.

requisite: required

enumeration: counting

No person shall be a Representative who shall not have attained to the age of 25 years, and been seven years a citizen of the United States, and who shall not, when elected, be an inhabitant of that State in which he shall be chosen.

Representatives and direct taxes shall be appointed among the several States which may be included within this Union, according to the respective numbers, which shall be determined by adding to the whole number of free persons, including those bound to service for a term of years, and excluding Indians not taxed, three fifths of all other persons. The actual enumeration shall be made within three years after the first meeting of the Congress of the United States, and within every subsequent term of ten years, in such manner as they shall by law direct. The number of Representatives shall not exceed one for every thirty thousand, but each State shall have at least one Representative; and until such enumeration shall be made, the State of New-Hampshire shall be entitled to choose three, Massachusetts eight, Rhode-Island and Providence Plantation one, Connecticut five, New-York six, New-Jersey four, Pennsylvania eight, Delaware one, Maryland six, Virginia ten, North-Carolina five, South-Carolina five, and Georgia three.

writs of election: acts calling for elections

When vacancies happen in the Representation from any State, the Executive authority thereof shall issue writs of election to fill such vacancies.

The House of Representatives shall choose their Speaker and other officers, and shall have the sole power of impeachment.

Sect. 3. The Senate of the United States shall be composed of two Senators from each State, chosen by the Legislature thereof, for six years; and each Senator shall have one vote.

Immediately after they shall be assembled in consequence of the first election, they shall be divided as equally as may be into three classes. The seats of the Senators of the first class shall be vacated at the expiration of the second year, of the second class at the expiration of the fourth year, and of the third class at the expiration of the sixth year; so that one third may be chosen every second year, and if vacancies happen, by resignation or otherwise, during the recess of the Legislature of any State, the Executive thereof may make temporary appointments until the next meeting of the Legislature, which shall then fill such vacancies.

No person shall be a Senator who shall not have attained to the age of thirty years, and been nine years a citizen of the United States and who shall not, when elected, be an inhabitant of that State for which he shall be chosen.

The Vice-President of the United States shall be President of the Senate, but shall have no vote, unless they be equally divided. The Senate shall choose their other officers, and also a President pro tempore, in the absence of the Vice-President, or when he shall exercise the office of President of the United States.

pro tempore: for a short time

The Senate shall have the sole power to try all impeachments. When sitting for that purpose, they shall be on oath or affirmation. When the President of the United States is tried, the Chief Justice shall preside; and no person shall be convicted without the concurrence of two thirds of the members present.

impeachments: charges of misconduct
affirmation: sworn statement
concurrence: agreement

Judgement in cases of impeachment, shall not extend further than to removal from office, and disqualification to hold and enjoy any office of honour, trust or profit, under the United States; but the party convicted shall nevertheless be liable and subject to indictment, trial, judgement and punishment, according to law.

indictment: accusation

Sect. 4. The times, places and manner, of holding elections for Senators and representatives, shall be prescribed in each State by the Legislature thereof; but the Congress may at any time, by law, make or alter such regulations, except as to the place of choosing Senators.

prescribed: established

The Congress shall assemble at least once in every year, and such meeting shall be on the first Monday in December, unless they shall by law appoint a different day.

Sect. 5. Each House shall be the judge of the elections, returns and qualification, of its own members, and a majority of each shall constitute a quorum to do business; but a smaller number may adjourn from day to day, and may be authorized to compel the attendance of absent members, in such manner, and under such penalties, as each House may provide.

returns: counting of votes

quorum: minimum
adjourn: stop for a while
compel: force

Each House may determine the rules of its proceedings, punish its members for disorderly behavior, and, with the concurrence of two thirds, expel a member.

Each House shall keep a journal of its proceedings, and from time to time publish the same, excepting such parts as may in their judgment require a secrecy; and the yeas and nays of the members of either House on any question shall, at the desire of one fifth of those present, be entered on the journal.

yeas and nays: votes for or against

Neither House, during the session of Congress, shall, without the consent of the other, adjourn for more than three days, nor to any other place than that in which the two Houses shall be sitting.

treason: crime against the state
felony: serious crime
breach: disruption

civil office: government job
emoluments: payment for employment

revenue: funds, money

Sect. 6. The Senators and Representatives shall receive a compensation for their services, to be ascertained by law, and paid out of the treasury of the United States. They shall in all cases, except treason, felony and breach of peace, be privileged from arrest during their attendance at the session of their respective Houses, and in going to and returning from the same; and for any speech or debate in either House, they shall not be questioned in any other place.

No Senator or Representative shall, during the time for which he was elected, be appointed to any civil office under the authority of the United States, which shall have been created, or the emoluments whereof shall have been encreased, during such time; and no person holding any officer under the United States shall be a member of either House, during his continuance in office.

Sect. 7. All bills for raising revenue shall originate in the House of Representatives; but the Senate may propose or concur with amendments, as on other bills.

Every bill which shall have passed the House of Representatives and the Senate shall, before it become a law, be presented to the President of the United States; if he approve, he shall sign it; but if not, he shall return it, with his objections, to that House in which it shall have originated, who shall enter the objections at large on their journal, and proceed to reconsider it. If after such reconsideration two thirds of that House shall agree to pass the bill, it shall be sent, together with the objections, to the other House, by which it shall likewise be reconsidered, and if approved by two thirds of that House, it shall become a law. But in all such cases the votes of both Houses shall be determined by yeas and nays, and the names of the persons voting for and against the bill shall be entered on the journal of each House respectively. If any bill shall not be returned by the President within ten days (Sundays excepted) after it shall have been presented to him, the same shall be a law in like manner as if he had signed it, unless the Congress by their adjournment prevent its return, in which case it shall not be a law.

Every order, resolution or vote, to which the concurrence of the Senate and House of Representatives may be necessary (except on a question of adjournment) shall be presented to the President of the United States; and before the same shall take effect, shall be approved by him, or being disapproved by him, shall be re-passed by two thirds of the Senate and House of Representatives, according to the rules and limitations prescribed in the case of a bill.

duties, imposts, and excises: kinds of taxes

Sect. 8. The Congress shall have power: To lay and collect taxes, duties, imposts and excises. To pay the debts and provide for the common defence and general welfare of the United States; but all duties, imposts and excises, shall be uniform throughout the United States;

To borrow money on the credit of the United States; To regulate commerce with foreign nations, and among the several States, and with the Indian tribes;

To establish a uniform rule of naturalization, and uniform laws on the subject of bankruptcies, throughout the United States;

naturalization: granting of citizenship
bankruptcies: financial failures

To coin money, regulate the value thereof, and of foreign coin, and fix the standard of weights and measures;

To provide for the punishment of counterfeiting the securities and current coin of the United States;

counterfeiting: faking
securities: papers showing ownership or documenting loans

To establish post-offices and post-roads;

To promote the progress of science and useful arts, by securing for limited times to authors and inventors the exclusive right to their respective writings and discoveries;

To constitute tribunals inferior to the Supreme Court;

tribunals: courts

To define and punish piracies and felonies committed on the high seas and offences against the law of nations;

To declare war, grant letters of marque and reprisal, and make rules concerning captures on land and water;

letters of marque or reprisal: permission granted to a citizen to seize goods or citizens of another country
appropriation: use

To raise and support armies, but no appropriation of money to that use shall be for a longer term than two years;

To provide and maintain a navy;

To make rules for the government and regulation of the land and naval forces;

To provide for calling forth the militia to execute the laws of the Union, suppress insurrections, and repel invasions;

suppress: keep down
insurrections: rebellions

To provide for organizing, arming and disciplining the militia, and for governing such part of them as may be employed in the service of the United States, reserving to the States respectively the appointment of the officers, and the authority of training the militia according to the discipline prescribed by Congress;

To exercise exclusive legislation, in all cases whatsoever, over such district (not exceeding ten miles square) as may, by cession of particular States, and the acceptance of Congress, become the seat of the government of the United States, and to exercise like authority over all places purchased by the consent of the Legislature of the State in which the same shall be, for the erection of forts, magazines, arsenals, dock-yards, and other needful buildings;—and,

cession: withdrawal

magazines: warehouses

To make all laws which shall be necessary and proper for carrying into execution the foregoing powers, and all other powers vested by this Constitution in the government of the United States, or in any department or officer thereof.

Sect. 9. The migration or importation of such persons as any of the States now existing shall think proper to admit, shall not be prohibited by the Congress prior to the year one thousand eight hundred and eight; but a tax or duty may be imposed on such importation, not exceeding ten dollars for each person.

writ: law, decree
habeas corpus: the right of anyone who is arrested to be brought before a judge and to make the arresting officer show that there is good enough reason for the arrest

The privilege of the writ of habeas corpus shall not be suspended, unless when in cases of rebellion or invasion the public safety may require it.

No bill of attainder, or ex post facto law, shall be passed.

bill of attainder: formal removal of a person's civil rights
ex post facto law: a law passed after the fact
capitation: per person tax
sensus: census, a count of the population

No capitation or other direct tax shall be laid, unless in proportion to the sensus or enumeration herein before directed to be taken.

No tax or duty shall be laid on articles exported from any State. No preference shall be given by any regulation of commerce or revenue to the ports of one State over those of another: Nor shall vessels bound to or from one State, be obliged to enter, clear, or pay duties, in another.

No money shall be drawn from the treasury, but in consequence of appropriations made by law; and a regular statement and account of the receipts and expenditures of all public money shall be published from time to time.

No title of nobility shall be granted by the United States: And no person holding any office of profit or trust under them shall, without the consent of the Congress, accept of any present, emolument, office or title, or any kind whatever from any King, Prince, or foreign State.

tender: offering

Sect. 10. No State shall enter into any treaty, alliance or confederation; grant letters of marque and reprisal; coin money; emit bills of credit; make any thing but gold and silver coin a tender in payment of debts; pass any bill of attainder, ex post facto law, or law impairing the obligation of contracts, or grant any title of nobility.

No State shall, without the consent of Congress, lay any imposts or duties on imports or exports, except what may be absolutely necessary for executing its inspection laws; and the new produce of all duties and imposts, laid by any State, on imports or exports, shall be for the use of the treasury of the United States; and all such laws shall be subject to the revision and controul of the Congress. No State shall, without the consent of Congress, lay any duty of tonage, keep troops or ships of war in time of peace, enter into any agreement or compact with another State, or with a foreign power, or engage in war, unless actually invaded, or in such imminent danger as will not admit of delay.

compact: agreement
imminent: near

ARTICLE II.

Sec. 1. The executive power shall be vested in a President of the United States of America. He shall hold his office during the term of four years, and, together with the Vice-President, chosen for the same term, be elected as follows.

Each State shall appoint, in such manner as the Legislature thereof may direct, a number of Electors, equal to the whole number of Senators and Representatives to which the State may be entitled in the Congress; but no Senator or Representative, or person holding an office of trust or profit under the United States, shall be appointed an Elector.

The Electors shall meet in their respective States, and vote by ballot for two persons, of whom one at least shall not be an inhabitant of the same state with themselves. And they shall make a list of all the persons voted for, and of the number of votes for each; which list they shall sign and certify, and transmit sealed to the seat of the government of the United States, directed to the President of the Senate. The President of the Senate shall, in the presence of the Senate and House of Representatives, open all the certificates, and the votes shall then be counted. The person having the greatest number of votes shall be the President, if such number be a majority of the whole number of Electors appointed; and if there be more than one who have such majority, and have an equal number of votes, then the House of Representatives shall immediately choose by ballot one of them for President; and if no person have a majority, then from the five highest on the list the said House shall in like manner choose a President. But in choosing the President the votes shall be taken by States, the representation from each State having one vote: a quorum for this purpose shall consist of a member or members from two thirds of the States, and a majority of all the States shall be necessary to a choice. In every case, after the choice of the President, the person having the greatest number of votes of the Electors, shall be the Vice-President. But if there should remain two or more who have equal votes, the Senate shall choose from them by ballot the Vice-President.

quorum: minimum

The Congress may determine the time of choosing the Electors, and the day on which they shall give their votes; which day shall be the same throughout the United States.

No person, except a natural born citizen, or a citizen of the United States at the time of the adoption of this Constitution, shall be eligible to the office of President; neither shall any person be eligible to that office, who shall not have attained to the age of thirty-five years, and been fourteen years a resident within the United States.

devolve on: fall to

In case of the removal of the President from office, or of his death, resignation, or inability to discharge the powers and duties of the said office, the same shall devolve on the Vice-President; and the Congress may by law provide for the case of removal, death, resignation, or inability, both of the President and Vice-President, declaring what officer shall then act as President, and such officer shall act accordingly, until the disability be removed, or a President shall be elected.

The President shall, at stated times, receive for his services a compensation, which shall neither be increased nor diminished during the period for which he shall have been elected, and he shall not receive within that period any other emolument from the United States, or any of them.

Before he enter on the execution of his office, he shall take the following oath or affirmation:

"I do solemnly swear (or affirm) that I will faithfully execute the office of President of the United States; and will, to the best of my ability, preserve, protect and defend, the Constitution of the United States."

Sect. 2. The President shall be Commander in Chief of the army and navy of the United States, and of the militia of the several states, when called into the actual service of the United States; he may require the opinion, in writing, of the principal officer in each of the executive departments, upon any subject relating to the duties of their respective offices, and he shall have power to grant reprieves and pardons for offences against the United States, except in cases of impeachment.

reprieves: delays of punishment

He shall have power, by and with the advice and consent of the Senate, to make treaties, provided two thirds of the Senators present concur; and he shall nominate, and by and with the advice and consent of the Senate shall appoint Ambassadors, other public Ministers, and Consuls, Judges of the Supreme Court, and all other offices of the United States, whose appointments are not herein otherwise provided for, and which shall be established by law. But the Congress may by law vest the appointment of such inferior officers as they think proper in the President alone, in the courts of law, or in the heads of departments.

vest: assign

The President shall have power to fill all vacancies that may happen during the recess of the Senate, by granting commissions, which shall expire at the end of their next session.

commissions: short-term appointments

Sect. 3. He shall from time to time give to the Congress information of the state of the Union, and recommend to their consideration such measures as he shall judge necessary and expedient; he may, on extraordinary occasions, convene both Houses, or either of them, and in case of disagreement between them, with respect to the time of adjournment, he may adjourn them to such time as he shall think proper; he shall receive Ambassadors and other public Ministers; he shall take care that the laws be faithfully executed, and shall commission all the officers of the United States.

Sect. 4. The President, Vice-President, and all civil officers of the United States, shall be removed from office, on impeachment for and conviction of treason, bribery, or other high crimes and misdemeanors.

ARTICLE III.

Sect. 1. The judicial power of the United States shall be vested in one Supreme Court, and in such Inferior Courts as the Congress may from time to time ordain and establish. The judges, both of the Supreme and Inferior Courts, shall hold their offices during good behavior; and shall, at stated times, receive for their services a compensation, which shall not be diminished during their continuance in office.

Sect. 2. The judicial power shall extend to all cases in law and equity, arising under this Constitution, the laws of the United States, and treaties made, or which shall be made, under their authority; to all cases affecting Ambassadors, other public Ministers, and Consuls; to all cases of admiralty and maritime jurisdiction; to controversies to which the United States shall be a party; to controversies between two or more States, between a State and citizen of another State, between citizens of different States, between citizens of the same State claiming lands under grants of different States, and between a State, or the citizens thereof, and foreign States, citizens or subjects.

"admiralty and maritime": naval and seafaring

In all cases affecting Ambassadors, other public Ministers and consuls, and those in which a State shall be party, the Supreme Court shall have original jurisdiction. In all the other cases before mentioned, the Supreme Court shall have appellate jurisdiction, both as to law and fact, with such exceptions and under such regulations as the Congress shall make.

appellate jurisdiction: authority for reviewing appeals

The trial of all crimes, except in cases of impeachment, shall be by jury; and such trial shall be held in the State where the said crimes shall have been committed; but when not committed within any State, the trial shall be at such place or places as the Congress may by law have directed.

levying: collecting

overt: open

"Congress shall have power . . . person attained.": Children and other relatives of individuals convicted of treason shall not inherit their parents' punishment.

immunities: protections

construed: understood

republican: representative

Sect. 3. Treason, against the United States, shall consist only in levying war against them, or in adhering to their enemies, giving them aid and comfort. No person shall be convicted of treason, unless on the testimony of two witnesses to the same overt act, or on concession in open court.

The Congress shall have power to declare the punishment of treason, but no attainder of treason shall work corruption of blood, or forfeiture, except during the life of the person attainted.

ARTICLE IV.
Sect. 1. Full faith and credit shall be given in each State to the public acts, records and judicial proceedings, of every other State. And the Congress may by general laws prescribe the manner in which such acts, records and proceedings, shall be proved, and the effect thereof.

Sect. 2. The citizens of each State shall be entitled to all privileges and immunities of citizens in the several states. A person, charged in any State with treason, felony, or other crime, who shall flee from justice, and be found in another State, shall, on demand of the executive authority of the State from which he fled, be delivered up, to be removed to the State having jurisdiction of the crime.

No person, held to service or labour in one State, under the laws thereof, escaping into another, shall, in consequence of any law or regulation therein, be discharged from such service or labour; but shall be delivered up, on claim of the party to whom such service or labour may be due.

Sect. 3. New States may be admitted by the Congress into this Union; but no new State shall be formed to erected within the jurisdiction of any other State; nor any State be formed by the junction of two or more States, or parts of States, without the consent of the Legislatures of the States concerned, as well as of the Congress.

The Congress shall have power to dispose of and make all needful rules and regulations, respecting the territory or other property belonging to the United States; and nothing in this Constitution shall be so construed, as to prejudice any claims of the United States, or of any particular State.

Sect. 4. The United States shall guarantee, to every State in this Union, a republican form of government, and shall protect each of them against invasion; and, on application of the Legislature, or of the Executive (when the Legislature cannot be convened) against domestic violence.

ARTICLE V.

The Congress, whenever two thirds of both Houses shall deem it necessary, shall propose amendments to this Constitution; or, on the application of the Legislatures of two thirds of the several States, shall call a Convention, for proposing amendments; which, in either case, shall be valid, to all intents and purposes, as part of this Constitution, when ratified by the Legislature of three fourths of the several States, or by conventions in three fourths thereof, as the one or the other mode of ratification may be proposed by the Congress: Provided, that no amendment which may be made prior to the year one thousand eight hundred and eight shall in any manner affect the first and fourth clauses, in the ninth section of the first article; and that no State, without its consent, shall be deprived of its equal suffrage in the Senate.

ratified: legally approved

suffrage: the right to vote

ARTICLE VI.

All debts contracted, and engagements entered into, before the adoption of this Constitution, shall be as valid against the United States under this Constitution, as under the Confederation.

engagements: agreements

This Constitution, and the laws of the United States which shall be made in pursuance thereof, and all treaties made, or which shall be made, under the authority of the United States, shall be the supreme law of the land; and the Judges in every State, shall be bound thereby; any thing in the constitution or laws of any State to the contrary notwithstanding.

The Senators and Representatives before mentioned; and the members of the several State Legislatures, and all executive and judicial officers, both of the United States and of the several States, shall be bound by oath or affirmation to support this Constitution; but no religious test shall ever be required as a qualification to any office, or public trust, under the United States.

ARTICLE VII.

The ratification of the Conventions of Nine States shall be sufficient for the establishment of this constitution, between the States so ratifying the same.

Done in Convention, by the unanimous consent of the States present, the seventeenth day of September, in the year of our Lord one thousand seven hundred and eighty-seven, and of the Independence of

unanimous: total

the United States of America the twelfth. In witness whereof, we have hereunto subscribed our names.

GEORGE WASHINGTON, President, and Deputy from Virginia.
New-Hampshire, John Langdon, Nicholas Gilman.
Massachusetts, Nathaniel Gorham, Rufus King.
Connecticut, William Samuel Johnson, Roger Sherman.
New-York, Alexander Hamilton.
New-Jersey, William Livingston, David Brearley, William Paterson, Jonathan Dayton.
Pennsylvania, Benjamin Franklin, Thomas Mifflin, Robert Morris, George Clymer, Thomas Fitzsimons, Jared Ingersoll, James Wilson, Gouverneur Morris.
Delaware, George Read, Gunning Bedford, jun., John Dickinson, Richard Bassett, Jacob Broom.
Maryland, James M'Henry, Daniel of St. Tho. Jenifer, Daniel Carrol.
Virginia. John Blair, James Madison, jun.
North-Carolina, William Blount, Richard Dobbs Spaight, Hugh Williamson.
South-Carolina, John Rutledge, Charles Cotesworth Pinckney, Charles Pinckney, Pierce Butler.
Georgia, William Few, Abraham Baldwin.

Attest, ... WILLIAM JACKSON, Secretary.

The Bill of Rights

Amendment I
Congress shall make no law respecting an establishment of religion, or prohibiting the free exercise thereof; or abridging the freedom of speech, or of the press; or the right of the people peaceably to assemble, and to petition the Government for a redress of grievances.

Amendment II
A well regulated Militia, being necessary to the security of a free State, the right of the people to keep and bear Arms, shall not be infringed.

Amendment III
No Soldier shall, in time of peace be quartered in any house, without the consent of the Owner, nor in time of war, but in a manner to be prescribed by law.

abridging: cutting

redress of grievances: address a complaint

quartered: placed in to live

Amendment IV

The right of the people to be secure in their persons, houses, papers, and effects, against unreasonable searches and seizures, shall not be violated, and no Warrants shall issue, but upon probable cause, supported by Oath or affirmation, and particularly describing the place to be searched, and the persons or things to be seized.

Warrants: authorizations

Amendment V

No person shall be held to answer for a capital, or otherwise infamous crime, unless on a presentment or indictment of a Grand Jury, except in cases arising in the land or naval forces, or in the Militia, when in actual service in time of War or public danger; nor shall any person be subject for the same offence to be twice put in jeopardy of life or limb; nor shall be compelled in any criminal case to be a witness against himself, nor be deprived of life, liberty, or property, without due process of law; nor shall private property be taken for public use, without just compensation.

capital: serious crime, often punished by death

due process: a course of formal actions based on standard, established rules

Amendment VI

In all criminal prosecutions, the accused shall enjoy the right to a speedy and public trial, by an impartial jury of the State and district wherein the crime shall have been committed, which district shall have been previously ascertained by law, and to be informed of the nature and cause of the accusation; to be confronted with the witnesses against him; to have compulsory process for obtaining witnesses in his favor, and to have the Assistance of Counsel for his defence.

impartial: not taking sides

compulsory process: the right to force a person to do something
counsel: lawyer

Amendment VII

In suits at common law, where the value in controversy shall exceed twenty dollars, the right of trial by jury shall be reserved, and no fact tried by a jury, shall be otherwise reexamined in any Court of the United States, than according to the rules of the common law.

Amendment VIII

Excessive bail shall not be required, nor excessive fines imposed, nor cruel and unusual punishments inflicted.

bail: money held in exchange for the temporary release of a prisoner before trial

Amendment IX

The enumeration in the Constitution, of certain rights, shall not be construed to deny or disparage others retained by the people.

Amendment X
The powers not delegated to the United States by the Constitution, nor prohibited by it to the States, are reserved to the States respectively, or to the people.

For more information see
Chapter 33, Book 3, *From Colonies to Country,* and Chapter 32, Book 4, *The New Nation.*

21. From *The Northwest Ordinance* (1787)

The Northwest Ordinance was the greatest achievement of the United States government under the Articles of Confederation. Enacted in 1787, this law set up regulations for settling and governing the West. It also ensured that territories would eventually be admitted to the union as states on equal footing with the original 13 states.

The Northwest Ordinance occupies a special place in American constitutional history. It was the first American law to prohibit slavery. It also was the first document voted on by all the states to guarantee freedom of speech and religion and the right of habeas corpus (the right of a prisoner to know the reason for his imprisonment). The Ordinance also declared that the Indians' "land and property shall never be taken from them without their consent."

And, for extending the fundamental principles of civil and religious liberty, which form the basis whereon these republics, their laws and constitutions are erected; to fix and establish those principles as the basis of all laws, constitutions, and governments, which forever hereafter shall be formed in the said territory; to provide also for the establishment of states, and permanent government therein, and for their admission to a share in the federal councils on an equal footing with the original states, at as early periods as may be consistent with the general interest:

It is hereby ordained and declared by the authority aforesaid, That the following articles shall be considered as articles of compact, between the original states and the people and states in the said territory and forever remain unalterable, unless by common consent, to wit:

Article 1. No person, demeaning himself in a peaceable and orderly manner, shall ever be molested on account of his mode of worship or religious sentiments in the said territory.

Article 2. The inhabitants of the said territory shall always be entitled to the benefits of the writ of habeas corpus and of the trial by jury; of a proportionate representation of the people in the legislature; and of judicial proceedings according to the course of the common law. All persons shall be bailable, unless for capital offenses, where the proof shall be evident, or the presumption great. All fines shall be moderate; and no cruel or unusual punishments shall be inflicted. No man shall be deprived of his liberty or property, but by the judgment of his peers or the law of the land; and should the public exigencies make it necessary, for the common preservation, to take any person's property, or to demand his particular services, full compensation shall be made for the same. And, in the just preservation of rights and property, it is understood and declared, that no law ought ever to be made or have force in the said territory, that shall, in any manner whatever, interfere with or affect private contracts or engagements, bona fide, and without fraud previously formed.

writ: law, decree
habeas corpus: the right of anyone who is arrested to be brought before a judge and to make the arresting officer show that there is good enough reason for the arrest
bailable: able to hold money in exchange for the temporary release of a prisoner before trial
capital offenses: crimes punishable by death
exigencies: urgent situations

bona fide: in good faith

Article 3. Religion, morality, and knowledge being necessary to good government and the happiness of mankind, schools and the means of education shall forever be encouraged. The utmost good faith shall always be observed towards the Indians; their lands and property shall never be taken from them without their consent; and in their property, rights, and liberty they shall never be invaded or disturbed, unless in just and lawful wars authorized by Congress; but laws founded in justice and humanity shall from time to time be made for preventing wrongs being done to them, and for preserving peace and friendship with them. . . .

Prohibition of Slavery

Article 6. There shall be neither slavery nor involuntary servitude in the said territory, otherwise than in punishment of crimes whereof the party shall have been duly convicted: *Provided, always*, That any person escaping into the same, from whom labor or service is lawfully claimed in any one of the original states, such fugitive may be lawfully reclaimed, and conveyed to the person claiming his or her labor or services as aforesaid.

involuntary servitude: slavery

fugitive: runaway

22. From Alexander Hamilton and James Madison, *The Federalist,* Nos. 1, 10, and 51 (1788)

The Federalist was a series of 85 essays that appeared in New York City newspapers in 1787 and 1788. Written by Alexander Hamilton, James Madison, and John Jay, but originally published under the pen name "Publius" (who was the founding father of the ancient Roman Republic), they were intended to explain and defend the yet-to-be-ratified Constitution. Thomas Jefferson regarded *The Federalist* as the best source of information on "the genuine meaning" of the U.S. Constitution.

At the time *The Federalist* essays were written, it was not clear if the states would ratify the Constitution. Nine states had ratified the document, but two of the larger states, Virginia and New York, had not. In Virginia, Patrick Henry spoke out loudly against the new Constitution, and in New York, Governor George Clinton opposed ratification. *The Federalist* convinced many Virginians and New Yorkers to support the Constitution. It argued that the new Constitution was necessary to provide the new country with an adequate defense, to guarantee public peace, and to regulate commerce. Opponents of the Constitution, who were known as Anti-Federalists, argued that the United States was too large to have a democratic system of government. Anti-Federalists also feared that the document created a President who would become a dictator and that a national army would crush dissent.

The Federalist addressed each of these concerns. In the following selections, Hamilton and Madison give their answers to questions facing the new nation as it invented a new system of government. They insist that the new Constitution was based on a realistic conception of how liberty might best be guaranteed in an imperfect world.

Federalist No. 1
Alexander Hamilton
October 27, 1787
General Introduction For the Independent Journal

unequivocal: clear, unmistakable
subsisting: surviving

After an unequivocal experience of the inefficiency of the subsisting federal government, you are called upon to deliberate on a new Constitution for the United States of America. The subject speaks its own importance; comprehending in its consequences nothing less than the existence of the UNION, the safety and welfare of the parts of which it is composed, the fate of an empire in many respects the most interesting in the world. It has been frequently remarked that it seems to have been reserved to the people of this country, by their conduct and example, to decide the important question, whether societies of men are really capable or not of establishing good government from reflection and choice, or whether they are forever destined to depend for their political constitutions on accident and force. If there be any truth in the remark, the crisis at which we are arrived may with propriety be regarded as the era in which that decision is to be made; and a wrong election of the part we shall act may, in this view, deserve to be considered as the general misfortune of mankind. . . .

propriety: correctness

Among the most formidable of the obstacles which the new Constitution will have to encounter may readily be distinguished the obvious interest of a certain class of men in every State to resist all changes which may hazard a diminution of the power, emolument, and consequence of the offices they hold under the State establishments; and the perverted ambition of another class of men, who will either hope to aggrandize themselves by the confusions of their country, or will flatter themselves with fairer prospects of elevation from the subdivision of the empire into several partial confederacies than from its union under one government. . . .

diminution: decrease
emolument: payment for employment
perverted: corrupted
aggrandize: gain a false glory

Federalist No. 10
James Madison
November 23, 1787
The Union as a Safeguard Against Domestic Faction and Insurrection

AMONG the numerous advantages promised by a well-constructed Union, none deserves to be more accurately developed than its tendency to break and control the violence of faction. The friend of popular governments never finds himself so much alarmed for their character and fate, as when he contemplates their propensity to this dangerous vice. . . . The instability, injustice, and confusion introduced into the public councils, have, in truth, been the mortal diseases under which popular governments have everywhere perished. . . . Complaints are everywhere heard from our most considerate and virtuous citizens . . . that our governments are too unstable, that the public good is disregarded in the conflicts of rival parties, and that measures are too often decided, not according to the rules of justice and the rights of the minor party, but by the

contemplates: thinks about
propensity: weakness with respect to
public councils: the legislatures

aggregate: combined

aliment: nutrient
folly: foolishness
annihilation: complete
destruction

expedient: method
fallible: likely to make errors

latent: hidden

speculation: guessing about the
future
contending: competing
preeminence: unquestioned
leadership or superiority
animosity: hostility
vex: annoy

superior force of an interested and overbearing majority. . . . [K]nown facts will not permit us to deny that they are in some degree true. . . .

By a faction, I understand a number of citizens, whether amounting to a majority or a minority of the whole, who are united and actuated by some common impulse of passion, or of interest, adversed to the rights of other citizens, or to the permanent and aggregate interests of the community.

There are two methods of curing the mischiefs of faction: the one, by removing its causes; the other, by controlling its effects.

There are again two methods of removing the causes of faction: the one, by destroying the liberty which is essential to its existence; the other, by giving to every citizen the same opinions, the same passions, and the same interests.

It could never be more truly said than of the first remedy, that it was worse than the disease. Liberty is to faction what air is to fire, an aliment without which it instantly expires. But it could not be less folly to abolish liberty, which is essential to political life, because it nourishes faction, than it would be to wish the annihilation of air, which is essential to animal life, because it imparts to fire its destructive agency.

The second expedient is as impracticable as the first would be unwise. As long as the reason of man continues fallible, and he is at liberty to exercise it, different opinions will be formed. . . . The diversity in the faculties of men, from which the rights of property originate, is not less an insuperable obstacle to a uniformity of interests. The protection of these faculties is the first object of government. From the protection of different and unequal faculties of acquiring property, the possession of different degrees and kinds of property immediately results; and from the influence of these on the sentiments and views of the respective proprietors, ensues a division of the society into different interests and parties.

The latent causes of faction are thus sown in the nature of man; and we see them everywhere brought into different degrees of activity, according to the different circumstances of civil society. A zeal for different opinions concerning religion, concerning government, and many other points, as well of speculation as of practice; an attachment to different leaders ambitiously contending for pre-eminence and power; or to persons of other descriptions whose fortunes have been interesting to the human passions, have, in turn, divided mankind into parties, inflamed them with mutual animosity, and rendered them much more disposed to vex and oppress each other than to co-operate for their common good. So strong is this propensity of mankind to fall into mutual animosities, that where no substantial occasion presents itself, the most frivolous and fanciful distinctions have been sufficient to kindle their unfriendly passions and excite their most violent conflicts. But the most common and durable source of factions has been the various and unequal distribution of property. Those who hold and those who are without property have ever formed distinct interests in society. Those who are creditors, and those who are debtors, fall under a like discrimination. A landed interest, a manufacturing interest, a mercantile interest, a moneyed interest, with many lesser interests, grow up of necessity in civilized nations, and divide them into different classes, actuated by different sentiments and views. The regulation of these various and interfering interests forms the principal task of modern legislation, and involves the spirit of party and faction in the necessary and ordinary operations of the government. . . .

mercantile: commercial

faction: division within a larger group

It is in vain to say that enlightened statesmen will be able to adjust these clashing interests, and render them all subservient to the public good. Enlightened statesmen will not always be at the helm. . . .

subservient to: less important than

The inference to which we are brought is, that the *causes* of faction cannot be removed, and that relief is only to be sought in the means of controlling its *effects*.

If a faction consists of less than a majority, relief is supplied by the republican principle, which enables the majority to defeat its sinister views by regular vote. . . . When a majority is included in a faction, the form of popular government, on the other hand, enables it to sacrifice to its ruling passion or interest both the public good and the rights of other citizens. To secure the public good and private rights against the danger of such a faction, and at the same time to preserve the spirit and the form of popular government, is then the great object to which our inquiries are directed. . . .

republican: representative
sinister: unwholesome

From this view of the subject it may be concluded that a pure democracy, by which I mean a society consisting of a small number of citizens, who assemble and administer the government in person, can admit of no cure for the mischiefs of faction. . . . Theoretic politicians, who have patronized this species of government, have erroneously supposed that by reducing mankind to a perfect equality in their political rights, they would, at the same time, be perfectly equalized and assimilated in their possessions, their opinions, and their passions.

assimilated: absorbed into a larger body

A republic, by which I mean a government in which the scheme of representation takes place, opens a different prospect, and promises the cure for which we are seeking. Let us examine the points in which it varies from pure democracy, and we shall comprehend both the

efficacy: proven capability

delegation: handing over

spheres: areas

unison: united effort

partition: division

nature of the cure and the efficacy which it must derive from the Union.

The two great points of difference between a democracy and a republic are: first, the delegation of the government, in the latter, to a small number of citizens elected by the rest; secondly, the greater number of citizens, and greater sphere of country, over which the latter may be extended.

The effect of the first difference is, on the one hand, to refine and enlarge the public views, by passing them through the medium of a chosen body of citizens, whose wisdom may best discern the true interest of their country, and whose patriotism and love of justice will be least likely to sacrifice it to temporary or partial considerations. . . .

The other point of difference is, the greater number of citizens and extent of territory which may be brought within the compass of republican than of democratic government; and it is this circumstance principally which renders factious combinations less to be dreaded in the former than in the latter. . . . Extend the sphere, and you take in a greater variety of parties and interests; you make it less probable that a majority of the whole will have a common motive to invade the rights of other citizens; or if such a common motive exists, it will be more difficult for all who feel it to discover their own strength, and to act in unison with each other. . . .

Hence, it clearly appears, that the same advantage which a republic has over a democracy, in controlling the effects of faction, is enjoyed by a large over a small republic,—is enjoyed by the Union over the States composing it. . . .

The Federalist No. 51
Hamilton or Madison
February 8, 1788

To what expedient, then, shall we finally resort, for maintaining in practice the necessary partition of power among the several departments, as laid down in the Constitution? The only answer that can be given is . . . by so contriving the interior structure of the government as that its several constituent parts may, by their mutual relations, be the means of keeping each other in their proper places. . . .

In order to lay a due foundation for that separate and distinct exercise of the different powers of government, which to a certain extent is admitted on all hands to be essential to the preservation of liberty, it is evident that each department should have a will of its own; and consequently should be so constituted that the members of each should have as little agency as possible in the appointment of the members of the others. . . .

It is equally evident, that the members of each department should be as little dependent as possible on those of the others. . . .

But the great security against a gradual concentration of the several powers in the same department, consists in giving to those who administer each department the necessary constitutional means and personal motives to resist encroachments of the others. . . .

encroachments: intrusion upon

Ambition must be made to counteract ambition. The interest of the man must be connected with the constitutional rights of the place. It may be a reflection on human nature, that such devices should be necessary to control the abuses of government. But what is government itself, but the greatest of all reflections on human nature? If men were angels, government would be necessary. If angels were to govern men, neither external nor internal controls on government would be necessary. In framing a government which is to be administered by men over men, the great difficulty lies in this: you must first enable the government to control the governed; and in the next place oblige it to control itself. A dependence on the people is, no doubt, the primary control on the government; but experience has taught mankind the necessity of auxiliary precautions. . . .

auxiliary: additional

But it is not possible to give to each department [of the State] an equal power of self-defense. In republican government, the legislative authority necessarily predominates. The remedy for this inconveniency is to divide the legislature into different branches; and to render them, by different modes of election and different principles of action, as little connected with each other as the nature of their common functions and their common dependence on the society will admit. It may even be necessary to guard against dangerous encroachments by still further precautions. As the weight of the legislative authority requires that it should be thus divided, the weakness of the executive may require, on the other hand, that it should be fortified. . . .

fortified: strengthened

There are, moreover, two considerations particularly applicable to the federal system of America, which place that system in a very interesting point of view.

First. In a single republic, all the power surrendered by the people is submitted to the administration of a single government; and the usurpations are guarded against by a division of the government into distinct and separate departments. In the compound republic of America, the power surrendered by the people is first divided between two distinct governments, and then the portion allotted to each subdivided among distinct and separate departments. Hence

usurpations: thefts of power

a double security arises to the rights of the people. The different governments will control each other, at the same time that each will be controlled by itself.

Second. It is of great importance in a republic not only to guard the society against the oppression of its rulers, but to guard one part of the society against the injustice of the other part. Different interests necessarily exist in different classes of citizens. If a majority be united by a common interest, the rights of the minority will be insecure. There are but two methods of providing against this evil. . . . The second method will be exemplified in the federal republic of the United States. Whilst all authority in it will be derived from and dependent on the society, the society itself will be broken into so many parts, interests, and classes of citizens, that the rights of individuals, or of the minority, will be in little danger from interested combinations of the majority. . . . Justice is the end of government. It is the end of civil society. It ever has been and ever will be pursued until it be obtained, or until liberty be lost in the pursuit. In a society under the forms of which the stronger faction can readily unite and oppress the weaker, anarchy may as truly be said to reign as in a state of nature, where the weaker individual is not secured against the violence of the stronger; and as, in the latter state, even the stronger individuals are prompted, by the uncertainty of their condition, to submit to a government which may protect the weak as well as themselves; so, in the former state, will the more powerful factions or parties be gradually induced, by a like motive, to wish for a government which will protect all parties, the weaker as well as the more powerful. . . .

anarchy: chaos

For more information see
Chapters 1–5, Book 4, *The New Nation.*

23. George Washington, *Inaugural Address* (1789)

When George Washington took office as President in 1789, the United States government consisted of 75 post offices, a large debt, a small number of unpaid clerks, and an army of just 46 officers and 672 soldiers. There was no federal court system, no navy, and no system for collecting taxes. The Constitution provided only a broad outline of the office and powers of the President. It would be up to President Washington to define the office.

In his first inaugural address, delivered at New York City's Federal Hall, Washington made it clear that he accepted the office of President reluctantly and only out of a sense of public obligation. He promised to represent all the

American people. To ensure that his actions would be motivated solely by the public good, Washington refused to accept a salary as President.

Fellow citizens of the Senate and of the House of Representatives: Among the vicissitudes incident to life, no event could have filled me with greater anxieties than that of which the notification was transmitted by your order, and received on the fourteenth day of the present month: On the one hand, I was summoned by my country, whose voice I can never hear but with veneration and love, from a retreat which I had chosen with the fondest predilection, and, in my flattering hopes, with an immutable decision, as the asylum of my declining years: a retreat which was rendered every day more necessary as well as more dear to me, by the addition of habit to inclination, and of frequent interruptions in my health to the gradual waste committed on it by time. On the other hand, the magnitude and difficulty of the trust to which the voice of my country called me, being sufficient to awaken in the wisest and most experienced of her citizens, a distrustful scrutiny into his qualifications, could not but overwhelm with despondence, one, who, inheriting inferior endowments from nature and unpracticed in the duties of civil administration, ought to be peculiarly conscious of his own deficiencies. In this conflict of emotions, all I dare aver, is, that it has been my faithful study to collect my duty from a just appreciation of every circumstance, by which it might be affected. All I dare hope, is, that, if in executing this task I have been too much swayed by a grateful remembrance of former instances, or by an affectionate sensibility to this transcendent proof, of the confidence of my fellow-citizens; and have thence too little consulted my incapacity as well as disinclination for the weighty and untried cares before me; my error will be palliated by the motives which misled me, and its consequences be judged by my Country, with some share of the partiality in which they originated.

Such being the impressions under which I have, in obedience to the public summons, repaired to the present station; it would be peculiarly improper to omit in this first official act, my fervent supplications to that Almighty Being who rules over the universe, who presides in the councils of nations, and whose providential aids can supply every human defect, that His benediction may consecrate to the liberties and happiness of the people of the United States, a government instituted by themselves for these essential purposes: and may enable every instrument employed in its administration to execute with success, the functions allotted to His charge. In tendering this homage to the Great Author of every public and private good, I assure myself that it expresses your sentiments not less than my

vicissitudes: ups and downs

veneration: respect
predilection: attraction to something dearly loved
immutable: unchanging
asylum: safe place

magnitude: greatness

scrutiny: careful watching
despondence: lack of hope
endowments: gifts

aver: state

palliated by: seem less serious

station: job
fervent: most sincere

providential: favorable
benediction: blessing

homage: praise

presage: predict

expedient: appropriate
acquit me from: free me from

congenial: sympathetic
actuate: point
rectitude: correctness

pledges: promises

animosities: feelings of hostility

immutable: unchanging
preeminence: unquestioned leadership

ardent: passionate

indissoluble: unbreakable

felicity: happiness

own; nor those of my fellow-citizens at large, less than either. No people can be bound to acknowledge and adore the invisible hand, which conducts the affairs of men more than the people of the United States. Every step, by which they have advanced to the character of an independent nation, seems to have been distinguished by some token of providential agency. And in the important revolution just accomplished in the system of their united government; the tranquil deliberations and voluntary consent of so many distinct communities, from which the event has resulted, cannot be compared with the means by which most governments have been established, without some return of pious gratitude along with an humble anticipation of the future blessings which the past seem to presage. These reflections, arising out of the present crisis, have forced themselves too strongly on my mind to be suppressed. You will join with me I trust in thinking, that there are none under the influence of which, the proceedings of a new and free Government can more auspiciously commence.

By the article establishing the executive department, it is made the duty of the president "to recommend to your consideration, such measures as he shall judge necessary and expedient." The circumstances under which I now meet you, will acquit me from entering into that subject, farther than to refer to the great constitutional charter under which you are assembled; and which, in defining your powers, designates the objects to which your attention is to be given. It will be more consistent with those circumstances, and far more congenial with the feelings which actuate me, to substitute, in place of a recommendation of particular measures, the tribute that is due to the talents, the rectitude, and the patriotism which adorn the characters selected to devise and adopt them. In these honorable qualifications, I behold the surest pledges, that as on one side, no local prejudices, or attachments; no separate views, nor party animosities, will misdirect the comprehensive and equal eye which ought to watch over this great assemblage of communities and interests: so, on another, that the foundations of our national policy will be laid in the pure and immutable principles of private morality; and the pre-eminence of free government, be exemplified by all the attributes which can win the affections of its citizens, and command the respect of the world. I dwell on this prospect with every satisfaction which an ardent love for my country can inspire: since there is no truth more thoroughly established, than that there exists in the economy and course of nature, an indissoluble union between virtue and happiness, between duty and advantage, between the genuine maxims of an honest and magnanimous policy, and the solid rewards of public prosperity and felicity: since we ought to be no less persuaded that the propitious smiles of Heaven, can never be expected on a nation that disregards the eternal rules of order and right, which Heaven itself has ordained: and since the preservation of the sacred fire of liberty, and the destiny of the Republican model of Government, are justly considered as deeply, perhaps as finally staked, on the experiment entrusted to the hands of the American people.

propitious: promising future blessings

Besides the ordinary objects submitted to your care, it will remain with your judgment to decide, how far an exercise of the occasional power delegated by the Fifth article of the Constitution is rendered expedient at the present juncture by the nature of objections which have been urged against the system, or by the degree of inquietude which has given birth to them.—Instead of undertaking particular recommendations on this subject, in which I could be guided by no lights derived from official opportunities, I shall again give way to my entire confidence in your discernment and pursuit of the public good: For I assure myself that whilst you carefully avoid every alteration which might endanger the benefits of an united and effective government, or which ought to await the future lessons of experience; a reverence for the characteristic rights of freemen, and a regard for the public harmony, will sufficiently influence your deliberations on the question how far the former can be more impregnably fortified, or the latter be safely and advantageously promoted.

juncture: crossroads
inquietude: discontent

discernment: good judgment

impregnably: unbeatably

To the preceding observations I have one to add, which will be most properly addressed to the House of Representatives. It concerns myself, and will therefore be as brief as possible. When I was first honored with a call into the service of my country, then on the eve of an arduous struggle for its liberties, the light in which I contemplated my duty required that I should renounce every pecuniary compensation. From this resolution I have in no instance departed. And being still under the impressions which produced it, I must decline as inapplicable to myself, any share in the personal emoluments, which may be indispensably included in a permanent provision for the Executive Department; and must accordingly pray that the pecuniary estimates for the station in which I am placed, may, during my continuance in it, be limited to such actual expenditures as the public good may be thought to require.

emoluments: payments for employment

pecuniary: financial

Having thus imparted to you my sentiments, as they have been awakened by the occasion which brings us together, I shall take my present leave; but not without resorting once more to the benign parent of the human race, in humble supplication that since he has been pleased to favor the American people with opportunities for deliberating in perfect tranquility, and dispositions for deciding with unparalleled unanimity on a form of government, for the security of their

benign: loving

conspicuous: evident, clear
temperate: calm

union, and the advancement of their happiness, so this divine bless- ing may be equally conspicuous in the enlarged views, the temperate consultations and the wise measures on which the success of this government must depend.

For more information see
Chapters 1–5, Book 4, *The New Nation.*

24. George Washington, *Letter to Moses Seixas* (1790)

President Washington's letter to the Jewish congregation of Newport, Rhode Island, is a classic statement of the new nation's commitment to religious free- dom. It was the first public declaration that Jews in the United States would be able to practice their religion free from government persecution. In his letter, the President states that America's government is one "which gives to bigotry no sanction, to persecution, no assistance." According to Washington, it is not enough to merely tolerate other religions. Religious freedom, he insists, is an "inherent natural right." A year after Washington wrote his letter, the principle of religious freedom was included in the First Amendment to the Constitution.

Gentlemen:

replete: full

cordial: pleasant, gracious

While I received with much satisfaction your address replete with expressions of esteem, I rejoice in the opportunity of assuring you that I shall always retain grateful remembrance of the cordial welcome I experienced on my visit to Newport from all classes of citizens.

The reflection on the days of difficulty and danger which are past is rendered the more sweet from a consciousness that they are suc- ceeded by days of uncommon prosperity and security.

If we have wisdom to make the best use of the advantages with which we are now favored, we cannot fail, under the just administra- tion of a good government, to become a great and happy people.

The citizens of the United States of America have a right to applaud Themselves for having given to mankind examples of an enlarged and liberal policy—a policy worthy of imitation. All possess alike liberty of conscience and immunities of citizenship.

immunities: protections
indulgence: pleasure or kindness

inherent: granted at birth

It is now no more that toleration is spoken of as if it were the indul- gence of one class of people that another enjoyed the exercise of their inherent natural rights, for, happily, the Government of the

United States, which gives to bigotry no sanction, to persecution no assistance, requires only that they who live under its protection should demean themselves as good citizens in giving it on all occasions their effectual support.

bigotry: intolerance, prejudice

demean: insult
effectual: capable

It would be inconsistent with the frankness of my character not to avow that I am pleased with your favorable opinion of my administration and fervent wishes for my felicity.

fervent: most sincere
felicity: happiness

May the children of the stock of Abraham who dwell in this land continue to merit and enjoy the good will of the other inhabitants—while every one shall sit in safety under his own vine and fig tree and there shall be none to make him afraid.

stock of Abraham: future generations of the Jewish people

May the father of all mercies scatter light, and not darkness, upon our paths, and make us all in our several vocations useful here, and in His own due time and way everlastingly happy.

25. George Washington, *Letter to the New Church in Baltimore* (1793)

For more information see
Chapters 1–5, Book 4, *The New Nation*.

In this 1793 letter to the members of Baltimore's New Church, President Washington expresses his pride at living in a country in which "every person may . . . worship God according to the dictates of his own heart." In the United States a person may reach for the highest government office, regardless of their religious beliefs.

We have abundant reason to rejoice that in this Land the light of truth and reason has triumphed over the power of bigotry and superstition, and that every person may here worship God according to the dictates of his own heart. In this enlightened Age and in this Land of equal liberty it is our boast, that a man's religious tenets will not forfeit the protection of the Laws, nor deprive him of the right of attaining and holding the highest Offices that are known in the United States.

bigotry: intolerance, prejudice

tenets: beliefs

Your prayers for my present and future felicity are received with gratitude; and I sincerely wish, Gentlemen, that you may in your social and individual capacities taste those blessings, which a gracious God bestows upon the Righteous.

For more information see

Chapters 1–5, Book 4, *The New Nation.*

26. From George Washington, *Farewell Address* (1796)

George Washington announced his retirement two months before the Presidential election of 1796. He had served two terms as President, and this decision established the tradition that two terms should be the limit. In his Farewell Address, published in a Philadelphia newspaper, the President called on Americans to put aside the differences between political parties and geographical regions and unite for the common good. In foreign policy, he advised Americans to "steer clear" of foreign entanglements. While the country should be open to commerce with all nations, he said, it should avoid permanent alliances with other countries. In fact, the United States did not join a peacetime alliance with foreign nations until 1949.

conduce: lead
apprise: inform
decline: decide against

Friends and fellow citizens: The period for a new election of a citizen to administer the executive government of the United States being not far distant, and the time actually arrived when your thoughts must be employed in designating the person who is to be clothed with that important trust, it appears to me proper, especially as it may conduce to a more distinct expression of the public voice, that I should now apprise you of the resolution I have formed to decline being considered among the number of those out of whom a choice is to be made.

In looking forward to the moment which is intended to terminate the career of my political life, my feelings do not permit me to suspend the deep acknowledgment of that debt of gratitude which I owe to my beloved country for the many honors it has conferred upon me; still more for the steadfast confidence with which it has supported me, and for the opportunities I have thence enjoyed of manifesting my inviolable attachment by services faithful and persevering, though in usefulness unequal to my zeal.

inviolable: unbreakable

solicitude: concern

Here, perhaps, I ought to stop. But a solicitude for your welfare, which cannot end but with my life, and the apprehension of danger natural to that solicitude urge me on an occasion like the present to offer to your solemn contemplation and to recommend to your frequent review some sentiments which are the result of much reflection, of no inconsiderable observation, and which appear to me all important to the permanency of your felicity as a people.

The unity of government which constitutes you one people is also now dear to you. It is justly so, for it is a main pillar in the edifice of

edifice: building

your real independence, the support of your tranquillity at home, your peace abroad, of your safety, of your prosperity, of that very liberty which you so highly prize.

But as it is easy to foresee that from different causes and from different quarters much pains will be taken, many artifices employed, to weaken in your minds the conviction of this truth, as this is the point in your political fortress against which the batteries of internal and external enemies will be most constantly and actively (though often covertly and insidiously) directed, it is of infinite moment that you should properly estimate the immense value of your national union to your collective and individual happiness.

artifices: clever tricks

batteries: attacks

The name of American, which belongs to you in your national capacity, must always exalt the just pride of patriotism more than any appellation derived from local discriminations. With slight shades of difference, you have the same religion, manners, habits, and political principles. You have in a common cause fought and triumphed together. The independence and liberty you possess are the work of joint councils and joint efforts, of common dangers, sufferings, and successes.

appellation: name
discriminations: differences

But these considerations, however powerfully they address themselves to your sensibility, are greatly outweighed by those which apply more immediately to your interest. Here every portion of our country finds the most commanding motives for carefully guarding and preserving the union of the whole.

sensibilities: emotions

In contemplating the causes which may disturb our Union, it occurs as matter of serious concern that any ground should have been furnished for characterizing parties by geographical discriminations—Northern and Southern, Atlantic and Western—whence designing men may endeavor to excite a belief that there is a real difference of local interests and views. One of the expedients of party to acquire influence within particular districts is to misrepresent the opinions and aims of other districts. You cannot shield yourselves too much against the jealousies and heartburnings which spring from these misrepresentations. They tend to render alien to each other those who ought to be bound together by fraternal affection.

designing: dishonest

fraternal: brotherly

To the efficacy and permanency of your Union a government for the whole is indispensable. No alliances, however strict, between the parts can be an adequate substitute. They must inevitably experience the infractions and interruptions which all alliances in all times have experienced. Sensible of this momentous truth, you have improved upon your first essay by the adoption of a constitution of government better calculated than your former for an intimate union, and for the efficacious management of your common concerns.

infractions: breaking of rules

efficacious: effective

requisite: required

discountenance: look upon with disfavor

specious: attractive, but misleading

baneful: causing death and destruction

dissension: conflict

despotism: tyranny

absolute power: complete and arbitrary power, like the power held by a dictator

subvert: bring down

pious: religious, showing faith
felicity: happiness

supposition: idea
conceded to: acknowledged as an outcome of

popular government: government by the people

diffusion: spread

Toward the preservation of your government and the permanency of your present happy state, it is requisite not only that you steadily discountenance irregular oppositions to its acknowledged authority, but also that you resist with care the spirit of innovation upon its principles, however specious the pretexts. One method of assault may be to effect in the forms of the Constitution alterations which will impair the energy of the system, and thus to undermine what cannot be directly overthrown.

I have already intimated to you the danger of parties in the state, with particular reference to the founding of them on geographical discriminations. Let me now take a more comprehensive view and warn you in the most solemn manner against the baneful effects of the spirit of party generally.

The alternate domination of one faction over another, sharpened by the spirit of revenge natural to party dissension, which in different ages and countries has perpetrated the most horrid enormities, is itself a frightful despotism. But this leads at length to a more formal and permanent despotism. The disorders and miseries which result gradually incline the minds of men to seek security and repose in the absolute power of an individual, and sooner or later the chief of some prevailing faction, more able or more fortunate than his competitors, turns this disposition to the purposes of his own elevation on the ruins of public liberty.

Of all the dispositions and habits which lead to political prosperity, religion and morality are indispensable supports. In vain would that man claim the tribute of patriotism who should labor to subvert these great pillars of human happiness, these firmest props of the duties of men and citizens. The mere politician, equally with the pious man, ought to respect and to cherish them. A volume could not trace all their connections with private and public felicity. Let it simply be asked: Where is the security for property, for reputation, for life, if the sense of religious obligation desert the oaths which are the instruments of investigation in courts of justice? And let us with caution indulge the supposition that morality can be maintained without religion. Whatever may be conceded to the influence of refined education on minds of peculiar structure, reason and experience both forbid us to expect that national morality can prevail in exclusion of religious principle.

'Tis substantially true that virtue or morality is a necessary spring of popular government. The rule indeed extends with more or less force to every species of free government. Who that is a sincere friend to it can look with indifference upon attempts to shake the foundation of the fabric? Promote, then, as an object of primary importance, institutions for the general diffusion of knowledge. In proportion as the structure of a government gives force to public opinion, it is essential that public opinion should be enlightened.

Observe good faith and justice toward all nations. Cultivate peace and harmony with all. Religion and morality enjoin this conduct; and can it be that good policy does not equally enjoin it? It will be worthy of a free, enlightened, and at no distant period, a great nation, to give to mankind the magnanimous and too novel example of a people always guided by an exalted justice and benevolence. Who can doubt that in the course of time and things the fruits of such a plan would richly repay any temporary advantages which might be lost by a steady adherence to it? Can it be that Providence has not connected the permanent felicity of a nation with its virtues? The experiment, at least, is recommended by every sentiment which ennobles human nature. Alas! is it rendered impossible by its vices?

magnanimous: generous
exalted: high, revered
benevolence: goodwill

adherence: sticking

In the execution of such a plan nothing is more essential than that permanent, inveterate antipathies against particular nations and passionate attachments for others should be excluded, and that in place of them just and amicable feelings toward all should be cultivated.

inveterate: deep-rooted, long established
antipathies: dislikes
amicable: friendly
intercourse: communication

Harmony, liberal intercourse with all nations are recommended by policy, humanity, and interest. But even our commercial policy should hold an equal and impartial hand, neither seeking nor granting exclusive favors or preferences. There can be no greater error than to expect or calculate upon real favors from nation to nation. 'Tis an illusion which experience must cure, which a just pride ought to discard.

In offering to you, my countrymen, these counsels of an old and affectionate friend, I dare not hope they will make the strong and lasting impression I could wish, that they will control the usual current of the passions or prevent our nation from running the course which has hitherto marked the destiny of nations. But if I may even flatter myself that they may be productive of some partial benefit, some occasional good—that they may now and then recur to moderate the fury of party spirit, to warn against the mischiefs of foreign intrigue, to guard against the impostures of pretended patriotism—this hope will be a full recompense for the solicitude for your welfare by which they have been dictated. . . .

counsels: words of advice

recur: be remembered

impostures: acts of deceit
recompense: payment

27. From Thomas Jefferson, *First Inaugural Address* (1801)

For more information see
Chapter 10, Book 4, *The New Nation.*

Thomas Jefferson was a strong defender of political, religious, and intellectual freedom. He took the motto on his family crest as his inspiration: "Resistance to tyrants is obedience to God." Having served the new United States as Secretary of State under President Washington and Vice President under John Adams, he was elected President in 1800. His inaugural address is a classic statement of democratic principles. The election of 1800 was the first transfer of political power from one party (the Federalists) to another (the Republicans). Jefferson's first concern was to ease Federalist fears that he would overturn all of their accomplishments of the preceding twelve years. "We are all Republicans," he insisted, "we are all Federalists."

Echoing George Washington's *Farewell Address,* Jefferson asked his listeners to set aside political differences and remember that "ever difference of opinion is not a difference of principle." Only a proper respect for the principle of majority rule and minority rights would allow the new nation to thrive. In the remainder of his address he laid out the principles that would guide his Presidency: a limited national government; respect for state's rights; and encouragement of agriculture. He committed his administration to repealing oppressive taxes, slashing government expenses, cutting military expenditures, and paying off the public debt.

presentiments: feelings about what will take place in the future

traversing: crossing

transcendent objects: supreme, almost unreachable ideals
auspices: omens, signs

zeal: devotion
sovereign: independent

Called upon to undertake the duties of the first executive office of our country, I avail myself of the presence of that portion of my fellow-citizens which is here assembled to express my grateful thanks for the favor with which they have been pleased to look toward me, to declare a sincere consciousness that the task is above my talents, and that I approach it with those anxious and awful presentiments which the greatness of the charge and the weakness of my powers so justly inspire. A rising nation, spread over a wide and fruitful land, traversing all the seas with the rich productions of their industry, engaged in commerce with nations who feel power and forget right, advancing rapidly to destinies beyond the reach of mortal eyes— when I contemplate these transcendent objects, and see the honor, the happiness, and the hopes of this beloved country committed to the issue and the auspices of this day, I shrink from the contemplation, and humble myself before the magnitude of the undertaking. Utterly, indeed, should I despair did not the presence of many whom I here see remind me that in the other high authorities provided by our Constitution I shall find resources of wisdom, of virtue, and of zeal on which to rely under all difficulties. To you, then, gentlemen, who are charged with the sovereign functions of legislation, and to those associated with you, I look with encouragement for that guidance and support which may enable us to steer with safety the vessel in which we are all embarked amidst the conflicting elements of a troubled world.

During the contest of opinion through which we have passed the animation of discussions and of exertions has sometimes worn an aspect which might impose on strangers unused to think freely and to speak and to write what they think; but this being now decided by the voice of the nation, announced according to the rules of the Constitution, all will, of course, arrange themselves under the will of the law, and unite in common efforts for the common good. All, too, will bear in mind this sacred principle, that though the will of the majority is in all cases to prevail, that will to be rightful must be reasonable; that the minority possess their equal rights, which equal law must protect, and to violate would be oppression. Let us, then, fellow-citizens, unite with one heart and one mind. Let us restore to social intercourse that harmony and affection without which liberty and even life itself are but dreary things. And let us reflect that, having banished from our land that religious intolerance under which mankind so long bled and suffered, we have yet gained little if we countenance a political intolerance as despotic, as wicked, and capable of as bitter and bloody persecutions. During the throes and convulsions of the ancient world, during the agonizing spasms of infuriated man, seeking through blood and slaughter his long-lost liberty, it was not wonderful that the agitation of the billows should reach even this distant and peaceful shore; that this should be more felt and feared by some and less by others, and should divide opinions as to measures of safety. But every difference of opinion is not a difference of principle. We have called by different names brethren of the same principle. We are all Republicans, we are all Federalists. If there be any among us who would wish to dissolve this Union or to change its republican form, let them stand undisturbed as monuments of the safety with which error of opinion may be tolerated where reason is left free to combat it. I know, indeed, that some honest men fear that a republican government can not be strong, that this Government is not strong enough; but would the honest patriot, in the full tide of successful experiment, abandon a government which has so far kept us free and firm on the theoretic and visionary fear that this Government, the world's best hope, may by possibility want energy to preserve itself? I trust not. I believe this, on the contrary, the strongest Government on earth. I believe it the only one where every man, at the call of the law, would fly to the standard of the law, and would meet invasions of the public order as his own personal concern. Sometimes it is said that man can not be trusted with

intercourse: communication

countenance: tolerate or approve
despotic: exercising unchecked power
throes: painful struggle or effort
convulsions: violent changes
billows: waves

brethren: brothers

theoretic: abstract
visionary: imaginary

exterminating: destructive
havoc: chaos
endure: put up with, survive
faculties: abilities
acquisitions: rewards, things
gained or won
benign: well intentioned

inculcating: bringing
temperance: moderate behavior
dispensations: gifts

frugal: economical

felicities: happinesses

compress: squeeze
compass: borders

bulwarks: defenses
antirepublican: opposed to
representative government

acquiescence: agreement or
cooperation
despotism: unchecked power

government of himself. Can he, then, be trusted with the government of others? Or have we found angels in the forms of kings to govern him? Let history answer this question.

Let us, then, with courage and confidence pursue our own Federal and Republican principles, our attachment to union and representative government. Kindly separated by nature and a wide ocean from the exterminating havoc of one quarter of the globe; too high-minded to endure the degradations of the others; possessing a chosen country, with room enough for our descendants to the thousandth and thousandth generation; entertaining a due sense of our own faculties, to the acquisitions of our own industry, to honor and confidence from our fellow-citizens, resulting not from birth, but from our actions and their sense of them; enlightened by a benign religion, professed, indeed, and practiced in various forms, yet all of them inculcating honesty, truth, temperance, gratitude, and the love of man; acknowledging and adoring an overruling Providence, which by all its dispensations proves that it delights in the happiness of man here and his greater happiness hereafter—with all these blessings, what more is necessary to make us a happy and prosperous people? Still one thing more, fellow-citizens—a wise and frugal Government, which shall restrain men from injuring one another, shall leave them otherwise free to regulate their own pursuits of industry and improvement, and shall not take from the mouth of labor the bread it has earned. This is the sum of good government, and this is necessary to close the circle of our felicities.

About to enter, fellow-citizens, on the exercise of duties which comprehend everything dear and valuable to you, it is proper you should understand what I deem the essential principles of our Government, and consequently those which ought to shape its Administration. I will compress them within the narrowest compass they will bear, stating the general principle, but not all its limitations. Equal and exact justice to all men, of whatever state or persuasion, religious or political; peace, commerce, and honest friendship with all nations, entangling alliances with none; the support of the State governments in all their rights, as the most competent administrations for our domestic concerns and the surest bulwarks against antirepublican tendencies; the preservation of the General Government in its whole constitutional vigor, as the sheet anchor of our peace at home and safety abroad; a jealous care of the right of election by the people—a mild and safe corrective of abuses which are lopped by the sword of revolution where peaceable remedies are unprovided; absolute acquiescence in the decisions of the majority, the vital principle of republics, from which is no appeal but to force, the vital principle and immediate parent of despotism; a well-disciplined militia, our best reliance in peace and for the first moments of war, till regulars may relieve them; the supremacy of the civil over the military authority; economy in the public expense, that labor may be lightly burthened; the honest payment of our debts and sacred preservation of the public faith; encouragement of agriculture, and of commerce as its handmaid; the diffusion of information and arraignment of all abuses at the bar of the public reason; freedom of religion; freedom of the press, and freedom of person under the protection of the habeas corpus, and trial by juries impartially selected. These principles form the bright constellation which has gone before us and guided our steps through an age of revolution and reformation. The wisdom of our sages and blood of our heroes have been devoted to their attainment. They should be the creed of our political faith, the text of civic instruction, the touchstone by which to try the services of those we trust; and should we wander from them in moments of error or of alarm, let us hasten to retrace our steps and to regain the road which alone leads to peace, liberty, and safety. . . .

diffusion: spread
arraignment: summons before a court to answer a charge
habeas corpus: the right of anyone who is arrested to be brought before a judge and to make the arresting officer show that there is good enough reason for the arrest

28. From Thomas Jefferson, *Letter to Danbury Baptist Association* (1802)

For more information see
Chapter 10, Book 4, *The New Nation.*

In 1802, an alliance of 26 Baptist churches sent a letter to Jefferson congratulating him on his election to the Presidency. In their letter, the Baptists also complained that Connecticut's government discriminated against religious minorities.

Jefferson used his response to voice his views on the proper relationship between religion and government. He wanted to explain why he, unlike earlier Presidents or governors, refused to designate days of public prayer, fasting, and thanksgiving. And he wanted to answer the Federalist charge that he was an enemy of religion because he opposed government support for churches. The President stated that religion is a matter lying solely between an individual and that person's God. In his view, the First Amendment absolutely prohibited the federal government from meddling in peoples' beliefs or from favoring a particular religious denomination.

In this letter, Jefferson called for a "wall of separation" between church and state. This phrase has profoundly influenced the way that 20th-century courts have understood the constitutional relationship between government and religion. It led the Supreme Court to restrict prayer in schools and regulate the display of religious symbols in public spaces.

solely: only

sovereign: highest

reciprocate: return
tender: offer

Believing with you that religion is a matter which lies solely between man and his God, that he owes account to none other for his faith or his worship, that the legislative powers of government reach actions only, and not opinions, I contemplate with sovereign reverence that act of the whole American people which declared that their legislature should "make no law respecting an establishment of religion, or prohibiting the free exercise thereof," thus building a wall of separation between Church and State. Adhering to this expression of the supreme will of the nation on behalf of the rights of conscience, I shall see with sincere satisfaction the progress of those sentiments which tend to restore to man all his natural rights, convinced he has no natural right in opposition to his social duties.

I reciprocate your kind prayers for the protection and blessing of the common Father and Creator of man, and tender you for yourselves and your religious association, assurance of my high respect and esteem.

For more information see
Chapter 9, Book 4, *The New Nation*.

29. From John Marshall, opinion in *Marbury* v. *Madison* (1803)

The case of *Marbury* v. *Madison* established the Supreme Court's authority to declare laws passed by Congress unconstitutional. By making the Court the ultimate judge of the Constitution, this decision helped transform the judiciary from the weakest branch of government into an equal branch.

In 1801, President John Adams appointed William Marbury justice of the peace in the District of Columbia. But Adams's term ended before Marbury took office, and James Madison, the new Secretary of State, refused to give Marbury the appointment. Marbury appealed to the Supreme Court. He said that the Judiciary Act, passed by Congress, granted the Court the power to force the President to appoint him. The Supreme Court rejected this argument, ruling that the Judiciary Act passed by Congress was not within the rights spelled out by the Constitution.

In his opinion, Chief Justice John Marshall stated that the Constitution is the "paramount law" and that it is "emphatically the province and duty of the judicial department to say what the law is."

repugnant: offensive

The question whether an act repugnant to the constitution can become the law of the land, is a question deeply interesting to the

United States. . . . That the people have an original right to establish for their future government such principles as, in their opinion, shall most conduce to their own happiness, is the basis on which the whole American fabric has been erected. . . .

conduce: lead

This original and supreme will organizes the government, and assigns to different departments their respective powers. It may either stop here or establish limits not to be transcended by those departments.

The government of the United States is of the latter description. The powers of the legislature are defined and limited; and that those limits may not be mistaken or forgotten, the constitution is written. . . . The distinction between a government with limited and unlimited powers is abolished if those limits do not confine the persons on whom they are imposed and if acts prohibited and acts allowed are of equal obligation. It is a proposition too plain to be contested, that the constitution controls any legislative act repugnant to it; or, that the legislature may alter the constitution by an ordinary act. Between these alternatives there is no middle ground. . . .

Certainly all those who have framed written constitutions contemplate them as forming the fundamental and paramount law of the nation, and consequently the theory of every such government must be that an act of the legislature repugnant to the Constitution is void.

paramount: highest

void: invalid and without authority

This theory is essentially attached to a written constitution, and is consequently to be considered, by this court as one of the fundamental principles of our society. . . .

The Constitution is either a superior, paramount law, unchangeable by ordinary means, or it is on a level with ordinary legislative acts, and, like other acts, is alterable when the legislature shall please to alter it.

If the former part of the alternative be true, then a legislative act contrary to the Constitution is not law: if the latter part be true, then written Constitutions are absurd attempts, on the part of the people, to limit a power in its own nature illimitable. . . .

It is emphatically the province and duty of the judicial department to say what the law is. Those who apply the rule to particular cases, must of necessity expound and interpret that rule. If two laws conflict with each other, the courts must decide on the operation of each. . . .

expound: analyze

If, then, the courts are to regard the Constitution, and the Constitution is superior to any ordinary act of the legislature, the Constitution, and not such ordinary act, must govern the case to which they both apply. . . .

For more information see

Chapter 12, Book 4, *The New Nation.*

30. From Red Jacket (Sagoyewatha), *Address to the Chiefs of the Iroquois Confederacy and Missionary Cram* (1805)

Sagoyewatha was a leader of the Senecas, the largest of the six Indian tribes in the Iroquois Confederacy in New York State. Like most Iroquois, he was convinced that the colonists' westward expansion threatened Iroquois homelands. Sagoyewatha sided with the British during the American Revolution, and his nickname, Red Jacket, came from the scarlet coat that he wore while carrying British dispatches. After the war, the Iroquois lost much of their land in New York through a succession of treaties with the Americans. The Senecas were confined to a series of small reservations in New York, and many of them became Christians.

Sagoyewatha played a pivotal role in the outcome of the War of 1812. When war broke out between the United States and Britain, several Mohawks from Canada urged the Indians in western New York to take up arms against the Americans. Sagoyewatha argued for neutrality and the council of the Six Nations agreed. But Britain invaded land claimed by the Seneca Nation during the war, and the Seneca and Tuscarora Nations responded by declaring war against Britain. Sagoyewatha led a successful surprise attack on a British fort in the region. A brilliant orator, he urged his people to maintain their traditional religious beliefs and practices. At the peak of his influence in the mid-1820s, he succeeded in pushing Protestant missionaries off the Seneca reservations, but his influence declined after his wife and other family members converted to Christianity.

Brother, listen to what we say. There was a time when our forefathers owned this great island. Their seats extended from the rising to the setting sun. The [Creator] had made it for the use of Indians. He had created the buffalo, the deer, and other animals for food. He made the bear and the beaver, and their skins served us for clothing. He had scattered them over the country, and taught us how to take them. He had caused the earth to produce corn for bread. All this he had done for his red children because he loved them. . . . But an evil day came upon us. Your forefathers crossed the great waters, and landed on this island. Their numbers were small. They found friends and not enemies. They told us they had fled from their own country for fear of wicked men, and come here to enjoy their religion. They asked for a small seat. We took pity on them, granted their request, and they sat down amongst us. We gave them corn and meat. They gave us poison in return. The white people had now found our country. Tidings were carried back, and more came amongst us. Yet we did not fear them. We took them to be friends.

They called us brothers. We believed them, and gave them a larger seat. At length their numbers had greatly increased. They wanted more land. They wanted our country.

Our eyes were opened, and our minds became uneasy. Wars took place. Indians were hired to fight against Indians, and many of our people were destroyed. They also brought strong liquors among us. It was strong and powerful, and has slain thousands.

Brother!—our seats were once large, and yours were very small. You have now become a great people, and we have scarcely a place left to spread our blankets. You have got our country, but are not satisfied. You want to force your religion upon us. . . . The [Creator] has made us all. But he has made a great difference between his white and red children. He has given us a different complexion and different customs. . . . Since he has made so great a difference between us in other things, why may we not conclude that he has given us a different religion according to our understanding? The [Creator] does right. He knows what is best for his children. We are satisfied. Brother!—We do not wish to destroy your religion, or take it from you. We only want to enjoy our own.

31. From Meriwether Lewis, *Report to Thomas Jefferson* (1806)

For more information see Chapter 11, Book 4, *The New Nation.*

The Lewis and Clark expedition may well have been the greatest feat of exploration in history. The voyage of *Apollo 11*, which carried astronauts to the moon's surface and back, lasted only about a week. The expedition led by Meriwether Lewis and William Clark lasted two years and five months. Their epic 8,500-mile journey took them from St. Louis across the Great Plains and the Rocky Mountains to the Pacific Ocean. Malaria, dysentery, and grizzly bears plagued the travelers. By the trek's end, they had classified 178 new plants and 122 new species and subspecies of animals (including the antelope, the coyote, the prairie dog, and the snow goose).

President Thomas Jefferson was the driving force behind the expedition. Fearful that Britain would lay claim to the Pacific Northwest, Jefferson chose Lewis, his personal secretary, to explore the newly acquired Louisiana Territory and establish U.S. claims to the Far Northwest. It was more than a year and a half into the trip before Lewis sent back his first report, in the form of this letter to Jefferson. The President allowed the report to circulate publicly, which sharpened many Americans' desire to explore and expand the West. It also marked the beginning of an era of wrenching changes for the Indians of the Plains and the Pacific Northwest.

The expedition was truly multiethnic. The party included American soldiers, French Canadian boatmen and trappers, the legendary Shoshone guide and translator Sacagawea and her infant son, and Clark's African-American slave, York. Lewis and Clark depended heavily on Native Americans—Sioux, Mandans, Nez Perce, and others—for information, food, and guidance.

affirm: declare

It is with pleasure that I announce to you the safe arrival of myself and party at 12 o'clock today at this place with our papers and baggage. In obedience to your orders we have penetrated the continent of North America to the Pacific Ocean, and sufficiently explored the interior of the country to affirm with confidence that we have discovered the most practicable route which does exist across the continent by means of the navigable branches of the Missouri and Columbia Rivers. . . .

We view this passage across the continent as affording immense advantages to the fur trade, but fear that the advantages which it offers as a communication for the productions of the East Indies to the United States and thence to Europe will never be found equal on an extensive scale to that by way of the Cape of Good Hope; still we believe that many articles not bulky, brittle nor of a very perishable nature may be conveyed to the United States by this route with more facility and at less expense than by that at present practiced.

The Missouri and all its branches from the Cheyenne upwards abound more in beaver and common otter, than any other streams on earth, particularly that proportion of them lying within the Rocky Mountains. The furs of all this immense tract of country including such as may be collected on the upper portion of the River St. Peters, Red River, and the Assinniboin with the immense country watered by the Columbia, may be conveyed to the mouth of the Columbia by the 1st of August in each year and from thence be shipped to, and arrive in Canton [China] earlier than the furs at present shipped from Montreal annually arrive in London. The British N. West Company of Canada were they permitted by the United States might also convey their furs collected in the Athabaske, on the Saskashawan, and south and west of Lake Winnipic by that route within the period before

tract: area

conveyed: transported

mentioned. The productions of nine-tenths of the most valuable fur country of America could be conveyed by the route proposed to the East Indies.

In the infancy of the trade across the continent, or during the period that the trading establishments shall be confined to the Missouri and its branches, the men employed in this trade will be compelled to convey the furs collected in that quarter as low on the Columbia as tide water [near the ocean], in which case they could not return to the falls of the Missouri until about the 1st of October, which would be so late in the season that there would be considerable danger of the river being obstructed by ice before they could reach this place and consequently that the commodities brought from the East Indies would be detained until the following spring; but this difficulty will at once vanish when establishments are also made on the Columbia, and a sufficient number of men employed at them to convey annually the productions of the East Indies to the upper establishment on the Kooskooske, and there exchange them with the men of the Missouri for their furs in the beginning of July. By this means the furs not only of the Missouri but those also of the Columbia may be shipped to the East Indies by the season before mentioned, and the commodities of the East Indies arrive at St. Louis or the mouth of the Ohio by the last of September in each year.

Although the Columbia does not as much as the Missouri abound in beaver and otter, yet it is by no means despicable in this respect, and would furnish a valuable fur trade distinct from any other consideration in addition to the otter and beaver which it could furnish. There might be collected considerable quantities of the skins of three species of bear affording a great variety of colours and of superior delicacy, those also of the tiger cat, several species of fox, martin and several others of an inferior class of furs, besides the valuable sea otter of the coast.

If the government will only aid, even in a very limited manner, the enterprise of her citizens I am fully convinced that we shall shortly derive the benefits of a most lucrative trade from this source, and that in the course of ten or twelve years a tour across the continent by the route mentioned will be undertaken by individuals with as little concern as a voyage across the Atlantic is at present. . . .

I have brought with me several skins of the sea otter, two skins of the native sheep of America, five skins and skeletons complete of the Bighorn or mountain ram, and a skin of the mule deer besides the skins of several other quadrapeds and birds native of the countries through which we have passed. I have also preserved a pretty extensive collection of plants, and collected nine other vocabularies [of Indian tribes].

compelled: forced

commodities: supplies or goods

abound in: have an abundance of
despicable: unworthy of respect

martin [marten]: a small, weasel-like mammal

lucrative: financially rewarding

quadrapeds: four-legged animals

I have prevailed on the great chief of the Mandan nation to accompany me to Washington; he is now with my friend and colleague Capt. Clark at this place, in good health and spirits, and very anxious to proceed. . . .

The route by which I purpose traveling from hence to Washington is by way of Cahokia, Vincennes, Louisville, Ky., the Crab Orchard, Abington, Fincastle, Stanton and Charlottesville. Any letters directed to me at Louisville ten days after the receipt of this will most probably meet me at that place. I am very anxious to learn the state of my friends in Albermarle, particularly whether my mother is yet living. I am with every sentiment of esteem your Obt. and very Humble servant.

For more information see
Chapters 9 and 18, Book 4, *The New Nation.*

32. From John Marshall, opinion in *McCulloch* v. *Maryland* (1819)

In the case of *McCullough* v. *Maryland,* the state of Maryland questioned Congress's right to create the Second Bank of the United States, and it imposed a heavy tax on the Bank's Baltimore branch. James McCulloch, a cashier for the bank, refused to pay the tax, and the case went to the Supreme Court.

In his opinion, Chief Justice John Marshall had to answer two questions. The first was whether Congress had the power to create a national bank, even though the Constitution did not specifically grant this authority. The Court's answer was "yes," since the Constitution gave Congress the power "to make all laws which shall be necessary" to carry out its functions, in this case its financial functions. The second question was whether a state could tax the national bank. The court's answer was "no," because the states could not tax any federal agency. In the Chief Justice's words, the American people "did not design to make their government dependent on the states."

In other words, the Supreme Court ruled that Congress has more powers than the ones specifically stated in the Constitution. The court also established the principle of national supremacy, that the U.S. Constitution and federal laws are superior to state laws and powers.

The government proceeds directly from the people; is "ordained and established," in the name of the people; and is declared to be ordained, "in order to form a more perfect union, establish justice, insure domestic tranquillity, and secure the blessings of liberty to themselves and to their posterity." The assent of the states, in their sovereign capacity, is implied, in calling a convention, and thus submitting that instrument to the people. But the people were at perfect liberty to accept or reject it; and their act was final. It required not the affirmance, and could not be negatived, by the state governments. The constitution, when thus adopted, was of complete obligation, and bound the state sovereignties.

sovereign: independent

affirmance: approval
negatived: voted down

It has been said, that the people had already surrendered all their powers to the state sovereignties, and had nothing more to give. But, surely, the question whether they may resume and modify the powers granted to government, does not remain to be settled in this country. Much more might the legitimacy of the general government be doubted, had it been created by the states. The powers delegated to the state sovereignties were to be exercised by themselves, not by a distinct and independent sovereignty, created by themselves. To the formation of a league, such as was the confederation, the state sovereignties were certainly competent. But when, "in order to form a more perfect union," it was deemed necessary to change this alliance into an effective government, possessing great and sovereign powers, and acting directly on the people, the necessity of referring it to the people, and of deriving its powers directly from them, was felt and acknowledged by all. The government of the Union, then (whatever may be the influence of this fact on the case), is, emphatically and truly, a government of the people. In form, and in substance, it emanates from them. Its powers are granted by them, and are to be exercised directly on them, and for their benefit. . . .

resume: take over
modify: change
legitimacy: lawfulness
delegated: given

emphatically: with great conviction
emanates: shines or radiates

assent: agreement

If any one proposition could command the universal assent of mankind, we might expect it would be this—that the government of the Union, though limited in its powers, is supreme within its sphere of action. This would seem to result, necessarily, from its nature. It is the government of all; its powers are delegated by all; it represents all, and acts for all. Though any one state may be willing to control its operations, no state is willing to allow others to control them. The nation, on those subjects on which it can act, must necessarily bind its component parts. But this question is not left to mere reason: the people have, in express terms, decided it . . . "this constitution, and the laws of the United States, which shall be made in pursuance thereof, shall be the supreme law of the land," and by requiring that the members of the state legislatures, and the officers of the executive and judicial departments of the states, shall take the fidelity: faithfulness

oath of fidelity to it. The government of the United States, then, though limited in its powers, is supreme; and its laws, when made in pursuance of the constitution, form the supreme law of the land, "anything in the constitution or laws of any state to the contrary notwithstanding."

For more information see

Chapters 16, Book 5, *Liberty for All?*

33. James Monroe, *The Monroe Doctrine* (1823)

The Monroe Doctrine declared that the United States opposed the establishment of new European colonies and nondemocratic governments in the Western Hemisphere. President James Monroe proclaimed this principle in 1823, at a time when the United States was concerned about Russian and European activity in the Americas. British leaders suggested that the United States and Britain issue a joint statement against European intervention in Latin America, but Secretary of State John Quincy Adams recommended that President Monroe issue a unilateral statement. The President did. President Monroe announced that the United States would not interfere in European affairs and regarded the Western Hemisphere closed to future European colonization. He pledged that the United States would regard any European attempt "to extend their system to any portion of this hemisphere as dangerous to our peace and safety."

During the early 20th century, the Monroe Doctrine was often used to justify American intervention in Central America and the Caribbean. During the Cold War, it was used to justify U.S. support for anti-Communist governments in Latin America and opposition to unfriendly governments in Cuba, Guatemala, Nicaragua, and elsewhere.

amicable: friendly

acceded: agreed

At the proposal of the Russian imperial government, made through the minister of the Emperor residing here, full power and instructions have been transmitted to the Minister of the United States at St. Petersburg, to arrange, by amicable negotiation, the respective rights and interests of the two nations on the northwest coast of this continent. A similar proposal has been made by his Imperial Majesty to the government of Great Britain, which has likewise been acceded to. The government of the United States has been desirous, by this friendly proceeding, of manifesting the great value which they have invariably attached to the friendship of the emperor, and their solicitude to cultivate the best understanding with his government. In the discussions to which this interest has given rise, and in the arrangements by which they may terminate, the occasion has been judged proper for asserting, as a principle in which the rights and interests of the United States are involved, that the American continents, by the free and independent condition which they have assumed and maintain, are henceforth not to be considered as subjects for future colonization by any European powers.

manifesting: demonstrating
solicitude: care
cultivate: grow

It was stated at the commencement of the last session, that a great effort was then making in Spain and Portugal, to improve the condition of the people of those countries; and that it appeared to be conducted with extraordinary moderation. It need scarcely be remarked, that the result has been, so far, very different from what was then anticipated. Of events in that quarter of the globe, with which we have so much intercourse, and from which we derive our origin, we have always been anxious and interested spectators. The citizens of the United States cherish sentiments the most friendly, in favor of the liberty and happiness of their fellow men on that side of the Atlantic. In the wars of the European powers, in matters relating to themselves, we have never taken any part, nor does it comport with our policy so to do. It is only when our rights are invaded, or seriously menaced, that we resent injuries, or make preparation for our defense. With the movements in this hemisphere, we are, of necessity, more immediately connected, and by causes which must be obvious to all enlightened and impartial observers. The political system of the allied powers is essentially different, in this respect, from that of America. This difference proceeds from that which exists in their respective governments. And to the defence of our own, which has been achieved by the loss of so much blood and treasure, and matured by the wisdom of their most enlightened citizens, and under which we have enjoyed unexampled felicity, this whole nation is devoted. We owe it, therefore, to candor, and to the amicable relations existing between the United States and those powers, to declare, that we should consider any attempt on their part to extend their system to any portion of this hemisphere, as dangerous to our peace and safety. With the existing colonies or dependencies of any European power, we have not interfered, and shall not interfere. But, with the governments who have declared their independence and maintained it, and whose independence we have, on great consideration, and on just principles, acknowledged, we could not view any interposition for the purpose of oppressing

colonization: made subservient to a foreign or distant land
commencement: beginning

derive: gain

comport: agree

hemisphere: half of the globe

impartial: not favoring one side or another

felicity: happiness
candor: honesty

interposition: getting involved with the affairs of another
oppressing: holding down or back

manifestation: sign
disposition: attitude
neutrality: lack of special
favorites
adhered: stuck
competent: appropriate

adduced: shown

interposed: interfered

agitated: stirred up

de facto: in reality, but not by law

eminently: importantly
conspicuously: clearly

subdue: beat

them, or controlling, in any other manner, their destiny, by any European power, in any other light than as the manifestation of an unfriendly disposition towards the United States. In the war between these new governments and Spain, we declared our neutrality at the time of their recognition, and to this we have adhered, and shall continue to adhere, provided no change shall occur, which, in the judgment of the competent authorities of this government, shall make a corresponding change, on the part of the United States, indispensable to their security.

The late events in Spain and Portugal, shew that Europe is still unsettled. Of this important fact, no stronger proof can be adduced than that the allied powers should have thought it proper, on any principle satisfactory to themselves, to have interposed, by force, in the internal concerns of Spain. To what extent such interposition may be carried, on the same principle, is a question, in which all independent powers, whose governments differ from theirs, are interested; even those most remote, and surely none more so than the United States. Our policy, in regard to Europe, which was adopted at an early stage of the wars which have so long agitated that quarter of the globe, nevertheless remains the same, which is, not to interfere in the internal concerns of any of its powers; to consider the government de facto as the legitimate government for us; to cultivate friendly relations with it, and to preserve those relations by a frank, firm, and manly policy, meeting, in all instances, the just claims of every power; submitting to injuries from none. But, in regard to those continents, circumstances are eminently and conspicuously different.

It is impossible that the allied powers should extend their political system to any portion of either continent, without endangering our peace and happiness; nor can any one believe that our Southern Brethren, if left to themselves, would adopt it of their own accord. It is equally impossible, therefore, that we should behold such interposition, in any form, with indifference. If we look to the comparative strength and resources of Spain and those new governments, and their distance from each other, it must be obvious that she can never subdue them. It is still the true policy of the United States, to leave the parties to themselves, in the hope that other powers will pursue the same course.

34. From *Memorial of the Cherokee Nation* (1830)

For more information see
**Chapters 23 and 24, Book 4,
The New Nation.

As late as the 1820s, the Creeks, Choctaws, Chickasaws, and Cherokees occupied much of the land that would become the South's Cotton Kingdom. After Andrew Jackson became President, Congress adopted the Indian Removal Act of 1830, providing funds to acquire tribal lands and relocate the tribes living there to Oklahoma and Arkansas. By 1840, almost all of these tribes had been moved west of the Mississippi River.

The Cherokees had little interest in moving west. In 1791, they had signed a treaty that recognized Cherokee territory in Georgia as independent. An 1832 Supreme Court decision, *Worcester* v. *Georgia*, ruled that "The Cherokee Nation is a distinct community occupying its own territory in which the laws of Georgia have no right to enter without the consent of the Cherokees." In 1835, however, President Jackson persuaded a minority of Cherokees to sign a treaty giving up their homelands in western Georgia for new Western lands. The tribe's leaders submitted the following *Memorial and Protest of the Cherokee Nation* to Congress in 1836. It showed that President Jackson had obtained the 1835 treaty by fraud. Nevertheless, the army evicted the Cherokees from their land in 1838. Thousands of Cherokees died from malnutrition, disease, and physical hardship as they followed the "Trail of Tears" westward.

We are aware that some persons suppose it will be for our advantage to remove beyond the Mississippi. We think otherwise. Our people universally think otherwise. Thinking that it would be fatal to their interests, they have almost to a man sent their memorial to Congress, deprecating the necessity of a removal. . . . It is incredible that Georgia should ever have enacted the oppressive laws to which reference is here made, unless she had supposed that something extremely terrific in its character was necessary in order to make the Cherokees willing to remove. We are not willing to remove; and if we could be brought to this extremity, it would be not by argument, nor because our judgment was satisfied, not because our condition will be improved; but only because we cannot endure to be deprived of our national and individual rights and subjected to a process of intolerable oppression.

We wish to remain on the land of our fathers. We have a perfect and original right to remain without interruption or molestation. The treaties with us, and laws of the United States made in pursuance of

deprecating: protesting against
oppressive: unjust in the application of power

prepossessions: preliminary opinions

agriculturalists: farmers

treaties, guaranty our residence and our privileges, and secure us against intruders. Our only request is, that these treaties may be fulfilled, and these laws executed.

But if we are compelled to leave our country, we see nothing but ruin before us. The country west of the Arkansas territory is unknown to us. From what we can learn of it, we have no prepossessions in its favor. All the inviting parts of it, as we believe, are preoccupied by various Indian nations, to which it has been assigned. They would regard us as intruders. . . . The far greater part of that region is, beyond all controversy, badly supplied with wood and water; and no Indian tribe can live as agriculturists without these articles. All our neighbors . . . would speak a language totally different from ours, and practice different customs. The original possessors of that region are now wandering savages lurking for prey in the neighborhood. . . . Were the country to which we are urged much better than it is represented to be, . . . still it is not the land of our birth, nor of our affections. It contains neither the scenes of our childhood, nor the graves of our fathers. . . .

We have been called a poor, ignorant, and degraded people. We certainly are not rich; nor have we ever boasted of our knowledge, or our moral or intellectual elevation. But there is not a man within our limits so ignorant as not to know that he has a right to live on the land of his fathers, in the possession of his immemorial privileges, and that this right has been acknowledged by the United States; nor is there a man so degraded as not to feel a keen sense of injury, on being deprived of his right and driven into exile. . . .

For more information see
Book 5, *Liberty for All?* and Book 6, *War, Terrible War.*

35. From William Lloyd Garrison, *The Liberator,* vol. 1, no. 1 (1831)

William Lloyd Garrison was the nation's most hated opponent of slavery. When he called for the immediate freedom of slaves without compensation to their owners, he was denounced in Congress and nearly lynched by a Boston mob. The Georgia legislature offered $5,000 to anyone who would bring him to the state to stand trial. Garrison was one of the first whites to denounce the popular idea of colonization, the gradual emancipation of slaves and their resettlement in Africa. He regarded it as an impractical and immoral solution to the problem of slavery. Garrison's opposition to slavery was based on his religious conviction that slavery was a vile sin. He believed that African Americans—free and slave—had the same natural rights as whites and were "entitled to all the privileges of American citizenship." Only by immediately freeing their slaves could slaveholders cleanse themselves of sin.

Garrison voiced his opinions in *The Liberator,* a newspaper that he founded on January 1, 1831. It was mainly supported by free blacks. On the first page of the first issue he thundered: "I am in earnest . . . I will not retreat a single inch—AND I WILL BE HEARD." As an editor, Garrison supported many radical causes including racial equality, women's rights, and "non-resistance," a movement that condemned war and any institution that depended on the threat of violence, including prisons.

In the month of August, I issued proposals for publishing *The Liberator* in Washington city; but the enterprise, though hailed in different sections of the country, was palsied by public indifference. Since that time, the removal of the *Genius of Universal Emancipation* to the Seat of Government has rendered less imperious the establishment of a similar periodical in that quarter.

indifference: lack of caring

periodical: magazine or newsletter

During my recent tour for the purpose of exciting the minds of the people by a series of discourses on the subject of slavery, every place that I visited gave fresh evidence of the fact, that a greater revolution in public sentiment was to be effected in the free states—*and particularly in New-England*—than at the south. I found contempt more bitter, opposition more active, detraction more relentless, prejudice more stubborn, and apathy more frozen, than among the slave owners themselves. Of course, there were individual exceptions to the contrary. This state of things afflicted, but did not dishearten me. I determined, at every hazard, to lift up the standard of emancipation in the eyes of the nation, *within sight of Bunker Hill and in the birth place of liberty*. That standard is now unfurled; and long may it float, unhurt by the spoliations of time or the missiles of a desperate foe—yea, till every chain be broken, and every bondman set free! Let southern oppressors tremble—let their secret abettors tremble—let their northern apologists tremble—let all the enemies of the persecuted blacks tremble.

contempt: harsh lack of respect
detraction: judging others negatively

afflicted: pained

spoliations: vandalism
bondman: slave
abettors: helpers
apologists: supporters

I deem the publication of my original Prospectus unnecessary, as it has obtained a wide circulation. The principles therein inculcated will be steadily pursued in this paper, excepting that I shall not array myself as the political partisan of any man. In defending the great cause of human rights, I wish to derive the assistance of all religions and of all parties.

Prospectus: proposal
inculcated: forced upon, taught or impressed
partisan: supporter
derive: get

Assenting to the "self-evident truth" maintained in the American Declaration of Independence, "that all men are created equal, and

strenuously: with great effort and energy
enfranchisement: voting rights
pernicious: very harmful

unequivocal: absolute
recantation: disavowal of earlier statement
brethren: brothers

ravisher: a man who forces himself physically on women
extricate: get out
equivocate: send mixed messages
apathy: lack of interest or commitment
retarding: slowing
coarseness: lack of delicacy
invective: angry words
precipitancy: rushed nature
measures: actions
perniciously: destructively
beneficially: for the good
posterity: future generations

endowed by their Creator with certain inalienable rights—among which are life, liberty and the pursuit of happiness," I shall strenuously contend for the immediate enfranchisement of our slave population. In Park-street Church, on the Fourth of July, 1829, in an address on slavery, I unreflectingly assented to the popular but pernicious doctrine of *gradual* abolition. I seize this opportunity to make a full and unequivocal recantation, and thus publicly to ask pardon of my God, of my country, and of my brethren the poor slaves, for having uttered a sentiment so full of timidity, injustice and absurdity. A similar recantation, from my pen, was published in the *Genius of Universal Emancipation* at Baltimore, at Baltimore, in September, 1829. My conscience is now satisfied.

I am aware that many object to the severity of my language; but is there not cause for severity? I *will be* as harsh as truth, and as uncompromising as justice. On this subject, I do not wish to think, or speak, or write, with moderation. No! no! Tell a man whose house is on fire, to give a moderate alarm; tell him to moderately rescue his wife from the hands of the ravisher; tell the mother to gradually extricate her babe from the fire into which it has fallen;—but urge me not to use moderation in a cause like the present. I am in earnest—I will not equivocate—I will not excuse—I will not retreat a single inch— AND I WILL BE HEARD. The apathy of the people is enough to make every statue leap from its pedestal, and to hasten the resurrection of the dead.

It is pretended, that I am retarding the cause of emancipation, by the coarseness of my invective, and the precipitancy of my measures. *The charge is not true.* On this question my influence,—humble as it is,—is felt at this moment to a considerable extent, and shall be felt in coming years—not perniciously, but beneficially—not as a curse, but as a blessing; and posterity will bear testimony that I was right. I desire to thank God, that he enables me to disregard "the fear of man which bringeth a snare," and to speak his truth in its simplicity and power. . . .

36. From *A North Carolina Law Forbidding the Teaching of Slaves to Read and Write* (1831)

This North Carolina law of 1831 made it a crime to teach slaves to read and write. Most other states in the pre-Civil War South had similar laws. The law was designed to keep blacks ignorant and unable to live outside of slavery. The fugitive slave and abolitionist Frederick Douglass believed that these laws were the greatest evil of slavery. At an early age, he managed to teach himself to read. After the Civil War, many former slaves were convinced that true liberation depended on learning how to read and write. Tens of thousands of freed men and women and their children flocked to Freedmen's Schools across the South.

Whereas the teaching of slaves to read and write, has a tendency to excite dissatisfaction in their minds, and to produce insurrection and rebellion, to the manifest injury of the citizens of this State: Therefore, *Be it enacted by the General Assembly of the State of North Carolina, and it is hereby enacted by the authority of the same*, That any free person, who shall hereafter teach, or attempt to teach, any slave within the State to read or write, the use of figures excepted, or shall give or sell to such slave or slaves any books or pamphlets, shall be liable to indictment in any court of record in this State having jurisdiction thereof, and upon conviction, shall, at the discretion of the court, if a white man or woman, be fined not less than one hundred dollars, nor more than two hundred dollars, or imprisoned; and if a free person of color, shall be fined, imprisoned, or whipped, at the discretion of the court, not exceeding thirty nine lashes, nor less than twenty lashes.

Be it further enacted, That if any slave shall hereafter teach, or attempt to teach, any other slave to read or write, the use of figures excepted, he or she may be carried before any justice of the peace and on conviction thereof, shall be sentenced to receive thirty nine lashes on his or her bare back.

insurrection: rebellion
manifest: clear, apparent

liable to: likely to endure
indictment: accusation
jurisdiction: area over which an authority has power

37. From Andrew Jackson, *Proclamation to the People of South Carolina* (1832)

In 1828 and 1832, Congress passed laws raising tax rates on foreign manufactured goods. The tax hurt Southerners most because they imported more manufactured goods than the North did. In 1832, South Carolina declared the federal tax null and void within the state. It threatened to leave the Union if the federal government tried to collect the tax at the port of Charleston. President Jackson was outraged at this defiance of federal authority. He persuaded Congress to pass a "Force Bill" allowing him to use the military to collect the tax. "The laws of the United States must be executed," he proclaimed. "Disunion by armed force is treason."

For more information see
Chapters 33–34, Book 4, *The New Nation;* Chapter 31 in Book 5, *Liberty for All?;* and Preface I in Book 6, *War, Terrible War.*

The crisis was resolved by compromise. Congress adopted a new law that gradually reduced taxes on foreign manufactured goods. Since no other southern state joined South Carolina and refused to pay the tax, the state's leaders accepted the compromise. As a final gesture of defiance the South Carolina legislature nullified the "Force Bill," but President Jackson ignored this act.

reposed: placed

To preserve this bond of our political existence from destruction, to maintain inviolate this state of national honor and prosperity, and to justify the confidence my fellow-citizens have reposed in me. I, Andrew Jackson, President of the United States, have thought proper to issue this my proclamation, stating my views of the Constitution and laws applicable to the measures adopted by the convention of South Carolina and to the reasons they have put forth to sustain them, declaring the course which duty will require me to pursue, and, appealing to the understanding and patriotism of the people, warn them of the consequences that must inevitably result from an observance of the dictates of the convention. . . .

dictates: orders
indefeasible: cannot be defeated

The [South Carolina] ordinance is founded, not on the indefeasible right of resisting acts which are plainly unconstitutional and too oppressive to be endured, but on the strange position that any one State may not only declare an act of Congress void, but prohibit its execution; that they may do this consistently with the Constitution; that the true construction of that instrument permits a State to retain its place in the Union and yet be bound by no other of its laws than those it may choose to consider as constitutional. . . . Look for a moment to the consequence. If South Carolina considers the revenue laws unconstitutional and has a right to prevent their execution in the port of Charleston, there would be a clear constitutional objection to their collection in every other port; and no revenue could be collected anywhere, for all imposts must be equal. . . .

prohibit: make illegal

instrument: document; here, the Constitution

imposts: taxes

If this doctrine had been established at an earlier day, the Union would have been dissolved in its infancy. . . .

If the doctrine of a State veto upon the laws of the Union carries with it internal evidence of its impracticable absurdity, our constitutional history will also afford abundant proof that it would have been repudiated with indignation had it been proposed to form a feature in our Government.

absurdity: ridiculousness

repudiated: refused

fatal: deadly

Our present Constitution was formed . . . in vain if this fatal doctrine prevails. It was formed for important objects that are announced in the preamble, made in the name and by the authority of the people of the United States, whose delegates framed and whose conventions approved it. The most important among these objects—that which is placed first in rank, on which all the others rest—is "*to form a more perfect union.*" Now, is it possible that even if there were no express provision giving supremacy to the Constitution and laws of the United States over those of the States, can it be conceived that an instrument made for the purpose of "*forming a more perfect union*" than that of the Confederation could be so constructed by the assembled wisdom of our country as to substitute for that Confederation a form of government dependent for its existence on the local interest, the party spirit, of a State, or of a prevailing faction in a State? Every man of plain, unsophisticated understanding who hears the question will give such an answer as will preserve the Union. Metaphysical subtlety, in pursuit of an impracticable theory, could alone have devised one that is calculated to destroy it.

Metaphysical subtlety: thinking based on philosophy

I consider, then, the power to annul a law of the United States, assumed by one State, *incompatible with the existence of the Union, contradicted expressly by the letter of the Constitution, unauthorized by its spirit, inconsistent with every principle on which it was founded, and destructive of the great object for which it was formed.*

incompatible: unable to be joined with

After this general view of the leading principle, we must examine the particular application of it which is made in the ordinance.

The preamble rests its justification on these grounds: It assumes as a fact that the obnoxious laws, although they purport to be laws for raising revenue, were in reality intended for the protection of manufactures, which purpose it asserts to be unconstitutional; that the operation of these laws is unequal; that the amount raised by them is greater than is required by the wants of the Government; and, finally, that the proceeds are to be applied to objects unauthorized by the Constitution. These are the only causes alleged to justify an open opposition to the laws of the country and a threat of seceding from the Union if any attempt should be made to enforce them. The first virtually acknowledges that the law in question was passed under a power expressly given by the Constitution to lay and collect imposts; but its constitutionality is drawn in question from the *motives* of those who passed it. . . . Admit this doctrine, and you give to the States an uncontrolled right to decide, and every law may be annulled under this pretext. If, therefore, the absurd and dangerous doctrine should be admitted that a State may annul an unconstitutional law, or one that it deems such, it will not apply to the present case.

The next objection is that the laws in question operate unequally. This objection may be made with truth to every law that has been or can be passed. The wisdom of man never yet contrived a system of taxation that would operate with perfect equality. If the unequal

abrogated: denied all existence

sophistical construction: clever argument
animosities: hostilities

expositions: explanations
reasonings: arguments
seceding: withdrawing

Fallacious: false
prejudices: already formed judgments
radical: deep

contravention: opposition

solecism: something that is not normal or accepted

operation of a law makes it unconstitutional, and if all laws of that description may be abrogated by any State for that cause, then, indeed, is the Federal Constitution unworthy of the slightest effort for its preservation. . . . No; we have not erred. The Constitution is still the object of our reverence, the bond of our Union, our defense in danger, the source of our prosperity in peace. It shall descend, as we have received it, uncorrupted by sophistical construction, to our posterity; and the sacrifices of local interest, of State prejudices, of personal animosities, that were made to bring it into existence, will again be patriotically offered for its support.

Here is a law of the United States, not even pretended to be unconstitutional, repealed by the authority of a small majority of the voters of a single State. Here is a provision of the Constitution which is solemnly abrogated by the same authority.

On such expositions and reasonings the ordinance grounds not only an assertion of the right to annul the laws of which it complains, but to enforce it by a threat of seceding from the Union if any attempt is made to execute them.

This right to secede is deduced from the nature of the Constitution, which, they say, is a compact between sovereign States who have preserved their whole sovereignty and therefore are subject to no superior; that because they made the compact they can break it when in their opinion it has been departed from by the other States. Fallacious as this course of reasoning is, it enlists State pride and finds advocates in the honest prejudices of those who have not studied the nature of our Government sufficiently to see the radical error on which it rests. . . .

The Constitution of the United States, then, forms a *government*, not a league; and whether it be formed by compact between the States or in any other manner, its character is the same. It is a Government in which all the people are represented, which operates directly on the people individually, not upon the States; they retained all the power they did not grant. But each State, having expressly parted with so many powers as to constitute, jointly with the other States, a single nation, can not, from that period, possess any right to secede, because such secession does not break a league, but destroys the unity of a nation; and any injury to that unity is not only a breach which would result from the contravention of a compact, but it is an offense against the whole Union. To say that any State may at pleasure secede from the Union is to say that the United States are not a nation, because it would be a solecism to contend that any part of a nation might dissolve its connection with the other parts, to their injury or ruin, without committing any offense. Secession, like any other revolutionary act, may be morally justified by the extremity of oppression; but to call it a constitutional right is confounding the meaning of terms, and can only be done through gross error or to deceive those who are willing to assert a right, but would pause before they made a revolution or incur the penalties consequent on a failure.

confounding: confusing

Because the Union was formed by a compact, it is said the parties to that compact may, when they feel themselves aggrieved, depart from it; but it is precisely because it is a compact that they can not. A compact is an agreement or binding obligation. It may by its terms have a sanction or penalty for its breach, or it may not. If it contains no sanction, it may be broken with no other consequence than moral guilt; if it have a sanction, then the breach incurs the designated or implied penalty. A league between independent nations generally has no sanction other than a moral one; or if it should contain a penalty, as there is no common superior it can not be enforced. A government, on the contrary, always has a sanction, express or implied; and in our case it is both necessarily implied and expressly given. An attempt, by force of arms, to destroy a government is an offense, by whatever means the constitutional compact may have been formed; and such government has the right by the law of self-defense to pass acts for punishing the offender, unless that right is modified, restrained, or resumed by the constitutional act. In our system, although it is modified in the case of treason, yet authority is expressly given to pass all laws necessary to carry its powers into effect, and under this grant provision has been made for punishing acts which obstruct the due administration of the laws. . . .

aggrieved: treated wrongly

sanction: punishment

incur: bring onto oneself
league: agreement

modified: changed
restrained: held back
treason: crime against the state

The States severally have not retained their entire sovereignty. It has been shown that in becoming parts of a nation, not members of a league, they surrendered many of their essential parts of sovereignty. The right to make treaties, declare war, levy taxes, exercise exclusive judicial and legislative powers, were all of them functions of sovereign power. The States, then, for all these important purposes were no longer sovereign. . . .

exclusive: sole

sovereignty: right of self-rule

If your leaders could succeed in establishing a separation, what would be your situation? Are you united at home? Those who told you that you might peaceably prevent their execution deceived you; they could not have been deceived themselves. They know that a forcible opposition could alone prevent the execution of the laws, and they know that such opposition must be repelled. Their object is disunion. But be not deceived by names. Disunion by armed force is *treason*. Are you really ready to incur its guilt? If you are, on the heads of the instigators of the act be the dreadful consequences; on their heads be the dishonor, but on yours may fall the punishment. On your unhappy State will inevitably fall all the evils of the conflict

disunion: separation

accede: agree

For more information see

Pages 24 and 123, Book 5, *Liberty For All?*

you force upon the Government of your country. It can not accede to the mad project of disunion, of which you would be the first victims. . . .

38. From Alexis de Tocqueville, *Democracy in America* (1835)

Alexis de Tocqueville was a French noble who spent nine months in America in 1831 and 1832. Only 26 years old when he toured the United States, he became famous for writing a two-volume study of democracy in America, a perceptive analysis of how the forces of democracy, individualism, and equality had altered every aspect of American life. In America, Tocqueville observed, there was no hereditary noble class, and distinctions in speech, manners, and clothing were far less noticeable than in Europe. But he feared that the "tyranny of the majority" pressured people to act like each other.

Tocqueville's study examined the impact of democracy on social institutions such as family roles and religion. He observed that in the United States a father's authority was not as strong as in Europe and that women and children were far more independent. He also recognized that in America there were many competing churches and religious denominations, all completely separate from the government—unlike Europe, where most nations had a single government-supported church.

America is the only country in which it has been possible to witness the natural and tranquil growth of society, and where the influence exercised on the future condition of states by their origin is clearly distinguishable.

At the period when the peoples of Europe landed in the New World, their national characteristics were already completely formed; each of them had a physiognomy of its own; and as they had already attained that stage of civilization at which men are led to study themselves, they have transmitted to us a faithful picture of their opinions, their manners, and their laws. The men of the sixteenth century are almost as well known to us as our contemporaries. America, consequently, exhibits in the broad light of day the phenomena which the ignorance or rudeness of earlier ages conceals from our researches. The men of our day seem destined to see further than their predecessors into human events; they are close

physiognomy: physical makeup

enough to the founding of the American settlements to known in detail their elements, and far enough away from that time already to be able to judge what these beginnings have produced. Providence has given us a torch which our forefathers did not possess, and has allowed us to discern fundamental causes in the history of the world which the obscurity of the past concealed from them. If we carefully examine the social and political state of America, after having studied its history, we shall remain perfectly convinced that not an opinion, not a custom, not a law, I may even say not an event is upon record which the origin of that people will not explain. The readers of this book will find in the present chapter the germ of all that is to follow and the key to almost the whole work.

Providence: divine guidance

obscurity: mystery, darkness

The emigrants who came at different periods to occupy the territory now covered by the American Union differed from each other in many respects; their aim was not the same, and they governed themselves on different principles.

emigrants: people who left their original homes to live somewhere else

These men had, however, certain features in common, and they were all placed in an analogous situation. The tie of language is, perhaps, the strongest and the most durable that can unite mankind. All the emigrants spoke the same language; they were all children of the same people. Born in a country which had been agitated for centuries by the struggles of faction, and in which all parties had been obliged in their turn to place themselves under the protection of the laws, their political education had been perfected in this rude school; and they were more conversant with the notions of right and the principles of true freedom than the greater part of their European contemporaries. At the period of the first emigrations the township system, that fruitful germ of free institutions, was deeply rooted in the habits of the English; and with it the doctrine of the sovereignty of the people had been introduced into the very bosom of the monarchy of the house of Tudor.

analogous: similar

faction: division

sovereignty: right of self-rule
monarchy: rule of kings
house of Tudor: English dynasty on the throne in the 16th century
rife: everywhere
vehemence: excessive energy or force
sedate: quiet
austere: overly plain

The religious quarrels which have agitated the Christian world were then rife. England had plunged into the new order of things with headlong vehemence. The character of its inhabitants, which had always been sedate and reflective, became argumentative and austere. General information had been increased by intellectual contests, and the mind had received in them a deeper cultivation. While religion was the topic of discussion, the morals of the people became more pure. All these national features are more or less discoverable in the physiognomy of those Englishmen who came to seek a new home on the opposite shores of the Atlantic.

Another observation, moreover, to which we shall have occasion to return later, is applicable not only to the English, but to the French, the Spaniards, and all the Europeans who successively

territorial aristocracy: social organization in which landowners are the upper class

established themselves in the New World. All these European colonies contained the elements, if not the development, of a complete democracy. Two causes led to this result. It may be said that on leaving the mother country the emigrants had, in general, no notion of superiority one over another. The happy and the powerful do not go into exile, and there are no surer guarantees of equality among men than poverty and misfortune. It happened, however, on several occasions, that persons of rank were driven to America by political and religious quarrels. Laws were made to establish a gradation of ranks; but it was soon found that the soil of America was opposed to a territorial aristocracy. It was realized that in order to clear this land, nothing less than the constant and self-interested efforts of the owner himself was essential; the ground prepared, it became evident that its produce was not sufficient to enrich at the same time both an owner and a farmer. The land was then naturally broken up into small portions, which the proprietor cultivated for himself. Land is the basis of an aristocracy, which clings to the soil that supports it; for it is not by privileges alone, nor by birth, but by landed property handed down from generation to generation that an aristocracy is constituted. A nation may present immense fortunes and extreme wretchedness; but unless those fortunes are territorial, there is no true aristocracy, but simply the class of the rich and that of the poor.

orders: classes

All the British colonies had striking similarities at the time of their origin. All of them, from their beginning, seemed destined to witness the growth, not of the aristocratic liberty of their mother country, but of that freedom of the middle and lower orders of which the history of the world had as yet furnished no complete example. . . .

For more information see

Chapters 27 and 28, Book 5, *Liberty for All?*

39. From Ralph Waldo Emerson, *Self-Reliance* (1841)

Trained as a Unitarian minister, Ralph Waldo Emerson quit his job at the age of 29 to become an essayist, poet, and orator. Between 1833 and 1860, he delivered more than 1,500 lectures in 20 states. His first book, *Nature*, maintained that God's presence can be found in nature and can be best sensed through feelings rather than reason. In "Self-Reliance," one of his most famous essays, he called on readers to strive for true individuality in the face of intense social pressure for everyone to be the same. "Society everywhere is in conspiracy against the manhood of every one of its members," he wrote. "Who would be a man must be a nonconformist." Emerson's stress on the individual, his defense of individuality, and his belief that God can be found in the examination of nature would heavily influence later American philosophers.

Trust thyself: every heart vibrates to that iron string. Accept the place the divine providence has found for you, the society of your contemporaries, the connection of events. Great men have always done so, and confided themselves childlike to the genius of their age, betraying their perception that the absolutely trustworthy was seated at their heart, working through their hands, predominating in all their being. And we are now men, and must accept in the highest mind the same transcendent destiny; and not minors and invalids in a protected corner, not cowards fleeing before a revolution, but guides, redeemers, and benefactors, obeying the Almighty effort, and advancing on Chaos and the Dark. . . .

divine providence: God

transcendent: going beyond what seems to be a limit
redeemers: people who rescue or save
benefactors: people who help other people

These are the voices which we hear in solitude, but they grow faint and inaudible as we enter into the world. Society everywhere is in conspiracy against the manhood of every one of its members. Society is a joint-stock company, in which the members agree, for the better securing of his bread to each shareholder, to surrender the liberty and culture of the eater. The virtue in most request is conformity. Self-reliance is its Aversion. It loves not realities and creators, but names and customs.

joint-stock company: a company with shares held in common by the stockholders
culture: individual customs
Aversion: strong dislike

Whoso would be a man must be a nonconformist. He who would gather immortal palms must not be hindered by the name of goodness, but must explore if it be goodness. Nothing is at last sacred but the integrity of your own mind. Absolve you to yourself, and you shall have the suffrage of the world. . . .

nonconformist: someone who does not act in step with others
palms: palm leaves, a symbol of victory
integrity: wholeness
Absolve: forgive
suffrage: vote
divines: religious leaders

A foolish consistency is the hobgoblin of little minds, adored by little statesmen and philosophers and divines. With consistency a great soul has simply nothing to do. He may as well concern himself with his shadow on the wall. Speak what you think now in hard words, and to-morrow speak what to-morrow thinks in hard words again, though it contradict every thing you said to-day.—"Ah, so you shall be sure to be misunderstood."—Is it so bad, then, to be misunderstood? Pythagoras was misunderstood, and Socrates, and Jesus, and Luther, and Copernicus, and Galileo, and Newton, and every pure and wise spirit that ever took flesh. To be great is to be misunderstood. . . .

The magnetism which all original action exerts is explained when we inquire the reason of self-trust. Who is the Trustee? What is the aboriginal Self, on which a universal reliance may be grounded? What is the nature and power of that science-baffling star, without parallax,

aboriginal: native, undeveloped
parallax: a seeming change of direction

tuitions: lessons

impiety: act of faithlessness
atheism: lack of faith in a higher power
discern: notice

phraseology: vocabulary

physiological: physical
impertinence: rudeness
apologue: moral fable
parable: short, symbolic tale

reverted: turned back
laments: mourns, regrets

without calculable elements, which shoots a ray of beauty even into trivial and impure actions, if the least mark of independence appear? The inquiry leads us to that source, at once the essence of genius, of virtue, and of life, which we call Spontaneity or Instinct. We denote this primary wisdom as Intuition, whilst all later teachings are tuitions. In that deep force, the last fact behind which analysis cannot go, all things find their common origin. For, the sense of being which in calm hours rises, we know not how, in the soul, is not diverse from things, from space, from light, from time, from man, but one with them, and proceeds obviously from the same source whence their life and being also proceed. We first share the life by which things exist, and afterwards see them as appearances in nature, and forget that we have shared their cause. Here is the fountain of action and of thought. Here are the lungs of that inspiration which giveth man wisdom, and which cannot be denied without impiety and atheism. We lie in the lap of immense intelligence, which makes us receivers of its truth and organs of its activity. When we discern justice, when we discern truth, we do nothing of ourselves, but allow a passage to its beams. . . .

If, therefore, a man claims to know and speak of God, and carries you backward to the phraseology of some old mouldered nation in another country, in another world, believe him not. Is the acorn better than the oak which is its fulness and completion? Is the parent better than the child into whom he has cast his ripened being? Whence, then, this worship of the past? The centuries are conspirators against the sanity and authority of the soul. Time and space are but physiological colors which the eye makes, but the soul is light; where it is, is day; where it was, is night; and history is an impertinence and an injury, if it be any thing more than a cheerful apologue or parable of my being and becoming.

Man is timid and apologetic; he is no longer upright; he dares not say "I think," "I am," but quotes some saint or sage. He is ashamed before the blade of grass or the blowing rose. These roses under my window make no reference to former roses or to better ones; they are for what they are; they exist with God to-day. There is no time to them. There is simply the rose; it is perfect in every moment of its existence. Before a leaf-bud has burst, its whole life acts; in the full-blown flower there is no more; in the leafless root there is no less. Its nature is satisfied, and it satisfies nature, in all moments alike. But man postpones or remembers; he does not live in the present, but with reverted eye laments the past, or, heedless of the riches that surround him, stands on tiptoe to foresee the future. He cannot be happy and strong until he too lives with nature in the present, above time. . . .

Henceforward I am the truth's. Be it known unto you that henceforward I obey no law less than the eternal law. I will have no covenants but proximities. I shall endeavour to nourish my parents, to support my family, to be the chaste husband of one wife,—but these relations I must fill after a new and unprecedented way. I appeal from your customs. I must be myself. I cannot break myself any longer for you, or you. If you can love me for what I am, we shall be the happier. If you cannot, I will still seek to deserve that you should. I will not hide my tastes or aversions. I will so trust that what is deep is holy, that I will do strongly before the sun and moon whatever inly rejoices me, and the heart appoints. If you are noble, I will love you; if you are not, I will not hurt you and myself by hypocritical attentions. If you are true, but not in the same truth with me, cleave to your companions; I will seek my own. I do this not selfishly, but humbly and truly. It is alike your interest, and mine, and all men's, however long we have dwelt in lies, to live in truth. Does this sound harsh to-day? You will soon love what is dictated by your nature as well as mine, and, if we follow the truth, it will bring us out safe at last.—But so you may give these friends pain. Yes, but I cannot sell my liberty and my power, to save their sensibility. Besides, all persons have their moments of reason, when they look out into the region of absolute truth; then will they justify me, and do the same thing. . . .

Insist on yourself; never imitate. Your own gift you can present every moment with the cumulative force of a whole life's cultivation; but of the adopted talent of another, you have only an extemporaneous, half possession. That which each can do best, none but his Maker can teach him. No man yet knows what it is, nor can, till that person has exhibited it. Where is the master who could have taught Shakspeare? Where is the master who could have instructed Franklin, or Washington, or Bacon, or Newton? Every great man is a unique. The Scipionism of Scipio is precisely that part he could not borrow. Shakspeare will never be made by the study of Shakspeare. Do that which is assigned you, and you cannot hope too much or dare too much. . . .

covenants: binding agreements
proximities: things that are close by
unprecedented: never before done

hypocritical: dishonest

cumulative: dishonest
extemporaneous: unpracticed

40. From John L. O'Sullivan, *Editorial on Manifest Destiny* (1845)

For more information see
Chapters 8–10, Book 5, *Liberty for All?*

In the July 1845 edition of *Democratic Review,* an editor named John L. O'Sullivan referred to America's "manifest destiny to overspread the continent allotted by Providence for the free development of our yearly multiplying millions." One of the most influential phrases ever coined, the words "manifest destiny" expressed the belief that led many Americans to risk their lives to settle the Far West. The idea that Americans had a special destiny to stretch across the continent inspired missionaries, farmers, and pioneers to dream of peacefully transforming western plains and valleys into farms and small towns. It also led many to demand that the United States lay claim to the Southwest and Pacific Northwest. Aggressive nationalists also used the idea of manifest destiny to justify war with Mexico in 1846.

It is time now for opposition to the Annexation of Texas to cease, all further agitation of the waters of bitterness and strife, at least in connexion with this question, even though it may perhaps be required of us as a necessary condition of the freedom of our institutions, that we must live on for ever in a state of unpausing struggle and excitement upon some subject of party division or other. But, in regard to Texas, enough has now been given to Party. It is time for the common duty of Patriotism to the Country to succeed; or if this claim will not be recognized, it is at least time for common sense to acquiesce with decent grace in the inevitable and the irrevocable.

Texas is now ours. Already, before these words are written, her Convention has undoubtedly ratified the acceptance, by her Congress, of our proffered invitation into the Union; and made the requisite changes in her already republican form of constitution to adopt it to its future federal relations. Her star and her stripe may already be said to have taken their place in the glorious blazon of our common nationality; and the sweep of our eagle's wing already includes within its circuit the wide extent of her fair and fertile land. She is no longer to us a mere geographical space a certain combination of coast, plain, mountain, valley, forest and stream. She is no longer to us a mere country on the map. She comes within the dear and sacred designation of Our Country. . . .

Why, were other reasoning wanting, in favor of now elevating this question of the reception of Texas into the Union, out of the lower region of our past party dissensions, up to its proper level of a high and broad nationality, it surely is to be found, found abundantly, in the manner in which other nations have undertaken to intrude themselves into it, between us and the proper parties to the case, in a spirit of hostile interference against us, for the avowed object of thwarting our policy and hampering our power, limiting our greatness and checking the fulfilment of our manifest destiny to over-

acquiesce: agree to
irrevocable: cannot be taken back

ratified: legally approved
proferred: to offer
republican: representative
Her star and her stripe: Texas's symbols in the American flag
blazon: design that proclaims identity
eagle's wing: the symbol of American unity

dissensions: disagreements

manifest destiny: inevitability of the United States gaining control of the lands to its west

spread the continent allotted by Providence for the free development of our yearly multiplying millions. . . .

Nor is there any just foundation of the charge that Annexation is a great pro-slavery measure calculated to increase and perpetuate that institution. Slavery had nothing to do with it. . . . The country which was the subject of Annexation in this case, from its geographical position and relations, happens to be or rather the portion of it now actually settled, happens to be a slave country. But a similar process might have taken place in proximity to a different section of our Union; and indeed there is a great deal of Annexation yet to take place, within the life of the present generation, along the whole line of our northern border. Texas has been absorbed into the Union in the inevitable fulfilment of the general law which is rolling our population westward; the connexion of which with that ratio of growth in population which is destined within a hundred years to swell our numbers to the enormous population of two hundred and fifty millions (if not more), is too evident to leave us in doubt of the manifest design of Providence in regard to the occupation of this continent. It was disintegrated from Mexico in the natural course of events, by a process perfectly legitimate on its own part, blameless on ours; and in which all the censures due to wrong, perfidy and folly, rest on Mexico alone. And possessed as it was by a population which was in truth but a colonial detachment from our own, and which was still bound by myriad ties of the very heartstrings to its old relations, domestic and political, their incorporation into the Union was not only inevitable, but the most natural, right and proper thing in the world and it is only astonishing that there should be any among ourselves to say it nay. . . .

California will, probably, next fall away from the loose adhesion which, in such a country as Mexico, holds a remote province in a slight equivocal kind of dependence on the metropolis. Imbecile and distracted, Mexico never can exert any real governmental authority over such a country. The impotence of the one and the distance of the other, must make the relation one of virtual independence; unless, by stunting the province of all natural growth, and forbidding that immigration which can alone develope its capabilities and fulfil the purposes of its creation, tyranny may retain a military dominion which is no government in the legitimate sense of the term. In the case of California this is now impossible. The Anglo-Saxon foot is already on its borders. Already the advance guard of the irresistible army of Anglo-Saxon emigration has begun to pour down upon it, armed with the plough and the rifle, and marking its trail with schools and colleges, courts and representative halls, mills and meeting-houses. A population will soon be in actual occupation of

Annexation: taking over a formerly independent area

proximity: closeness

disintegrated: pulled apart

censures: blame
perfidy: faithless act

myriad: very many

adhesion: union

equivocal: weak, uncertain
metropolis: city
Imbecile: stupid
impotence: lack of power

Anglo-Saxon: person of British descent

121

spontaneous: unplanned
elemental: basic

California, over which it will be idle for Mexico to dream of dominion. They will necessarily become independent. All this without agency of our government, without responsibility of our people in the natural flow of events, the spontaneous working of principles, and the adaptation of the tendencies and wants of the human race to the elemental circumstances in the midst of which they find themselves placed. And they will have a right to independence to self-government to the possession of the homes conquered from the wilderness by their own labors and dangers, sufferings and sacrifices a better and a truer right than the artificial title of sovereignty in Mexico a thousand miles distant, inheriting from Spain a title good only against those who have none better.

Their right to independence will be the natural right of self-government belonging to any community strong enough to maintain it distinct in position, origin and character, and free from any mutual obligations of membership of a common political body, binding it to others by the duty of loyalty and compact of public faith. This will be their title to independence; and by this title, there can be no doubt that the population now fast streaming down upon California will both assert and maintain the independence. Whether they will then attach themselves to our Union or not, is not to be predicted with any certainty. Unless the projected rail-road across the continent to the Pacific be carried into effect, perhaps they may not; though even in that case, the day is not distant when the Empires of the Atlantic and Pacific would again flow together into one, as soon as their inland border should approach each other. But that great work,

colossal: huge

colossal as appears the plan on its first suggestion, cannot remain long unbuilt. Its necessity for this very purpose of binding and holding together in its iron clasp our fast settling Pacific region with that of the Mississippi valley the natural facility of the route the ease with which any amount of labor for the construction can be drawn in from the overcrowded populations of Europe, to be paid in the lands made valuable by the progress of the work itself and its immense utility to the commerce of the world with the whole eastern coast of Asia, alone almost sufficient for the support of such a road these considerations give assurance that the day cannot be distant which shall wit-

conveyance: transportation

ness the conveyance of the representatives from Oregon and California to Washington within less time than a few years ago was devoted to a similar journey by those from Ohio; while the magnetic telegraph will enable the editors of the "San Francisco Union," the "Astoria Evening Post," or the "Nootka Morning News" to set up in type the first half of the President's Inaugural, before the echoes of the latter half shall have died away beneath the lofty porch of the Capitol, as spoken from his lips.

Away, then, with all idle French talk of balances of power on the American Continent. There is no growth in Spanish America! Whatever progress of population there may be in the British Canadas, is only for their own early severance of their present colonial relation to the little island three thousand miles across the Atlantic; soon to be followed by Annexation, and destined to swell the still accumulating momentum of our progress. And whatsoever may hold the balance, though they should cast into the opposite scale all the bayonets and cannon, not only of France and England, but of Europe entire, how would it kick the beam against the simple solid weight of the two hundred and fifty or three hundred millions and American millions destined to gather beneath the flutter of the stripes and stars, in the fast hastening year of the Lord 1845?

severance: cutting off
colonial: having to do with the state of being dominated by a foreign land
accumulating: building up

41. From Horace Mann, *12th Annual Report to the Massachusetts Board of Education* (1848)

For more information see
Chapter 20, Book 5, *Liberty for All?*

Horace Mann led the struggle for free universal public education in Massachusetts. As head of the Massachusetts State Board of Education, he lengthened the school year, classified students by age and ability, and won state support for training teachers. Mann had great faith in the power of public schools to solve social problems. In his 12th Annual Report to the Massachusetts Board of Education in 1848, he argued that public schools would promote economic growth, create enlightened and responsible citizens, help immigrants adjust to their new home in America, and overcome class differences. In 1848, revolutions swept across much of Europe. Mann believed that education could solve the social problems that led to revolutionary violence in other countries.

Without undervaluing any other human agency, it may be safely affirmed that the common school, improved and energized as it can easily be, may become the most effective and benignant of all the forces of civilization. Two reasons sustain this position. In the first place, there is an universality in its operation, which can be affirmed of no other institution whatever. If administered in the spirit of justice and conciliation, all the rising generation may be brought within the circle of its reformatory and elevating influences. And, in the second place, the materials upon which it operates are so pliant and

benignant: having a good effect

conciliation: solving conflicts
reformatory: improving

plaint: bendable

ductile: stretchable
susceptible of: likely to

republican: representative

despotism: unchecked power
anarchy: chaos

solecism: something that is not
normal or accepted
barbarism: uncivilized action

partition: division

vindicate: justify

primal: first
homicidal: murderous

ductile as to be susceptible of assuming a greater variety of forms than any other earthly work of the Creator. . . .

[T]he true business of the schoolroom connects itself, and becomes identical, with the great interests of society. The former is the infant, immature state of those interests; the latter their developed, adult state. As "the child is father to the man," so may the training of the schoolroom expand into the institutions and fortunes of the State. . . .

According to the European theory, men are divided into classes—some to toil and earn, others to seize and enjoy. According to the Massachusetts theory, all are to have an equal chance for earning, and equal security in the enjoyment of what they earn. . . .

[A] republican form of government, without intelligence in the people, must be, on a vast scale, what a mad-house without superintendent or keepers would be on a small one—the despotism of a few succeeded by universal anarchy, and anarchy by despotism, with no change but from bad to worse. . . .

However elevated the moral character of a constituency may be, however well-informed in matters of general science or history, yet they must, if citizens of a republic, understand something of the true nature and functions of the government under which they live. That any one, who is to participate in the government of a country when he becomes a man, should receive no instruction respecting the nature and functions of the government he is afterwards to administer, is a political solecism. . . . [I]t would be . . . proof of restored or never-removed barbarism amongst us to empower any individual to use the elective franchise without preparing him for so momentous a trust. Hence the Constitution of the United States, and of our own State, should be made a study in our public school. The partition of the powers of government into the three co-ordinate branches—legislative, judicial, and executive,—with the duties appropriately devolving upon each; the mode of electing or of appointing all officers, with the reasons on which it was founded; and, especially, the duty of every citizen, in a government of laws, to appeal to the courts for redress in all cases of alleged wrong, instead of undertaking to vindicate his own rights by his own arm; and, in a government where the people are the acknowledged sources of power, the duty of changing laws and rulers by an appeal to the ballot, and not by rebellion,—should be taught to all the children until they are fully understood.

Moral education is a primal necessity of social existence. The unrestrained passions of men are not only homicidal, but suicidal; and a community without a conscience would soon extinguish itself. Even with a natural conscience, how often has evil triumphed over good! From the beginning of time, wrong has followed right, as the shadow the substance. . . .

But to all doubters, disbelievers, or despairers in human progress, it may still be said, there is one experiment which has never yet been tried. It is an experiment, which, even before its inception, offers the highest authority for its ultimate success. Its formula is intelligible to all; and it is as legible as though written in starry letters on an azure sky. It is expressed in these few and simple words: *"Train up a child in the way he should go; and, when he is old, he will not depart from it."* This declaration is positive. If the conditions are complied with, it makes no provision for failure. Thought pertaining to morals, yet, if the terms of the direction are observed, there is no more reason to doubt the result than there would be in an optical or a chemical experiment. . . .

inception: beginning

The establishment of a republican government, without well-appointed and efficient means for the universal education of the people, is the most rash and foolhardy experiment ever tried by man. . . . It may be an easy thing to make a republic, but it is a very laborious thing to make republicans; and woe to the republic that rests upon no better foundations than ignorance, selfishness, and passion! . . .

Such, then, . . . is the Massachusetts system of common schools. Reverently it recognizes and affirms the sovereign rights of the Creator, sedulously and sacredly it guards the religious rights of the creature. . . . In a social and political sense, it is a free school system. It knows no distinction of rich and poor, of bond and free, or between those, who, in the imperfect light of this world, are seeking, through different avenues, to reach the gate of heaven. Without money and without price, it throws open its doors, and spreads the table of its bounty, for all the children of the State. Like the sun, it shines not only upon the good, but upon the evil, that they may become good; and, like the rain, its blessings descend not only upon the just, but upon the unjust, that their injustice may be depart from them, and be known no more.

sedulously: working hard

42. From Elizabeth Cady Stanton, *"Let Us Consider Man's Superiority": Address to the Seneca Falls Conference* (1848)

For more information see
Chapter 23, Book 5, *Liberty for All?* Chapters 26–27, Book 7, *Reconstruction and Reform.*

An early advocate of women's right to vote, Elizabeth Cady Stanton also fought for property rights for married women, equal education for women, and reform of divorce laws. The mother of seven children, she married the abolitionist

Henry Brewster Stanton in 1840 against her father's wishes. She had the minister omit the promise to obey from their wedding vows. The couple honeymooned in London, where she attended the World Antislavery Convention but was refused a seat on the floor. Instead, she and other women delegates were confined to a curtained balcony. Many male delegates feared that women's presence might "lower the dignity of the convention."

Eight years later, Stanton helped organize the first women's rights convention in the United States. She drew up a list of resolutions calling for equality of the sexes. The most controversial of the resolutions demanded voting rights for women. In a speech before the convention, Stanton attacked the notion that men were intellectually, morally, or physically superior to women. She also rejected the idea that the sexes were different but equal, saying that men "soon run this difference into the old groove of superiority."

. . . . Let us consider . . . man's superiority, intellectually, morally, physically.

Man's intellectual superiority cannot be a question until woman has had a fair trial. When we shall have had our freedom to find out our own sphere, when we shall have had our colleges, our professions, our trades, for a century, a comparison then may be justly instituted. When woman . . . shall be just to herself before she is generous to others; improving the talents God has given her, and leaving her neighbor to do the same for himself, we shall not hear so much about this boasted superiority. . . .

In consideration of man's claim to moral superiority. . . . In my opinion, he is infinitely woman's inferior in every moral quality, not by nature, but made so by a false education. In carrying out his own selfishness, man has greatly improved woman's moral nature, but by an almost total shipwreck of his own.

Woman has now the noble virtues of the martyr. She is early schooled to self-denial and suffering. But man is not so wholly buried in selfishness that he does not sometimes get a glimpse of the narrowness of his soul, as compared with woman. Then he says, by way of an excuse for his degradation, "God made woman more self-denying than man. It is her nature. It does not cost her as much to give up her wishes, her will, her life, even, as it does him. He is naturally selfish. God made him so."

No, I think not. . . . God's commands rest upon man as well as woman. It is as much his duty to be kind, self-denying and full of good works, as it is hers. . . . I would have the same code of morals for both. . . .

Let us now consider man's claim to physical superiority. . . . We cannot accord to man even this much, and he has no right to claim it until the fact has been fully demonstrated. . . . We cannot say what the woman might be physically, if the girl were not allowed all the freedom of the boy in romping, climbing, swimming, playing whoop and ball. Among some of the Tartar tribes of the present day, women manage a horse, hurl a javelin, hunt wild animals, and fight an enemy as well as a man. . . . Physically, as well as intellectually, it is use that produces growth and development. . . .

And, strange as it may seem to many, we now demand our right to vote according to the declaration of the government under which we live. . . . We have no objection to discuss the question of equality, for we feel that the weight of the argument lies wholly with us, but we wish the question of equality kept distinct from the question of rights, for the proof of the one does not determine the truth of the other.

All white men in this country have the same rights, however they may differ in mind, body or estate. The right is ours. The question now is, how shall we get possession of what rightfully belongs to us. We should not feel so sorely grieved if no man who had not attained the full stature of a Webster, Clay, Van Buren, or Gerrit Smith could claim the right of the elective franchise. But to have drunkards, idiots, horse-racing, rum-selling rowdies . . . fully recognized, while we ourselves are thrust out from all the rights that belong to citizens, it is too grossly insulting to the dignity of woman to be longer quietly submitted to. . . .

But what would woman gain by voting? Men must know the advantages of voting, for they all seem very tenacious about the right. Think you, if woman had a vote in this government, that all those laws affecting her interests would so entirely violate every principle of right and justice? . . .

"But you are already represented by your fathers, husbands, brothers and sons?" Let your statute books answer the question. We have had enough of such representation. In nothing is woman's true happiness consulted. Men like to call her an angel—to feed her on what they think sweet food—nourishing her vanity: to make her believe that her organization is so much finer than theirs, that she is not fitted to struggle with the tempests of public life, but needs their care and protection!! Care and protection—such as the wolf gives the lamb—such as the eagle the hare he carries to his eyrie!! Most cunningly he entraps her, and then takes from her all [her] rights. . . .

tempests: storms

eyrie: eagle's nest

For more information see

Chapter 23, Book 5, *Liberty for All?*; Chapters 26–27, Book 7, *Reconstruction and Reform.*

43. From *Declaration of Sentiments* (1848)

Seneca Falls, New York, is the birthplace of the women's rights movement in the United States. On July 19, 1848, the first convention dedicated to equal treatment of women opened in this fast-growing village of 4,000. Some 300 people, including 40 men, attended the meeting at the red-brick Wesleyan Methodist Chapel.

After a series of brief speeches by other delegates, Elizabeth Cady Stanton read a bold statement of purpose. Modeled on the Declaration of Independence, this Declaration of Sentiments stated, "We hold these truths to be self-evident, that all men and women are created equal." It listed a series of injuries that men had inflicted on women. It concluded by accusing men of "endeavoring to destroy" a woman's "confidence in her own powers, to lessen her self-respect, and to make her willing to lead a dependent and abject life."

The convention then voted on a series of resolutions. One by one the resolutions were approved, until the convention reached the ninth, demanding the vote for women. Opponents considered this demand impractical, but a speech by the abolitionist Frederick Douglass persuaded many delegates that rights could not be restricted by gender. When the meeting was over, exactly 100 people—68 women and 32 men—signed the Declaration of Sentiments. Only two women who signed the document lived long enough to see women gain the right to vote in 1920.

hitherto: so far

inalienable: unable to be separated from

When, in the course of human events, it becomes necessary for one portion of the family of man to assume among the people of the earth a position different from that which they have hitherto occupied, but one to which the laws of nature and of nature's God entitle them, a decent respect to the opinions of mankind requires that they should declare the causes that impel them to such a course.

We hold these truths to be self-evident: that all men and women are created equal; that they are endowed by their Creator with certain inalienable rights; that among these are life, liberty, and the pursuit of happiness; that to secure these rights governments are instituted, deriving their just powers from the consent of the governed. Whenever any form of government becomes destructive of these ends, it is the right of those who suffer from it to refuse allegiance to it, and to insist upon the institution of a new government, laying its foundation on such principles, and organizing its powers in such form, as to them shall seem most likely to effect their safety and happiness. Prudence, indeed, will dictate that governments long established should not be changed for light and transient causes; and accordingly all experience hath shown that mankind are more disposed to suffer, while evils are sufferable, than to right themselves by abolishing the forms to which they were accustomed. But when a long train of abuses and usurpations, pursuing invariably the same object, evinces a design to reduce them under absolute despotism, it is their duty to throw off such government, and to provide new guards for their future security. Such has been the patient sufferance of the women under this government, and such is now the necessity which constrains them to demand the equal station to which they are entitled.

Prudence: common sense
transient: changing

usurpations: acts of theft
evinces: shows
despotism: unchecked power

The history of mankind is a history of repeated injuries and usurpations on the part of man toward woman, having in direct object the establishment of an absolute tyranny over her. To prove this, let facts be submitted to a candid world.

He has never permitted her to exercise her inalienable right to the elective franchise.

elective franchise: vote

He has compelled her to submit to laws, in the formation of which she had no voice. . . .

Having deprived her of this first right of a citizen, the elective franchise, thereby leaving her without representation in the halls of legislation, he has oppressed her on all sides.

He has made her, if married, in the eye of the law, civilly dead.

He has taken from her all right in property, even to the wages she earns. . . .

He has monopolized nearly all the profitable employments, and from those she is permitted to follow, she receives but a scanty remuneration. He closes against her all the avenues to wealth and distinction which he considers most honorable to himself. As a teacher of theology, medicine, or law, she is not known.

monopolized: taken control of
scanty: very little
remuneration: pay, compensation

He has denied her the facilities for obtaining a thorough education, all colleges being closed against her. . . .

He has endeavored, in every way that he could, to destroy her confidence in her own powers, to lessen her self-respect, and to make her willing to lead a dependent and abject life.

abject: without dignity or liberty

Now, in view of this entire disfranchisement of one-half the people of this country, their social and religious degradation—in view of the unjust laws above mentioned, and because women do feel themselves aggrieved, oppressed, and fraudulently deprived of their most sacred rights, we insist that they have immediate admission to all the rights and privileges which belong to them as citizens of the United States.

degradation: humiliation

aggrieved: pained
oppressed: held down or back

instrumentality: method
tracts: pamphlets

In entering upon the great work before us, we anticipate no small amount of misconception, misrepresentation, and ridicule; but we shall use every instrumentality within our power to effect our object. We shall employ agents, circulate tracts, petition the State and National legislatures, and endeavor to enlist the pulpit and the press in our behalf. We hope this Convention will be followed by a series of Conventions embracing every part of the country.

For more information see
Chapter 28, Book 5, *Liberty for All?;* Chapter 32, Book 6, *War, Terrible War.*

44. From Henry David Thoreau, *Civil Disobedience* (1849)

Henry David Thoreau's doctrine of "civil disobedience," the nonviolent refusal to obey unjust laws, has inspired leaders around the world to stand up against injustice, from Mohandas Gandhi in India to the Rev. Dr. Martin Luther King, Jr. in the United States. In 1845, the 28-year-old Thoreau moved into a one-room cabin at Walden Pond, near Concord, Massachusetts. Convinced that his life was being wasted on trivial details, he went into the woods to see whether a person could live in harmony with nature and "front only the essential facts of life." The most important incident during his 26 months at Walden Pond came in 1846, when he spent a night in jail for refusing to pay his taxes. He withheld payment because he felt that he could not support a government that endorsed slavery and was waging an unjust war against Mexico.

This experience led Thoreau to write the classic defense of nonviolent direct action, "Civil Disobedience." In it, he said that it was the duty of every individual to protest unjust government policies, even if the policies had been adopted with the support of a majority. Thoreau called on people to engage in acts of nonviolent protest that disrupt the everyday workings of society. These acts of civil disobedience, he argued, would awaken people's consciences.

Ralph Waldo Emerson visited Thoreau in jail, and asked: "Henry, why are you here?" Thoreau replied, "Why are you not here?"

I heartily accept the motto, "That government is best which governs least"; and I should like to see it acted up to more rapidly and systematically. Carried out, it finally amounts to this, which also I believe—"That government is best which governs not at all"; and when men are prepared for it, that will be the kind of government which they will have. Government is at best but an expedient; but

expedient: a means to an end

most governments are usually, and all governments are sometimes, inexpedient. The objections which have been brought against a standing army, and they are many and weighty, and deserve to prevail, may also at last be brought against a standing government. The standing army is only an arm of the standing government. The government itself, which is only the mode which the people have chosen to execute their will, is equally liable to be abused and perverted before the people can act through it. Witness the present Mexican war, the work of comparatively a few individuals using the standing government as their tool; for in the outset, the people would not have consented to this measure.

This American government— what is it but a tradition, though a recent one, endeavoring to transmit itself unimpaired to posterity, but each instant losing some of its integrity? It has not the vitality and force of a single living man; for a single man can bend it to his will. It is a sort of wooden gun to the people themselves. But it is not the less necessary for this; for the people must have some complicated machinery or other, and hear its din, to satisfy that idea of government which they have. Governments show thus how successfully men can be imposed upon, even impose on themselves, for their own advantage. It is excellent, we must all allow. Yet this government never of itself furthered any enterprise, but by the alacrity with which it got out of its way. It does not keep the country free. It does not settle the West. It does not educate. The character inherent in the American people has done all that has been accomplished; and it would have done somewhat more, if the government had not sometimes got in its way. For government is an expedient, by which men would fain succeed in letting one another alone; and, as has been said, when it is most expedient, the governed are most let alone by it. Trade and commerce, if they were not made of india-rubber, would never manage to bounce over obstacles which legislators are continually putting in their way; and if one were to judge these men wholly by the effects of their actions and not partly by their intentions, they would deserve to be classed and punished with those mischievous persons who put obstructions on the railroads.

But, to speak practically and as a citizen, unlike those who call themselves no-government men, I ask for, not at one no government, but at once a better government. Let every man make known what kind of government would command his respect, and that will be one step toward obtaining it.

After all, the practical reason why, when the power is once in the hands of the people, a majority are permitted, and for a long period continue, to rule is not because they are most likely to be in the right, nor because this seems fairest to the minority, but because they are

prevail: win

liable: likely

posterity: future generations

imposed upon: burdened

alacrity: eagerness

inherent: natural to

fain: happily

whit: tiny bit

unscrupulous: unprincipled

reminiscence: memory

constables: police
posse comitatus: temporary
group formed to help a sheriff

physically the strongest. But a government in which the majority rule in all cases can not be based on justice, even as far as men understand it. Can there not be a government in which the majorities do not virtually decide right and wrong, but conscience?—in which majorities decide only those questions to which the rule of expediency is applicable? Must the citizen ever for a moment, or in the least degree, resign his conscience to the legislator? Why has every man a conscience then? I think that we should be men first, and subjects afterward. It is not desirable to cultivate a respect for the law, so much as for the right. The only obligation which I have a right to assume is to do at any time what I think right. It is truly enough said that a corporation has no conscience; but a corporation of conscientious men is a corporation with a conscience. Law never made men a whit more just; and, by means of their respect for it, even the well-disposed are daily made the agents on injustice. A common and natural result of an undue respect for the law is, that you may see a file of soldiers, colonel, captain, corporal, privates, powder-monkeys, and all, marching in admirable order over hill and dale to the wars, against their wills, ay, against their common sense and consciences, which makes it very steep marching indeed, and produces a palpitation of the heart. They have no doubt that it is a damnable business in which they are concerned; they are all peaceably inclined. Now, what are they? Men at all? or small movable forts and magazines, at the service of some unscrupulous man in power? Visit the Navy Yard, and behold a marine, such a man as an American government can make, or such as it can make a man with its black arts—a mere shadow and reminiscence of humanity, a man laid out alive and standing, and already, as one may say, buried under arms with funeral accompaniment. . . .

The mass of men serve the state thus, not as men mainly, but as machines, with their bodies. They are the standing army, and the militia, jailers, constables, posse comitatus, etc. In most cases there is no free exercise whatever of the judgement or of the moral sense; but they put themselves on a level with wood and earth and stones; and wooden men can perhaps be manufactured that will serve the purpose as well. Such command no more respect than men of straw or a lump of dirt. They have the same sort of worth only as horses and dogs. Yet such as these even are commonly esteemed good citizens. Others—as most legislators, politicians, lawyers, ministers, and office-holders—serve the state chiefly with their heads; and, as they rarely make any moral distinctions, they are as likely to serve the devil, without intending it, as God. A very few—as heroes, patriots, martyrs, reformers in the great sense, and men—serve the state with their consciences also, and so necessarily resist it for the most part; and they are commonly treated as enemies by it. A wise man will only be useful as a man, and will not submit to be "clay. . . ."

How does it become a man to behave toward the American government today? I answer, that he cannot without disgrace be associated with it. I cannot for an instant recognize that political organization as my government which is the slave's government also. . . .

Under a government which imprisons unjustly, the true place for a just man is also a prison. The proper place today, the only place which Massachusetts has provided for her freer and less despondent spirits, is in her prisons, to be put out and locked out of the State by her own act, as they have already put themselves out by their principles. It is there that the fugitive slave, and the Mexican prisoner on parole, and the Indian come to plead the wrongs of his race should find them; on that separate but more free and honorable ground, where the State places those who are not with her, but against her—the only house in a slave State in which a free man can abide with honor. If any think that their influence would be lost there, and their voices no longer afflict the ear of the State, that they would not be as an enemy within its walls, they do not know by how much truth is stronger than error, nor how much more eloquently and effectively he can combat injustice who has experienced a little in his own person. Cast your whole vote, not a strip of paper merely, but your whole influence. A minority is powerless while it conforms to the majority; it is not even a minority then; but it is irresistible when it clogs by its whole weight. If the alternative is to keep all just men in prison, or give up war and slavery, the State will not hesitate which to choose. If a thousand men were not to pay their tax bills this year, that would not be a violent and bloody measure, as it would be to pay them, and enable the State to commit violence and shed innocent blood. This is, in fact, the definition of a peaceable revolution, if any such is possible. If the tax-gatherer, or any other public officer, asks me, as one has done, "But what shall I do?" my answer is, "If you really wish to do anything, resign your office." When the subject has refused allegiance, and the officer has resigned from office, then the revolution is accomplished. But even suppose blood shed when the conscience is wounded? Through this wound a man's real manhood and immortality flow out, and he bleeds to an everlasting death. I see this blood flowing now. . . .

The authority of government, even such as I am willing to submit to—for I will cheerfully obey those who know and can do better than I, and in many things even those who neither know nor can do so well—is still an impure one: to be strictly just, it must have the sanction and consent of the governed. It can have no pure right over my

despondent: without hope

fugitive: runaway
parole: early release from prison with supervision

eloquently: with force and elegance
combat: fight

allegiance: loyalty

sanction: agreement

concede: agree to give
limited monarchy: system where there is a king but he does not have absolute power

person and property but what I concede to it. The progress from an absolute to a limited monarchy, from a limited monarchy to a democracy, is a progress toward a true respect for the individual. Even the Chinese philosopher was wise enough to regard the individual as the basis of the empire. Is a democracy, such as we know it, the last improvement possible in government? Is it not possible to take a step further towards recognizing and organizing the rights of man? There will never be a really free and enlightened State until the State comes to recognize the individual as a higher and independent power, from which all its own power and authority are derived, and treats him accordingly. I please myself with imagining a State at last which can afford to be just to all men, and to treat the individual with respect as a neighbor; which even would not think it inconsistent with its own repose if a few were to live aloof from it, not meddling with it, nor embraced by it, who fulfilled all the duties of neighbors and fellow men. A State which bore this kind of fruit, and suffered it to drop off as fast as it ripened, would prepare the way for a still more perfect and glorious State, which I have also imagined, but not yet anywhere seen.

repose: rest
aloof: apart

For more information see

Chapter 32, Book 5, *Liberty for All?*

45. From John C. Calhoun, *"Proposal to Preserve the Union": Speech on the Compromise of 1850* (1850)

In 1849, California applied for admission to the Union as a free, or nonslave, state. If California became a free state, there would be 16 free states and only 15 slave states. The free states, which already had a commanding majority in the House of Representatives, would then hold a majority in the Senate as well. The South feared that it would not be able to stop the Union from passing laws that were unfavorable to slave states. Henry Clay, a senator from Kentucky, proposed that California be admitted as a free state, but that the status of slavery in other parts of the Southwest be left to the settlers of those territories. He also suggested that the slave trade be abolished in the District of Columbia and that Congress pass a strict law to return runaway slaves.

Senator John C. Calhoun of South Carolina led Southern opposition to this compromise. In the following speech, he warned the North that the only way to save the Union was to "cease the agitation of the slavery question." The North, he argued, had to concede "to the South an equal right" to the western territories. Otherwise, the South's only option would be to leave the Union.

I have, Senators, believed from the first that the agitation of the subject of slavery would, if not prevented by some timely and effective measure, end in disunion. . . . The agitation has been permitted to proceed, with almost no attempt to resist it, until it has reached a period when it can no longer be disguised or denied that the Union is in danger. You have thus had forced upon you the greatest and the gravest question that can ever come under your consideration: How can the Union be preserved? . . .

agitation: stirring up

The first question, then, presented for consideration, in the investigation I propose to make, in order to obtain such knowledge, is: What is it that has endangered the Union?

To this question there can be but one answer: That the immediate cause is the almost universal discontent which pervades all the States composing the southern section of the Union. . . .

pervades: spreads through

It is a great mistake to suppose, as is by some, that it originated with demagogues. . . . No; some cause, far deeper and more powerful than the one supposed must exist to account for discontent so wide and deep. The question, then, recurs: What is the cause of this discontent? It will be found in the belief of the people of the southern States, as prevalent as the discontent itself, that they cannot remain, as things now are, consistently with honor and safety, in the Union. The next question to be considered is: What has caused this belief?

demagogues: powerful and manipulative speakers

One of the causes is, undoubtedly, to be traced to the long-continued agitation of the slave question on the part of the North, and the many aggressions which they have made on the rights of the South during the time. . . .

There is another, lying back of it, with which this is intimately connected, that may be regarded as the great and primary cause. That is to be found in the fact that the equilibrium between the two sections in the Government, as it stood when the Constitution was ratified and the Government put in action has been destroyed. At that time there was nearly a perfect equilibrium between the two, which afforded ample means to each to protect itself against the aggression of the other; but, as it now stands, one section has the exclusive power of controlling the Government, which leaves the other without any adequate means of protecting itself against its encroachment and oppression. . . .

ratified: legally approved

equilibrium: state of equal influence

encroachment: coming threateningly near

[The] great increase of Senators, added to the great increase of the House of Representatives and the electoral college on the part of the North, which must take place under the next decade, will effectually and irretrievably destroy the equilibrium which existed when the Government commenced. . . .

What was once a constitutional federal republic is now converted, in reality, into one as absolute as that of the Autocrat of Russia, and

commenced: began
Autocrat: tyrant, unconstrained ruler

135

despotic: exercising unchecked power
absolute: completely arbitrary
manifest: clear

hazard: danger

hostile: opposed

as despotic in its tendency as any absolute Government that ever existed.

As, then, the North has the absolute control over the Government, it is manifest that on all questions between it and the South, where there is a diversity of interests, the interests of the latter will be sacrificed to the former, however oppressive the effects may be. . . . But if there was no question of vital importance to the South, in reference to which there was a diversity of views between the two sections, this state of things might be endured without the hazard of destruction to the South. But such is not the fact. . . .

I refer to the relation between the two races in the southern section, which constitutes a vital portion of her social organization. Every portion of the North entertains views and feelings more or less hostile to it. . . .

If the agitation goes on, the same force, acting with increased intensity, as has been shown, will finally snap every cord, when nothing will be left to bind the States together except force. . . .

How can the Union be saved? To this I answer, there is but one way by which it can be, and that is by adopting such measures as will satisfy the States belonging to the southern section that they can remain in the Union consistently with their honor and their safety.

For more information see
Chapter 24, Book 5, *Liberty for All?* and Chapter 27, Book 7, *Reconstruction and Reform.*

46. From Sojourner Truth, *"Aren't I a Woman": Address to the Women's Rights Convention,* Akron, Ohio (1851)

As a slave in New York's Hudson River valley, Sojourner Truth was known simply as Isabella. But a decade and a half after escaping bondage, she adopted a new name. As Sojourner Truth, she became a legend in the struggle to abolish slavery and achieve equal rights for women. In this speech, delivered at a women's rights convention in Akron, Ohio, in 1851, she demanded recognition that hard labor made enslaved and working women the equals of men. "I have plowed and reaped and husked and chopped and mowed," she said, "and can any man do more than that?"

At her death in 1883, Sojourner Truth was rightly remembered as one of America's most eloquent opponents of discrimination in all forms. She never learned to write, and so she never wrote down her speeches herself. But Frances Gage, the president of the convention, wrote this speech down in shorthand. It records Truth's language in the dialect whites commonly used to represent the speech of African Americans in the 19th century, a practice that Truth found condescending.

Well, children, where there is so much racket there must be something out o'kilter. I think that 'twixt the Negroes of the South and the women of the North all a-talking about rights, the white men will be in a fix pretty soon.

But what's all this here talking about? That man over there says that women need to be helped into carriages, and lifted over ditches, and to have the best place everywhere. Nobody ever helps me into carriages, or over mud puddles or gives me any best place (*and raising herself to her full height and her voice to a pitch like rolling thunder, she asked*), and aren't I a woman? Look at me! Look at my arm! (*And she bared her right arm to the shoulder, showing her tremendous muscular power.*) I have plowed, and planted, and gathered into barns, and no man could head me—and aren't I a woman? I could work as much and eat as much as a man (when I could get it), and bear the lash as well—and aren't I a woman? I have borne thirteen children and seen them almost all sold off into slavery, and when I cried out with a mother's grief, none but Jesus heard—and aren't I a woman? Then they talk about this thing in the head—what's this they call it? (*"Intellect," whispered someone near.*) That's it honey. What's that got to do with woman's rights or Negroes' rights? If my cup won't hold but a pint and yours holds a quart, wouldn't you be mean not to let me have my little half-measure full? (*And she pointed her significant finger and sent a keen glance at the minister who had made the argument. The cheering was long and loud.*)

Then that little man in black there, he says women can't have as much rights as man, 'cause Christ wasn't a woman. Where did your Christ come from? (*Rolling thunder could not have stilled that crowd as did those deep, wonderful tones, as she stood there with outstretched arms and eye of fire. Raising her voice still louder, she repeated,*) Where did your Christ come from? From God and a woman. Man had nothing to do with him. (*Oh! what a rebuke she gave the little man.*)

(*Turning again to another objector, she took up the defense of mother Eve. I cannot follower [sic] her through it all. It was pointed, and witty, and solemn, eliciting at almost every sentence deafening applause; and she ended [sic] by asserting that*) If the first woman God ever made was strong enough to turn the world upside down, all alone, these together (*and she glanced her eye over us*), ought to be

eliciting: drawing out

able to turn it back and get it right side up again; and now they are asking to do it, the men better let them. *(Long-continued cheering.)*

'Bliged to you for hearing on me, and now old Sojourner hasn't got anything more to say.

For more information see
Chapter 31, Book 4, *The New Nation.*

47. From Frederick Douglass, *Fourth of July Oration* (1852)

Frederick Douglass was the first fugitive slave to speak out publicly against slavery. As a traveling lecturer, Douglass electrified audiences with his first-hand accounts of slavery. His speeches combated the notion that slaves were content. When many Northerners refused to believe that this eloquent orator could possibly have been a slave, he responded by writing an autobiography that identified his previous owners by name.

Women's rights advocate Elizabeth Cady Stanton recalled her first glimpse of Douglass: "He stood there like an African prince, majestic in his wrath, as with wit, satire, and indignation he graphically described the bitterness of slavery and the humiliation of subjection." Toward the end of his life, Douglass was asked what advice he had for a young man. "Agitate! Agitate! Agitate!" he replied. Despite old age, Douglass never stopped agitating. He died in 1895, at the age of 77, after attending a women's rights meeting with Susan B. Anthony.

tumultuous: wildly noisy

Fellow citizens above your national, tumultuous joy, I hear the mournful wail of millions! whose chains, heavy and grievous yesterday, are, today, rendered more intolerable by the jubilee shouts that reach them. If I do forget, if I do not faithfully remember those bleeding children of sorrow this day, "may my right hand forget her cunning, and may my tongue cleave to the roof of my mouth"! To forget them, to pass lightly over their wrongs, and to chime in with the popular theme would be treason most scandalous and shocking, and would make me a reproach before God and the world. My subject, then, fellow citizens, is *American Slavery*. I shall see this day and its popular characteristics from the slave's point of view. Standing there identified with the American bondman, making his wrongs mine. I do not hesitate to declare with all my soul that the character and conduct of this nation never looked blacker to me than on this Fourth of July! Whether we turn to the declarations of the past or to the pro-

professions: statements of belief

fessions of the present, the conduct of the nation seems equally hideous and revolting. America is false to the past, false to the present, and solemnly binds herself to be false to the future. Standing with God and the crushed and bleeding slave on this occasion, I will, in the name of humanity which is outraged, in the name of liberty which is fettered, in the name of the Constitution and the Bible which are disregarded and trampled upon, all the emphasis I can command, everything that serves to perpetuate slavery the great sin and shame of America! "I will not equivocate, I will not excuse"; I will use the severest of language I can command; and yet not one word shall escape that any man, whose judgment is not blinded by prejudice, or who is not at heart a slaveholder, shall not confess to be right and just.

fettered: bound, constrained

equivocate: send mixed messages

But I fancy I hear someone of my audience say, "It is just in this circumstance that you and your brother abolitionists fail to make a favorable impression on the public mind. Would you argue more and denounce less, would you persuade more and rebuke less, your cause would be much more likely to succeed." But, I submit, where all is plain, there is nothing to be argued. What point in the antislavery creed would you have me argue? On what branch of the subject do the people of this country need light? Must I undertake to prove that the slave is a man? That point is conceded already. Nobody doubts it. The slaveholders themselves acknowledge it the enactment of laws for their government. They acknowledge it when they punish disobedience on the part of the slave. There are seventy-two crimes in the state of Virginia which, if committed by a black man (no matter how ignorant he be), subject him to the punishment of death, while only two of the same crimes will subject a white man to the like punishment. What is this but the acknowledgment that the slave is a moral, intellectual, and responsible being? The manhood of the slave is conceded. It is admitted in the fact that the Southern statute books are covered with enactments forbidding, under severe fines and penalties, the teaching of the slave to read or to write. When you can point to any such laws in reference to the beasts of the field, then I may consent to argue the manhood of the slave. When the dogs in your streets, when the fowls of the air, when the cattle on your hills, when the fish of the sea and the reptiles that crawl shall be unable to distinguish the slave from a brute, then will I argue with you that the slave is a man!

rebuke: tell off

conceded: granted

statute: law
enactments: regulations

For the present, it is enough to affirm the equal manhood of the Negro race. It is not astonishing that, while we are plowing, planting, and reaping, using all kinds of mechanical tools erecting houses, constructing bridges, building ships, working in metals of brass, iron, copper and silver, and gold; that, while we are reading, writing, and ciphering, acting as clerks, merchants and secretaries, having among

affirm: openly declare

us lawyers, doctors, ministers, poets, authors, editors, orators, and teachers; that, while we are engaged in all manner of enterprises common to other men, digging gold in California, capturing the whale in the Pacific, feeding sheep and cattle on the hillside, living, moving, acting, thinking, planning, living in families as husbands, wives, and children, and, above all, confessing and worshipping the Christian's God, and looking hopefully for life and immortality beyond the grave, we are called upon to prove that we are men!

Would you have me argue that man is entitled to liberty? That he is the rightful owner of his own body? You have already declared it. Must I argue the wrongfulness of slavery? Is that a question for **republicans**? Is it to be settled by the rules of logic and **argumentation**, as a matter beset with great difficulty, involving a doubtful application of the principle of justice, hard to be understood? How should I look today, in the presence of Americans, dividing and subdividing a discourse, to show that men have a natural right to freedom? speaking of it relatively and positively, negatively and affirmatively? To do so would be to make myself ridiculous and to offer an insult to your understanding. There is not a man beneath the canopy of heaven that does not know that slavery is wrong for him.

What, am I to argue that is wrong to make men brutes, to rob them of their liberty, to work them without wages, to keep them ignorant of their relations to their fellow men, to beat them with sticks, to flay their flesh with the lash, to load their limbs with irons, to hunt them with dogs, to sell them at auction, to **sunder** their families, to knock out their teeth, to burn their flesh, to starve them into obedience and submission to their masters? Must I argue that a system marked with blood, and stained with pollution, is wrong? No! I will not. I have better employment for my time and strength than such arguments would **imply**.

What, then remains to be argued? Is it that slavery is not divine; that God did not establish it; that our doctors of divinity are mistaken? There is **blasphemy** in the thought. That which is inhuman cannot be divine? Who can reason on such a proposition? They that can may; I cannot. The time for such argument is past.

At a time like this, scorching iron, not convincing argument, is needed. O! had I the ability, and could I reach the nation's ear, I would today pour out a fiery stream of biting ridicule, blasting reproach, withering sarcasm, and stern rebuke. For it is not light that is needed, but fire; it is not the gentle shower, but thunder. We need the storm, the whirlwind, and the earthquake. The feeling of the nation must be quickened, the conscience of the nation must be startled; the **hypocrisy** of the nation must be exposed; and its crimes against God and man must be proclaimed and denounced.

republicans: citizens of a representative government
argumentation: debate

sunder: divide

imply: suggest

blasphemy: disrespect or irreverence towards God

hypocrisy: dishonesty

What, to the American slave is your Fourth of July? I answer: a day that reveals to him, more than all other days in the year, the gross injustice and cruelty to which he is the constant victim. To him, your celebration is a sham; your boasted liberty an unholy license; your national greatness, swelling vanity; your sound of rejoicing are empty and heartless; your denunciation of tyrants, brass-fronted impudence; your shouts of liberty and equality, hollow mockery; your prayers and hymns, your sermons and thanksgivings with all your religious parade and solemnity, are, to Him, mere bombast, fraud, deception, impiety, and hypocrisy, a thin veil to cover up crimes which would disgrace a nation of savages. There is not a nation on earth guilty of practices more shocking and bloody than are the people of the United States at this very hour.

Go where you may, search where you will, roam through all the monarchies and despotisms of the Old World, travel through South America, search out every abuse, and when you have found the last, lay your facts by the side of the everyday practices of this nation, and you will say with that, for revolting barbarity and shameless hypocrisy, America reigns without a rival.

sham: fake

denunciation: public condemnation
impudence: rudeness
bombast: showing off

despotisms: acts of unchecked power

barbarity: savagery

48. From Roger Taney, opinion in *Dred Scott* v. *Sandford* (1857)

In 1857, the Supreme Court answered the question of whether Congress could prohibit slavery in the western territories. The case originated in 1846, when a Missouri slave, Dred Scott, sued for his freedom. Scott had been the slave of an army surgeon and had lived in Illinois, a free state, and Wisconsin, a free territory. He argued that his residence on free soil had made him a free person.

The Supreme Court ruled that Scott had no right to sue in federal court because neither slaves nor free blacks were citizens of the United States. Chief Justice Roger Taney delivered the majority opinion of the court. At the time the Constitution was adopted, the Chief Justice wrote, blacks were "regarded as beings of an inferior order" with "no rights which the white man was bound to respect." (In fact, some states did recognize free blacks as citizens at the time the Constitution was adopted.) Taney also declared that Congress had no right to prohibit slavery in the western territories. Any law excluding slaves from the territories violated the Constitution, which prohibited Congress from seizing property without just compensation and due process of law. The court's ruling divided the nation and pushed the country closer to civil war.

The Dred Scott ruling was overturned by the first sentence of the 14th Amendment, which was ratified in 1868. It states that "All persons born . . . in the United States . . . [are] citizens of the United States and of the State wherein they reside."

ancestors: all the generations of relatives who lived before

The question is simply this: Can a negro, whose ancestors were imported into this country, and sold as slaves, become a member of the political community formed and brought into existence by the Constitution of the United States, and as such become entitled to all the rights, and privileges, and immunities, guarantied by [the Constitution] to the citizen? One of which rights is the privilege of suing in a court of the Unites States in the cases specified in the Constitution. . . .

[T]he plea applies to that class of persons only whose ancestors were negroes of the African race, and imported into this country, and sold and held as slaves. The only matter in issue before the court, therefore, is, whether the descendants of such slaves, when they shall be emancipated, or who are born of parents who had become free before their birth, are citizens of a State, in the sense in which the word citizen is used in the Constitution of the United States. . . .

descendants: all the generations of relatives who will live after
emancipated: freed

colonial: controlled by a foreign power
amalgamated: combined, mixed

The situation of this population was altogether unlike that of the Indian race. The latter . . . formed no part of the colonial communities, and never amalgamated with them in social connections or in government. But although they were uncivilized, they were yet a free and independent people, associated together in nations or tribes, and governed by their own laws. Many of these political communities were situated in territories to which the white race claimed the ultimate right of dominion. But that claim was acknowledged to be subject to the right of the Indians to occupy it as long as they thought proper, and neither the English nor colonial Governments claimed or exercised any dominion over the tribe or nation by whom it was occupied, nor claimed the right to the possession of the territory, until the tribe or nation consented to cede it. These Indian Governments were regarded and treated as foreign Governments, as much so as if an ocean had separated the red man from the white; and their freedom has constantly been acknowledged, from the time of the first emigration to the English colonies to the present day, by the different Governments which succeeded each other. Treaties have been negotiated with them, and their alliance sought for in war; and the people who compose these Indian political communities have always been treated as foreigners not living under our

dominion: power

cede: give up

emigration: departure

Government. It is true that the course of events has brought the Indian tribes within the limits of the United States under subjection to the white race; and it has been found necessary, for their sake as well as our own, to regard them as in a state of pupilage, and to legislate to a certain extent over them and the territory they occupy. But they may, without doubt, like the subjects of any other foreign Government, be naturalized by the authority of Congress, and become citizens of a State, and of the United States; and if an individual should leave his nation or tribe, and take up his abode among the white population, he would be entitled to all the rights and privileges which would belong to an emigrant from any other foreign people. . . .

pupilage: learning

The question before us is, whether [freed slaves or children of freed slaves] . . . compose a portion of this people [of the United States]. . . . We think they are not, and that they are not included, and were not intended to be included, under the word "citizens" in the Constitution, and can therefore claim none of the rights and privileges which [it] . . . secures to the citizens of the United States. On the contrary, they were at that time considered as a subordinate and inferior class of beings, who had been subjugated by the dominant race, and, whether emancipated or not, yet remained subject to their authority, and had no rights or privileges but such as those who held the power and the Government might choose to grant them. . . .

subjugated: forced down

In discussing this question, we must not confound the rights of citizenship which a State may confer within its own limits, and the rights of citizenship as a member of the Union. It does not by any means follow, because he has all the rights and privileges of a citizen of a State, that he must be a citizen of the United States. He may have all the rights and privileges of the citizen of a State, and yet not be entitled to the rights and privileges of a citizen in any other State. . . .

confound: confuse

The question then arises, whether the provisions of the Constitution, in relation to the personal rights and privileges to which the citizen of a State should be entitled, embraced the negro African race, at that time in this country, or who might afterwards be imported, who had then or should afterwards be made free in any State; and to put it in the power of a single State to make him a citizen of the United States, and endue him with the full rights of citizenship in every other State without their consent? . . .

endue: give

The court think the affirmative of these propositions cannot be maintained. And if it cannot, the plaintiff in error could not be a citizen of the State of Missouri . . . and consequently, was not entitled to sue in its courts.

propositions: statements

It is true, every person, and every class and description of persons, who were at the time of the adoption of the Constitution recognized as citizens in the several States, became also citizens of this new political body. . . . And it gave to each citizen rights and privileges outside of his own State . . . and placed him in every other State upon a perfect equality with its own citizens . . . ; it made him a citizen of the United States.

It becomes necessary . . . to determine who were citizens of the several States when the Constitution was adopted. . . . We must inquire who, at that time, were recognized as the people or citizens of a State. . . .

[The] legislation and histories of the times, and the language used in the Declaration of Independence, show, that neither the . . . slaves, nor their descendants, whether they had become free or not, were then acknowledged as a part of the people, nor intended to be included . . .

It is difficult at this day to realize the state of public opinion in relation to that unfortunate race, which prevailed in the civilized and enlightened portions of the world at the time of the Declaration of Independence, and when the Constitution of the United States was framed and adopted. But the public history of every European nation displays it in a manner too plain to be mistaken.

They had for more than a century been regarded as beings of an inferior order, and altogether unfit to associate with the white race, either in social or political relations; and so far inferior, that they had no rights which the white man was bound to respect; and that the negro might justly and lawfully be reduced to slavery for his benefit. He was bought and sold, and treated as an ordinary article of merchandise and traffic, whenever a profit could be made by it. This opinion was at that time fixed and universal in the civilized portion of the white race. It was regarded as an axiom in morals as well as in politics, which no one thought of disputing, or supposed to be open to dispute; and men in every grade and position in society daily and habitually acted upon it in their private pursuits, as well as in matters of public concern, without doubting for a moment the correctness of this opinion.

And in no nation was this opinion more firmly fixed or more uniformly acted upon than by the English Government and English people. They not only seized them on the coast of Africa, and sold them or held them in slavery for their own use; but they took them as ordinary articles of merchandise to every country where they could make a profit on them, and were far more extensively engaged in this commerce than any other nation in the world.

The opinion thus entertained and acted upon in England was naturally impressed upon the colonies they founded on this side of the

axiom: true statement

Atlantic. And accordingly, a negro of the African race was regarded by them as an article of property, and held, and bought and sold . . . in every one of the thirteen colonies . . .

[Laws passed in the thirteen colonies] show that a perpetual and impassable barrier was intended to be erected between the white race and the one which they had reduced to slavery, and governed as subjects with absolute and despotic power, and which they then looked upon as so far below them in the scale of created beings, that intermarriages between white persons and negroes or mulattoes were regarded as unnatural and immoral, and punished as crimes, not only in the parties, but in the person who joined them in marriage. And no distinction in this respect was made between the free negro or mulatto and the slave, but this stigma, of the deepest degradation, was fixed upon the whole race. . . .

The language of the Declaration of Independence is . . . conclusive:. . . .

[It declares]: "We hold these truths to be self-evident: that all men are created equal: that they are endowed by their Creator with certain unalienable rights; that among them is life, liberty, and the pursuit of happiness; that to secure these rights, Governments are instituted, deriving their just powers from the consent of the governed."

[These words] would seem to embrace the whole human family, and if they were used in a similar instrument at this day, would be so understood. But it is too clear for dispute, that the enslaved African race were not intended to be included, and formed no part of the people who framed and adopted this declaration; for if the language, as understood in that day, would embrace them, the conduct of the distinguished men who framed the Declaration of Independence would have been utterly and flagrantly inconsistent with the principles they asserted; and instead of the sympathy of mankind, to which they so confidently appealed, they would have deserved and received universal rebuke and reprobation.

Yet the men who framed the declaration were great men—high in literary acquirements—high in their sense of honor, and incapable of asserting principles inconsistent with those on which they were acting. They perfectly understood the meaning of the language they used, and how it would be understood by others; and they knew that it would not in any part of the civilized world be supposed to embrace the negro race, which, by common consent, had been excluded from Governments and the family of nations, and doomed to slavery. They spoke and acted according to the then established doctrines and principles, and in the ordinary language of the day,

perpetual: lasting forever

despotic: exercising unchecked power
mulattoes: people of mixed African and European descent

stigma: mark of pain or shame

unalienable: unable to be taken away
deriving: gaining

embrace: include

rebuke: strong disapproval
reprobation: criticism
framed: wrote

indelible: unable to be erased

and no one misunderstood them. The unhappy black race were separated from the white by indelible marks, and laws long before established, and were never thought of or spoken of except as property, and when the claims of the owner and the profit of the trader were supposed to need protection. . . .

[T]here are two clauses of the Constitution which point directly to the negro race as a separate class of persons, and show clearly that they were not regarded as a portion of the people or citizens of the Government then formed.

One of these clauses reserves to each of the thirteen States the right to import slaves until the year 1808. . . . And by the other provision the States pledge themselves to each other to maintain the right of property of the master, by delivering up to him any slave who may have escaped from his service, and be found within their respective territories. . . .

Undoubtedly, a person may be a citizen . . . although he exercises no share of the political power, and is incapacitated from holding particular offices. Women and minors, who form a part of the political family, cannot vote; and when a property qualification is required to vote or hold a particular office, those who have not the necessary qualification cannot vote or hold the office, yet they are citizens. . . .

minors: people not yet of legal or adult age

The only two provisions [of the Constitution] which point to [slaves] and include them, treat them as property, and make it the duty of the Government to protect it; on other power, in relation to this race, is to be found in the Constitution. . . .

presume: feel sure

No one, we presume, supposes that any change in public opinion or feeling, in relation to this unfortunate race, in the civilized nations of Europe or in this country, should induce the court to give to the words of the Constitution a more liberal construction in their favor than they were intended to bear when the instrument was framed and adopted. . . . [A]s long as it continues to exist in its present form, it speaks not only in the same words, but with the same meaning and intent with which it spoke when it came from the hands of the framers. . . .

induce: lead
liberal construction: broad interpretation

abatement: lessening

[T]he court is of the opinion, that, upon the facts stated in the plea of abatement, Dred Scott was not a citizen of Missouri within the meaning of the Constitution of the United States, and not entitled as such to sue in its courts. . . .

49. From Abraham Lincoln, *"A House Divided": Address to the Illlinois Republican Convention* (1858)

For more information see
Chapters 32 and 33, Book 6, *War, Terrible War.*

In 1858, Abraham Lincoln accepted the Republican nomination for the U.S. Senate with the famous words: "A house divided against itself cannot stand." In his speech, Lincoln argued that the Kansas-Nebraska Act of 1854 and the Dred Scott decision of 1857 were part of a conspiracy to make slavery lawful "in all the States, old as well as new—North as well as South." He feared that slave-holders wanted to reduce all laborers, white as well as black, to a state of virtual slavery. By the late 1850s, a growing number of Northerners were convinced that a ruthless Southern "slave power" had perverted the Constitution and threatened to subvert republican ideals of liberty and equality.

Mr. President and Gentlemen of the Convention:

If we could first know where we are, and whither we are tending, we could better judge what to do, and how to do it. We are now far into the fifth year since a policy was initiated with the avowed object and confident promise of putting an end to slavery agitation. Under the operation of that policy that agitation has not only not ceased but has constantly augmented. In my opinion, it will not cease until a crisis shall have been reached and passed.

slavery agitation: social unrest concerning slavery

"A house divided against itself cannot stand." I believe this government cannot endure permanently half slave and half free. I do not expect the Union to be dissolved; I do not expect the house to fall; but I do expect it will cease to be divided. It will become all one thing, or all the other. Either the opponents of slavery will arrest the further spread of it, and place it where the public mind shall rest in the belief that it is in the course of ultimate extinction, or its advocates will push it forward till it shall become alike lawful in all the states, old as well as new, North as well as South.

extinction: dying out
advocates: supporters

Have we no tendency to the latter condition?

Let anyone who doubts carefully contemplate that now almost complete legal combination—piece of machinery, so to speak—compounded of the Nebraska doctrine and the Dred Scott decision. Let him consider not only what work the machinery is adapted to do, and how well adapted, but also let him study the history of its construction, and trace, if he can, or rather fail, if he can, to trace the evidences of design, and concert of action, among its chief architects, from the beginning.

contemplate: consider

deferred: postponed

secured: won
reputed: supposed

vehemently: with too much passion
construe: interpret

immunities: protections

enhance: increase

The new year of 1854 found slavery excluded from more than half the states by state constitutions, and from most of the national territory by congressional prohibition. Four days later commenced the struggle which ended in repealing that congressional prohibition. This opened all the national territory to slavery and was the first point gained. . . .

While the Nebraska Bill was passing through Congress, a law case, involving the question of a Negro's freedom, by reason of his owner having voluntarily taken him first into a free state, and then into a territory covered by the congressional prohibition, and held him as a slave for a long time in each, was passing through the United States Circuit Court for the District of Missouri; and both Nebraska Bill and lawsuit were brought to a decision in the same month of May 1854. The Negro's name was Dred Scott, which name now designates the decision finally made in the case. Before the then next presidential election, the law case came to, and was argued in, the Supreme Court of the United States; but the decision of it was deferred until after the election.

The election came. Mr. Buchanan was elected, and the endorsement, such as it was, secured. That was the second point gained.

The reputed author of the Nebraska Bill finds an early occasion to make a speech at this capital endorsing the Dred Scott decision, and vehemently denouncing all opposition to it. The new president, too, seizes the early occasion of the Silliman letter to endorse and strongly construe that decision, and to express his astonishment that any different view had ever been entertained!

The several points of the Dred Scott decision, in connection with Senator Douglas's "care not" policy, constitute the piece of machinery, in its present state of advancement. This was the third point gained. The working points of that machinery are:

Firstly, That no Negro slave, imported as such from Africa, and no descendant of such slave, can ever be a citizen of any state, in the sense of that term as used in the Constitution of the United States. This point is made in order to deprive the Negro, in every possible event, of the benefit of that provision of the United States Constitution which declares that "the citizens of each state shall be entitled to all privileges and immunities of citizens in the several states."

Secondly, That, "subject to the Constitution of the United States," neither Congress nor a territorial legislature can exclude slavery from any United States territory. This point is made in order that individual men may fill up the territories with slaves, without danger of losing them as property, and thus to enhance the chances of permanency to the institution through all the future.

Thirdly, That whether the holding a Negro in actual slavery in a free state makes him free, as against the holder, the United States courts will not decide, but will leave to be decided by the courts of any slave state the Negro may be forced into by the master. This point is made, not to be pressed immediately; but, if acquiesced in for a while, and apparently endorsed by the people at an election, then to sustain the logical conclusion that what Dred Scott's master might lawfully do with Dred Scott in the free state of Illinois, every other master may lawfully do with any other one, or one thousand slaves, in Illinois, or in any other free state.

acquiesced in: agreed to
endorsed: supported
sustain: hold up

It will throw additional light on the latter, to go back and run the mind over the string of historical facts already stated. Several things will now appear less dark and mysterious than they did when they were transpiring. The people were to be left "perfectly free," "subject only to the Constitution." What the Constitution had to do with it out-siders could not then see. Plainly enough now, it was an exactly fitted niche for the Dred Scott decision afterward to come in and declare that perfect freedom of the people to be just no freedom at all. Why was the amendment expressly declaring the right of the people to exclude slavery voted down? Plainly enough now, the adoption of it would have spoiled the niche for the Dred Scott decision. . . .

transpiring: happening

niche: holding place

While the opinion of the court, by Chief Justice Taney, in the Dred Scott case, and the separate opinions of all the concurring judges, expressly declare that the Constitution of the United States neither permits Congress nor a territorial legislature to exclude slavery from any United States territory, they all omit to declare whether or not the same Constitution permits a state, or the people of a state, to exclude it. We may, ere long, see another Supreme Court decision declaring that the Constitution of the United States does not permit a state to exclude slavery from its limits. And this may especially be expected if the doctrine of "care not whether slavery be voted down or voted up" shall gain upon the public mind sufficiently to give promise that such a decision can be maintained when made.

concurring: agreeing

omit: leave out

Such a decision is all that slavery now lacks of being alike lawful in all the states. Welcome, or unwelcome, such decision is probably coming, and will soon be upon us, unless the power of the present political dynasty shall be met and overthrown. We shall lie down pleasantly dreaming that the people of Missouri are on the verge of making their state free, and we shall awake to the reality instead that the Supreme Court has made Illinois a slave state. To meet and over-throw the power of that dynasty is the work now before all those who would prevent that consummation. That is what we have to do. How can we best do it? . . .

dynasty: many generations of a powerful family

consummation: final event

impulse: quick decision to act
discordant: lacking harmony
hostile: opposing, warlike
elements: individual pieces
pampered: spoiled
dissevered: divided into parts
belligerent: warlike
counsels: advice
accelerate: speed up

For more information see

Chapter 7, Book 6, *War, Terrible War.*

Our cause, then, must be entrusted to, and conducted by, its own undoubted friends—those whose hands are free, whose hearts are in the work, who do care for the result. Two years ago the Republicans of the nation mustered over thirteen hundred thousand strong. We did this under the single impulse of resistance to a common danger, with every external circumstance against us. Of strange, discordant, and even hostile elements, we gathered from the four winds, and formed and fought the battle through, under the constant hot fire of a disciplined, proud, and pampered enemy. Did we brave all then to falter now? Now, when that same enemy is wavering, dissevered, and belligerent? The result is not doubtful. We shall not fail—if we stand firm, we shall not fail. Wise counsels may accelerate or mistakes delay it, but, sooner or later, the victory is sure to come.

50. From Abraham Lincoln, *Debate with Stephen Douglas* (1858)

The critical issues dividing the nation in the late 1850s were brought into sharp focus in a series of debates during the 1858 campaign for U.S. senator from Illinois. Democratic Senator Stephen Douglas and Republican challenger Abraham Lincoln traveled nearly 10,000 miles during the campaign and participated in seven face-to-face debates before crowds of up to 15,000. Douglas pictured Lincoln as a fanatic whose goal was to provoke civil war, emancipate the slaves, and make African Americans the social and political equals of whites. Lincoln denied that he was a radical. He said that he supported the Fugitive Slave Law and opposed any interference with slavery in the states where it already existed.

Lincoln and Douglas presented two sharply contrasting views of slavery. Douglas argued that slavery was a dying institution that could not thrive in the climate and soil of the western territories. Lincoln, in contrast, regarded slavery as an institution hungry for new territory. The sharpest difference between the candidates involved the rights of African Americans. Douglas said that he wanted "citizenship for whites only." Lincoln insisted that African Americans were equal to "every living man" in their right to life, liberty, and the fruits of their own labor. In the following selection from the seventh and last debate, Lincoln argues that the struggle against slavery is part of "the eternal struggle between . . . right and wrong—throughout the world."

I have stated upon former occasions, and I may as well state again, what I understand to be the real issue in this controversy between Judge Douglas and myself. . . . The real issue in this controversy—the one pressing upon every mind—is the sentiment on the part of one class that looks upon the institution of slavery *as a wrong*, and of another class that *does not* look upon it as a wrong. The sentiment that contemplates the institution of slavery in this country as a wrong is the sentiment of the Republican party. It is the sentiment around which all their actions, all their arguments, circle, from which all their propositions radiate. They look upon it as being a moral, social, and political wrong; and while they contemplate it as such, they nevertheless have due regard for its actual existence among us, and the difficulties of getting rid of it in any satisfactory way, and to all the constitutional obligations thrown about it. Yet, having a due regard for these, they desire a policy in regard to it that looks to its not creating any more danger. They insist that it should, as far as may be, *be treated* as a wrong; and one of the methods of treating it as a wrong is to *make provision that it shall grow no larger*. They also desire a policy that looks to a peaceful end of slavery at some time, as being wrong. These are the views they entertain in regard to it as I understand them; and all their sentiments, all their arguments and propositions, are brought within this range. I have said, and I repeat it here, that if there be a man amongst us who does not think that the institution of slavery is wrong in any one of the aspects of which I have spoken, he is misplaced, and ought not to be with us. And if there be a man amongst us who is so impatient of it as a wrong as to disregard its actual presence among us and the difficulty of getting rid of it suddenly in a satisfactory way, and to disregard the constitutional obligations thrown about it, that man is misplaced if he is on our platform. We disclaim sympathy with him in practical action. He is not placed properly with us.

On this subject of treating it as a wrong, and limiting its spread, let me say a word. Has anything ever threatened the existence of this Union save and except this very institution of slavery? What is it that we hold most dear amongst us? Our own liberty and prosperity. What has ever threatened our liberty and prosperity, save and except this institution of slavery? If this is true, how do you propose to improve the condition of things by enlarging slavery,— by spreading it out and making it bigger? You may have a wen or cancer upon your person, and not be able to cut it out, lest you bleed to death; but surely it is no way to cure it, to engraft it and spread it over your whole body. That is no proper way of treating what you regard a wrong. You see this peaceful way of dealing with

controversy: conflict

sentiment: feeling

contemplates: looks on

propositions: ideas for action
radiate: shine out from

make provision: make sure

disclaim: do not admit to

wen: a cyst

engraft: plant

tolerate: put up with

indifferent: neither good nor bad

contends: argues

eternal: never-ending

avow: swear to
perpetuation: continuation

it as a wrong,—restricting the spread of it, and not allowing it to go into new countries where it has not already existed. That is the peaceful way, the old-fashioned way, the way in which the fathers themselves set us the example.

On the other hand, I have said there is a sentiment which treats it as *not* being wrong. That is the Democratic sentiment of this day. . . .

The Democratic policy in regard to that institution will not tolerate the merest breath, the slightest hint, of the least degree of wrong about it. Try it by some of Judge Douglas's arguments. He says he "don't care whether it is voted up or voted down" in the Territories. I do not care myself, in dealing with that expression, whether it is intended to be expressive of his individual sentiments on the subject, or only of the national policy he desires to have established. It is alike valuable for my purpose. Any man can say that who does not see anything wrong in slavery; but no man can logically say it who does see a wrong in it, because no man can logically say he don't care whether a wrong is voted up or voted down. He may say he don't care whether an indifferent thing is voted up or down, but he must logically have a choice between a right thing and a wrong thing. He contends that whatever community wants slaves has a right to have them. So they have, if it is not a wrong. But if it is a wrong, he cannot say people have a right to do wrong. He says that upon the score of equality slaves should be allowed to go in a new Territory, like other property. This is strictly logical if there is no difference between it and other property. If it and other property are equal, this argument is entirely logical. But if you insist that one is wrong and the other right, there is no use to institute a comparison between right and wrong. You may turn over everything in the Democratic policy from beginning to end, whether in the shape it takes on the statute book, in the shape it takes in the Dred Scott decision, in the shape it takes in conversation, or the shape it takes in short maxim-like arguments,—it everywhere carefully excludes the idea that there is anything wrong in it.

That is the real issue. That is the issue that will continue in this country when these poor tongues of Judge Douglas and myself shall be silent. It is the eternal struggle between these two principles—right and wrong—throughout the world. They are the two principles that have stood face to face from the beginning of time, and will ever continue to struggle. The one is the common right of humanity, and the other the divine right of kings. . . . And whenever we can get rid of the fog which obscures the real question, when we can get Judge Douglas and his friends to avow a policy looking to its perpetuation,—we can get out from among that class of men and bring them to the side of those who treat it as a wrong. Then there will soon be an end of it, and that end will be its "ultimate extinction." Whenever the issue can be distinctly made, and all extraneous matter thrown out so that men can fairly see the real difference between the parties, this controversy will soon be settled, and it will be done peaceably too. There will be no war, no violence. It will be placed again where the wisest and best men of the world placed it. . . .

extraneous: extra, irrelevant

51. John Brown, *Last Statement to the Court* (1859)

On Sunday, October 16, 1859, John Brown led a raid on the federal weapons storehouse at Harpers Ferry, Virginia, hoping to steal arms for a slave rebellion. Brown believed that it was impossible to abolish slavery by passing laws. Instead, he supported a violent uprising. Less than 36 hours into the battle, Brown was taken prisoner by U.S marines under the command of Colonel Robert E. Lee. Ten of Brown's raiders, including two of his sons, were killed in the fighting. In his brief trial, Brown refused to plead insanity and was found guilty of treason and sentenced to death. Before mounting the scaffold, he wrote: "The crimes of this guilty land will never be purged away but with blood."

Even in his own time, Brown was one of the most hotly debated figures in American history. Ralph Waldo Emerson compared him to Jesus Christ and said he had made "the gallows as glorious as the cross." Abraham Lincoln refused to pardon Brown's acts of "violence, bloodshed, and treason," even though his goal of ending slavery was a noble one.

I have, may it please the Court, a few words to say. In the first place, I deny everything but what I have all along admitted: of a design on my part to free slaves. I intended certainly to have made a clean thing of that matter, as I did last winter, when I went into Missouri and there took slaves without the snapping of a gun on either side, moving them through the country, and finally leaving them in Canada. I designed to have done the same thing again on a larger scale. That was all I intended. I never did intend murder, or treason, or the destruction of property, or to exercise or incite slaves to rebellion, or to make insurrection.

treason: crime against the state
incite: stir up
insurrection: rebellion

I have another objection, and that is that it is unjust that I should suffer such a penalty. Had I interfered in the manner which I admit, and which I admit has been fairly proved—for I admire the

candor: honesty

endeavored: tried

enactments: laws

disposition: likelihood

induced: persuaded

truthfulness and candor of the greater portion of the witnesses who have testified in this case—Had I so interfered in behalf of the rich, the powerful, the intelligent, the so-called great, or in behalf of any of their friends, either father, mother, brother, sister, wife or children, or any of that class, and suffered and sacrificed what I have in this interference, it would have been all right. Every man in this Court would have deemed it an act worthy of reward rather than punishment.

This Court acknowledges, too, as I suppose, the validity of the law of God. I see a book kissed, which I suppose to be the Bible, or at least the New Testament, which teaches me that all things whatsoever I would that men should do to me, I should do even so to them. It teaches me, further, to remember them that are in bonds as bound with them. I endeavored to act up to that instruction. I say I am yet too young to understand that God is any respecter of persons. I believe that to have interfered as I have done, as I have always freely admitted I have done, in behalf of His despised poor, I did no wrong, but right. Now, if it is deemed necessary that I should forfeit my life for the furtherance of the ends of justice, and mingle my blood further with the blood of my children and with the blood of millions in this slave country whose rights are disregarded by wicked, cruel, and unjust enactments, I say, let it be done.

Let me say one word further. I feel entirely satisfied with the treatment I have received on my trial. Considering all the circumstances, it has been more generous than I expected. But I feel no consciousness of guilt. I have stated from the first what was my intention, and what was not. I never had any design against the liberty of any person, nor any disposition to commit treason or incite slaves to rebel or make any general insurrection. I never encouraged any man to do so, but always discouraged any idea of that kind.

Let me say, also, in regard to the statements made by some of those who were connected with me. I hear it has been stated by some of them that I have induced them to join me. But the contrary is true. I do not say this to injure them, but as regretting their weakness. Not one but joined me of his own accord, and the greater part at their own expense. A number of them I never saw, and never had a word of conversation with, till the day they came to me, and that was for the purpose I have stated.

Now, I have done.

52. From *The Homestead Act* (1862)

The Homestead Act allowed any citizen, or any person who had filed papers to become a citizen, to buy 160 acres of public land in the West for just 10 dollars. In return, the settlers were required to live on the land for five years and make a few improvements. Between 1862 and 1900, the Homestead Act provided land to more than 400,000 families. Women qualified for the purchase as well as men, and many widows and unmarried women moved West to become farmers.

Homesteading proved to be very difficult. About a third of those who tried to develop homesteads eventually failed. On the Great Plains, rain was scarce and a farm or ranch of 160 acres was too small to be economical.

An act to secure homesteads to actual settlers on the public domain.

Be it enacted, That any person who is the head of a family, or who has arrived at the age of twenty-one years, and is a citizen of the United States, or who shall have filed his declaration of intention to become such, as required by the naturalization laws of the United States, and who has never borne arms against the United States Government or given aid and comfort to its enemies, shall, from and after the first of January, eighteen hundred and sixty-three, be entitled to enter one quarter-section or a less quantity of unappropriated public lands, upon which said person may have filled a pre-emption claim, or which may, at the time the application is made, be subject to pre-emption at one dollar and twenty-five cents, or less, per acre; or eighty acres or less of such unappropriated lands, at two dollars and fifty cents per acre, to be located in a body, in conformity to the legal subdivisions of the public lands, and after the same shall have been surveyed: *Provided*, That any person owing or residing on land may, under the provisions of this act, enter other land lying contiguous to his or her said land, which shall not, with the land so already owned and occupied, exceed in the aggregate one hundred and sixty acres. . . .

naturalization: granting of citizenship

one quarter-section: 160 acres; a section is a square mile
pre-emption: right to purchase before others
unappropriated: unclaimed and unused
conformity to: accord with
surveyed: measured and valued
contiguous: next

aggregate: sum

53. Abraham Lincoln, *Gettysburg Address* (1863)

> **For more information see**
> Chapter 25, Book 6, *War, Terrible War.*

The Battle of Gettysburg, fought on July 3, 1863, was the bloodiest battle of the Civil War. It resulted in 50,000 casualties, including 8,000 deaths. In November

1863, with the war still raging, President Lincoln went to Gettysburg to dedicate a military cemetery. He hoped to use the occasion to restate the nation's ideals and to define the aims of the war. Although Lincoln said nothing specifically about slavery or the Emancipation Proclamation, he explained in just 272 words that the "honored dead" had fought for certain fundamental democratic principles, especially the idea of human equality.

Instead of recounting the details of the battle, Lincoln said that the Battle of Gettysburg was a test of constitutional government. Before the Civil War, Americans typically spoke of the United States in the plural—"The United States are." But in his address, Lincoln refers to the United States in the singular, as one nation rededicated to the ideals of the Declaration of Independence.

Fourscore and seven: 87; a score is 20 years

Fourscore and seven years ago our fathers brought forth, on this continent, a new nation, conceived in Liberty, and dedicated to the proposition that all men are created equal.

Now we are engaged in a great civil war, testing whether that nation, or any nation so conceived, and so dedicated, can long endure. We are met on a great battlefield of that war. We have come to dedicate a portion of that field, as a final resting-place for those who here gave their lives, that that nation might live. It is altogether fitting and proper that we should do this.

consecrate: make sacred
hallow: worship

But, in a larger sense, we can not dedicate—we can not consecrate—we can not hallow—this ground. The brave men, living and dead, who struggled here, have consecrated it far above our poor power to add or detract. The world will little note, nor long remember what we say here, but it can never forget what they did here. It is for us the living, rather, to be dedicated here to the unfinished work which they who fought here have thus far so nobly advanced. It is rather for us to be here dedicated to the great task remaining before us—that from these honored dead we take increased devotion to that cause for which they here gave the last full measure of devotion—that we here highly resolve that these dead shall not have died in vain—that this nation, under God, shall have a new birth of freedom—and that government of the people, by the people, for the people, shall not perish from the earth.

54. Abraham Lincoln, *Emancipation Proclamation* (1863)

For more information see
Chapter 20, Book 6, *War, Terrible War.*

The Emancipation Proclamation declared all slaves residing in areas in rebellion against the Union to be free. The proclamation did not affect the status of slaves in slaveholding states that remained in the Union. It also did not apply to Tennessee and portions of Louisiana and Virginia. But the proclamation did officially and immediately free slaves in South Carolina's sea islands, Florida, and some other locations occupied by Union troops. It also transformed the Union forces into an army of liberation.

Lincoln believed that only a constitutional amendment could free all slaves. But as commander-in-chief, he could take any measure necessary to preserve the Union. Freeing the slaves in the rebellious states, he felt, would undermine the Confederate war effort. At the time he issued the preliminary Emancipation Proclamation in September 1862, Lincoln defended it as just such a war measure.

When Lincoln issued the final proclamation on January 1, 1863, he described it not only as "a fit and necessary war measure for suppressing said rebellion," but an "act of justice." In July 1863, Hannah Johnson, the daughter of a fugitive slave, heard a false report that Lincoln was going to reverse the Emancipation Proclamation. She wrote the President: "Don't do it. When you are dead and in Heaven, in a thousand years that action of yours will make the Angels sing your praises. . . ."

January 1, 1863, by the President of the United States of America: A proclamation: Whereas, on the twenty-second day of September, in the year of our Lord one thousand eight hundred and sixty-two, a proclamation was issued by the President of the United States, containing, among other things, the following to wit:

That on the first day of January, in the year of our Lord one thousand eight hundred and sixty-three, all persons held as slaves within any State or designated part of a State, the people whereof shall then be in rebellion against the United States, shall be then, thenceforward, and forever free; and the Executive Government of the United States, including the military and naval authority thereof, will recognize and maintain the freedom of such persons, and will do no act or acts to repress such persons, or any of them, in any efforts they may make for their actual freedom.

aforesaid: mentioned before

countervailing: having the opposite effect

suppressing: holding down, stifling

That the Executive will, on the first day of January aforesaid, by proclamation, designate the States and parts of States, if any, in which the people thereof, shall on that day be, in good faith, represented in the Congress of the United States by members chosen thereto at elections wherein a majority of the qualified voters of such State shall have participated, shall in the absence of strong countervailing testimony, be deemed conclusive evidence that such State, and the people thereof, are not then in rebellion against the United States.

Now, therefore, I, Abraham Lincoln, President of the United States, by virtue of the power in me invested as Commander-in-Chief of the Army and Navy of the United States in time of actual armed rebellion against authority and government of the United States, and as a fit and necessary war measure for suppressing said rebellion, do, on this first day of January, in the year of our Lord one thousand eight hundred and sixty three, and in accordance with my purpose so to do publicly proclaimed for the full period of one hundred days, from the day first above mentioned, order and designate as the States and parts of States wherein the people thereof respectively, are this day in rebellion against the United States the following to wit:

Arkansas, Texas, Louisiana (except the Parishes of St. Bernard, Plaquemines, Jefferson, St. Johns, St. Charles, St. James, Ascension, Assumption, Terrebone, Lafourche, St. Mary, St. Martin, and Orleans, including the City of New Orleans), Mississippi, Alabama, Florida, Georgia, South-Carolina, North Carolina, and Virginia (except the forty-eight counties designated as West Virginia, and also the counties of Berkley, Accomac, Northampton, Elizabeth City, York, Princess Ann, and Norfolk, including the cities of Norfolk and Portsmouth, and which excepted parts are, for the present, left precisely as if this proclamation were not issued).

designated: chosen
henceforward: from now on

And by virtue of the power, and for the purpose aforesaid I do order and declare that all persons held as slaves within said designated States, and parts of States, are, and henceforward shall be free; and the Executive government of the United States, including the military and naval authorities thereof, will recognize and maintain the freedom of said persons.

abstain from: give up

And I hereby enjoin upon the people so declared to be free to abstain from all violence, unless in necessary self-defence; and I recommend to them that, in all cases when allowed, they labor faithfully for reasonable wages.

And I further declare and make known that such persons of suitable condition will be received into the armed service of the United

States to garrison forts, positions, stations, and other places, and to man vessels of all sorts in said service.

garrison: defend

And upon this act, sincerely believed to be an act of justice, warranted by the Constitution, upon military necessity, I invoke the considerate judgment of mankind, and the gracious favor of Almighty God.

invoke: call forth

In witness whereof, I have hereunto set my hand and caused the seal of the United States to be affixed.

Done at the City of Washington, the first day of January, in the year of our Lord one thousand eight hundred and sixty-three, and of the Independence of the United States of America the eighty-seventh.

55. Abraham Lincoln, *Second Inaugural Address* (1865)

For more information see Chapter 27, Book 6, *War, Terrible War.*

Delivered in March 1865, only a month before the end of the Civil War, Lincoln's Second Inaugural Address was intended to reunite the nation. His address stressed the similarities between the North and the South—that they "both read the same Bible, and pray to the same God"—and it cautioned the North against feeling superior. "Let us judge not," he says, "that we be not judged." Speaking to an audience deeply familiar with the Bible, Lincoln asked Northerners and Southerners to regard the war as atonement for the sin of slavery. Since both Northerners and Southerners had tolerated slavery, both sections had to pay the price for their sin in blood. Lincoln closed his address with a plea for harmony and a commitment to care for all the war's victims.

Fellow Countrymen:

At this second appearing to take the oath of the presidential office, there is less occasion for an extended address than there was at the first. Then a statement, somewhat in detail, of a course to be pursued, seemed fitting and proper. Now, at the expiration of four years, during which public declarations have been constantly called forth on every point and phase of the great contest which still absorbs the attention, and engrosses the energies of the nation, little that is new could be presented. The progress of our arms, upon which all else chiefly depends, is as well known to the public as to myself; and it is, I trust, reasonably satisfactory and encouraging to all. With high hope for the future, no prediction in regard to it is ventured.

expiration: end

engrosses: takes up all of

impending: coming soon
avert: avoid

insurgent: rebelling against the government

colored: African-American

perpetuate: make last

magnitude: greatness
duration: length of time

invokes: calls forth

providence: divine direction

discern: recognize

ascribe: see as belonging
scourge: great suffering
bond-man: slave
unrequited: unpaid

On the occasion corresponding to this four years ago, all thoughts were anxiously directed to an impending civil-war. All dreaded it—all sought to avert it. While the inaugural address was being delivered from this place, devoted altogether to *saving* the Union without war, insurgent agents were in the city seeking to *destroy* it without war—seeking to dissolve the Union, and divide effects, by negotiation. Both parties deprecated war; but one of them would *make* war rather than let the nation survive; and the other would *accept* war rather than let it perish. And the war came.

One eighth of the whole population were colored slaves, not distributed generally over the Union, but localized in the Southern part of it. These slaves constituted a peculiar and powerful interest. All knew that this interest was, somehow, the cause of the war. To strengthen, perpetuate, and extend this interest was the object for which the insurgents would rend the Union, even by war; while the government claimed no right to do more than to restrict the territorial enlargement of it. Neither party expected for the war, the magnitude, or the duration, which it has already attained. Neither anticipated that the *cause* of the conflict might cease with, or even before, the conflict itself should cease. Each looked for an easier triumph, and a result less fundamental and astounding. Both read the same Bible, and pray to the same God; and each invokes His aid against the other. It may seem strange that any men should dare to ask a just God's assistance in wringing their bread from the sweat of other men's faces; but let us judge not that we be not judged. The prayers of both could not be answered; that of neither has been answered fully. The Almighty has His own purposes. "Woe unto the world because of offences! for it must needs be that offences come; but woe to that man by whom the offence cometh!" If we shall suppose that American Slavery is one of those offences which, in the providence of God, must needs come, but which, having continued through His appointed time, He now wills to remove, and that He gives to both North and South, this terrible war, as the woe due to those by whom the offence came, shall we discern therein any departure from those divine attributes which the believers in a Living God always ascribe to Him? Fondly do we hope—fervently do we pray—that this mighty scourge of war may speedily pass away. Yet, if God wills that it continue, until all the wealth piled by the bond-man's two hundred and fifty years of unrequited toil shall be sunk, and until every drop of blood drawn with the lash, shall be paid by another drawn with the sword, as was said three thousand years ago, so still it must be said "the judgments of the Lord, are true and righteous altogether."

With malice toward none; with charity for all; with firmness in the right, as God gives us to see the right, let us strive on to finish the work we are in; to bind up the nation's wounds; to care for him who shall have borne the battle, and for his widow, and his orphan—to do all which may achieve and cherish a just, and a lasting peace, among ourselves, and with all nations.

malice: a desire to harm others

56. Ulysses S. Grant and Robert E. Lee, *Letters Setting Terms of Lee's Surrender at Appomattox* (1865)

> **For more information see**
> Chapter 29 Book 6, *War, Terrible War.*

On April 9, 1865, at Appomattox Court House, a village in central Virginia, Confederate General Robert E. Lee surrendered his army to Union General Ulysses S. Grant. The formal surrender ceremony took place on April 12, four years to the day after the war began. These two letters—from General Grant to General Lee, and Lee's reply—give the terms under which Lee surrendered his army.

For ten months, Lee's men withstood a siege by Grant's troops at Petersburg, Virginia, near the Confederate capital of Richmond. But Grant's forces finally broke through Lee's defenses, and for a week, Lee's tired and exhausted army retreated in a last-ditch effort to find supplies and join up with another Confederate army in North Carolina. When Grant overtook Lee's forces at Appomattox, the Confederate general had only 20,000 men left, while Grant had 60,000 soldiers.

Grant treated Lee's army with dignity. He allowed the Confederates to to take their horses with them and sent 25,000 rations to feed the Confederate soldiers.

Appomattox Court-House, Virginia
April 9, 1865

General: In accordance with the substance of my letter to you of the 8th instant, I propose to receive the surrender of the army of Northern Virginia on the following terms, to wit: Rolls of all the officers and men to be made in duplicate, one copy to be given to an officer to be designated by me, the other to be retained by such officer or officers as you may designate. The officers to give their individual

instant: of the current month
Rolls: lists

161

paroles: words of honor, promises

paroles not to take up arms against the government of the United States until properly exchanged; and each company or regimental commander to sign a like parole for the men of their commands. The arms, artillery, and public property to be parked and stacked, and turned over to the officers appointed by me to receive them. This will not embrace the side-arms of the officers nor their private horses or baggage. This done, each officer and man will be allowed to return to his home, not to be disturbed by United States authority so long as they observe their paroles and the laws in force where they may reside.

U. S. Grant, Lieutenant-General

Head-Quarters, Army of Northern Virginia
April 9, 1865

General: I received your letter of this date containing the terms of the surrender of the army of Northern Virginia, as proposed by you. As they are substantially the same as those expressed in your letter of the 8th instant, they are accepted. I will proceed to designate the proper officers to carry the stipulations into effect.

R. E. Lee, General

stipulations: terms of the agreement

For more information see
Chapter 29, Book 6, *War, Terrible War.*

57. Robert E. Lee, *Farewell to His Army* (1865)

In his farewell message to the Army of Northern Virginia, Confederate General Robert E. Lee intentionally omitted any words that could be viewed as political. After the war, Lee tried to set an "example of submission" by swearing allegiance to the United States. He was offered the presidencies of two universities and was invited to become the director of several prominent companies. He accepted the presidency of Washington College in Lexington, Virginia, which was on the verge of closing. Lee redesigned the college program, introducing courses such as chemistry and engineering. After his death, the institution was renamed Washington & Lee University.

Lee never forgot the respect with which Ulysses S. Grant had treated his army. Once, when a professor at the college criticized Grant, Lee said forcefully, "Sir, if you ever again presume to speak disrespectfully of General Grant in my presence, either you or I will sever his connection with this university."

Head-Quarters, Army of Northern Virginia
April 10, 1865

After four years of arduous service, marked by unsurpassed courage and fortitude, the Army of Northern Virginia has been compelled to yield to overwhelming numbers and resources. I need not tell the survivors of so many hard-fought battles, who have remained steadfast to the last, that I have consented to this result from no distrust of them: but, feeling that valour and devotion could accomplish nothing that could compensate for the loss that would have attended the continuation of the contest, I have determined to avoid the useless sacrifice of those whose past services have endeared them to their countrymen. By the terms of the agreement, officers and men can return to their homes and remain there until exchanged. You will take with you the satisfaction that proceeds from the consciousness of duty faithfully performed; and I earnestly pray that a merciful God will extend to you His blessing and protection. With an increasing admiration of your constancy and devotion to your country, and a grateful remembrance of your kind and generous consideration of myself, I bid you an affectionate farewell.

R. E. Lee, General

arduous: difficult, demanding
unsurpassed: unmatched
fortitude: strength

valour: bravery

endeared: made beloved

constancy: faithfulness

58. From Susan B. Anthony, *"Are Women Persons?": Address after Her Arrest for Illegal Voting* (1873)

For more information see
Chapter 27, Book 7, *Reconstruction and Reform*.

In 1869, Susan B. Anthony and Elizabeth Cady Stanton set up the National Woman Suffrage Association. In 1872 and 1873 Anthony tried to vote in congressional elections in Rochester, New York, and was taken to court on charges of vote fraud. During the six months she waited for her trial, Anthony gave many speeches on women's rights. In the speech below, she uses the language of the Constitution to prove that it is wrong for any state to deny women the right to vote. At her trial, she was found guilty and fined $100. She refused to pay the fine, but authorities did not enforce the sentence. It took 72 years and more than 800 campaigns directed at state legislatures, party conventions, state referendums, and Congress before women won the right to vote.

indictment: accusation
alleged: asserted, but not proven

domestic: national or local, but also within a home
tranquility: peace and quiet
posterity: future generations

mockery: something not taken seriously

disfranchisement: inability to vote
bill of attainder: formal removal of a person's civil rights
ex post facto law: a law created after the fact
odious: deserving of hatred
aristocracy: government by a privileged few
oligarchy: rule of the elite

sovereigns: rulers
subjects: servants
dissension: conflict

hardihood: daring, rudeness

abridge: cut short
immunities: protections

Friends and Fellow Citizens:—I stand before you tonight under indictment for the alleged crime of having voted at the last presidential election, without having a lawful right to vote. It shall be my work this evening to prove to you that in thus voting, I not only committed no crime, but, instead, simply exercised my *citizen's rights*, guaranteed to me and all United States citizens by the National Constitution, beyond the power of any State to deny.

The preamble of the Federal Constitution says:

"We, the people of the United States, in order to form a more perfect union, establish justice, insure *domestic* tranquillity, provide for the common defense, promote the general welfare, and secure the blessings of liberty to ourselves and our posterity, do ordain and establish this Constitution for the United States of America."

It was we, the people; not we, the white male citizens; nor yet we, the male citizens; but we, the whole people, who formed the Union. And we formed it, not to give the blessings of liberty, but to secure them; not to the half of ourselves and the half of our posterity, but to the whole people—women as well as men. And it is a downright mockery to talk to women of their enjoyment of the blessings of liberty while they are denied the use of the only means of securing them provided by this democratic-republican government—the ballot.

For any State to make sex a qualification that must ever result in the disfranchisement of one entire half of the people is to pass a bill of attainder, or an *ex post facto* law, and is therefore a violation of the supreme law of the land. By it the blessings of liberty are for ever withheld from women and their female posterity. To them this government has not just powers derived from the consent of the governed. To them this government is not a democracy. It is not a republic. It is an odious aristocracy; a hateful oligarchy of sex; the most hateful aristocracy ever established on the face of the globe; an oligarchy of wealth, where the rich govern the poor. An oligarchy of learning, where the educated govern the ignorant . . . might be endured; but this oligarchy of sex, which makes father, brothers, husband, sons, the oligarchs over the mother and sisters, the wife and daughters of every household—which ordains all men sovereigns, all women subjects, carries dissension, discord and rebellion into every home of the nation.

Webster, Worcester and Bouvier all define a citizen to be a person in the United States, entitled to vote and hold office.

The only question left to be settled now is: Are women persons? And I hardly believe any of our opponents will have the hardihood to say they are not. Being persons, then, women are citizens; and no State has a right to make any law, or to enforce any old law, that shall abridge their privileges or immunities. Hence, every discrimination against women in the constitutions and laws of the several States is to-day null and void, precisely as in every one against negroes.

59. *Preamble to the Constitution of the Knights of Labor* (1878)

For more information see Chapters 16–21, Book 8, *An Age of Extremes*.

The Knights of Labor began in 1869 in Philadelphia as a secret organization of tailors. It had a strongly Protestant religious orientation. A decade later, when a Catholic, Terence V. Powderly, was elected as its head, the Knights became a national organization open to all workers, regardless of their skills, sex, nationality, or race. The only occupations excluded from membership were bankers, gamblers, lawyers, and saloon keepers. At its height in 1885, the Knights claimed to have 700,000 members. The American Federation of Labor, a union of skilled workers, gradually replaced the Knights as the nation's largest labor organization.

The Knights of Labor wanted to organize workers into "one big brotherhood" rather than into separate unions made up of workers who had a common skill or who worked in a particular industry. The Knights campaigned for an eight-hour workday, the abolition of child labor, improved safety in factories, equal pay for men and women, and compensation for job-related injuries.

The recent alarming development and aggression of aggregated wealth, which, unless checked, will invariably lead to the pauperization and hopeless degradation of the toiling masses, render it imperative, if we desire to enjoy the blessings of life, that a check should be placed upon its power and upon unjust accumulation, and a system adopted which will secure to the laborer the fruits of his toil; and as this much-desired object can only be accomplished by the thorough unification of labor, and the united efforts of those who obey the divine injunction that "In the sweat of thy brow shalt thou eat bread," we have formed the ***** with a view of securing the organization and direction, by co-operative effort, of the power of the industrial classes; and we submit to the world the object sought to be accomplished by our organization, calling upon all who believe in securing "the greatest good to the greatest number" to aid and assist us:—

aggregated: combined
pauperization: impoverishment
imperative: absolutely necessary

accumulation: hoarding of money and other resources

unification: bringing together
divine injunction: order from God
*****: the name of the organization (Knights of Labor) omitted for secrecy

I. To bring within the folds of organization every department of productive industry, making knowledge a standpoint for action, and

folds: groups

165

industrial and moral worth, not wealth, the true standard of individual and national greatness.

II. To secure to the toilers a proper share of the wealth that they create; more of the leisure that rightfully belongs to them; more societary advantages; more of the benefits, privileges, and emoluments of the world; in word, all those rights and privileges necessary to make them capable of enjoying, appreciating, defending, and perpetuating the blessing of good government.

III. To arrive at the true condition of the producing masses in their educational, moral, and financial condition, by demanding from the various governments the establishment of bureaus of Labor Statistics.

IV. The establishment of co-operative institutions, productive and distributive.

V. The reserving of the public lands—the heritage of the people—for the actual settler;—not another acre for railroads or speculators.

VI. The abrogation of all laws that do not bear equally upon capital and labor, the removal of unjust technicalities, delays, and discriminations in the administration of justice, and the adopting of measures providing for the health and safety of those engaged in mining, manufacturing, or building pursuits.

VII. The enactment of laws to compel chartered corporations to pay their employees weekly, in full, for labor performed during the preceding week, in the lawful money of the country.

VIII. The enactment of laws giving mechanics and laborers a first lien on their work for their full wages.

IX. The abolishment of the contract system on national, state, and municipal work.

X. The substitution of arbitration for strikes, whenever and wherever employers and employees are willing to meet on equitable grounds.

XI. The prohibition of the employment of children in workshops, mines, and factories before attaining their fourteenth year.

XII. To abolish the system of letting out by contract the labor of convicts in our prisons and reformatory institutions.

XIII. To secure for both sexes equal pay for equal work.

XIV. The reduction of the hours of labor to eight per day, so that the laborers may have more time for social enjoyment and intellectual improvement, and be enabled to reap the advantages conferred by the labor-saving machinery which their brains have created.

XV. To prevail upon governments to establish a purely national circulating medium, based upon the faith and resources of the nation, and issued directly to the people, without the intervention of any

societary: social, public
emoluments: payment for employment
perpetuating: making last longer

productive: for making goods
distributive: for selling or sharing goods
speculators: people who make risky land purchases hoping to make a big profit
abrogation: throwing out
capital: money, investment
technicalities: unimportant rules
discriminations: unfair judgments
chartered: established
mechanics: a skilled manual worker
lien: the right to hold or sell the property of someone in debt as security for the debt
municipal: city
arbitration: resolution of a conflict by a third party

conferred: given

circulating medium: a standard form of money that is commonly traded

system of banking corporations, which money shall be a legal tender in payment of all debts, public or private.

legal tender: legitimate money

60. From John Wesley Powell, *Report on the Arid Region of the West* (1878)

For more information see
Chapter 11, Book 7, *Recon-struction and Reform.*

In the years following the Civil War, John Wesley Powell was America's leading student of the Far West. He understood that the distinctive feature of the region was its limited water supply and that one of the most important questions was how to properly allocate this scarce resource. His *Report on the Arid Region of the West* was the first government study to examine such environmental issues as how to fairly ration water resources, regulate grazing, manage forests, and prevent misuse of the nation's rangelands.

Powell spent considerable time among the Indian tribes of southern Utah and northern Arizona. Convinced that these cultures deserved study and understanding, he founded and served as director of the Smithsonian Institution's Bureau of American Ethnology. Powell was convinced that the federal government needed to inventory the West's natural resources and develop the region in an orderly, democratic, and balanced manner. He convinced the federal government to create the U.S. Geological Survey in 1879, and served as the survey's director from 1881 until 1894.

. . . If the whole of the Arid Region was yet unsettled, it might be wise for the Government to undertake the parceling of the lands and employ skilled engineers to do the work, whose duties could be performed in advance of settlement. . . . Many of the lands surveyed along the minor streams have been entered, and the titles to these lands are in the hands of actual settlers. Many pasturage farms, or ranches, as they are called locally, have been established throughout the country. These remarks are true of every state and territory in the Arid Region. In the main these ranches or pasturage farms are on Government land, and the settlers are squatters, and some are not expecting to make permanent homes. . . . It is now too late for the Government to parcel the pasturage lands in advance of the wants of settlers in the most available way, so as to closely group residences and give water privileges to the several farms. Many of the farmers are actually on the ground, and are clamoring for some means by

pasturage: land that animals graze on

clamoring: making a fuss

vogue: fashion

rapacity: greedy destructiveness

cultivation: farming
scant: few

subsistence: survival
stock: farm animals
irrigable: capable of being
watered and made fertile
inhere: exist naturally
equitable: fair

severed: cut off
tract: area

monopoly: control by a single
party
magnitude: greatness

which they can obtain titles to pasturage farms of an extent adequate to their wants, and the tens of thousands of individual interests would make the problem a difficult one for the officers of the Government to solve. A system less arbitrary than that of the rectangular surveys now in vogue, and requiring unbiased judgement, overlooking the interests of single individuals and considering only the interests of the greatest number, would meet with local opposition. . . .

Under these circumstances it is believed that it is best to permit the people to divide their lands for themselves—not in a way by which each man may take what he pleases for himself, but by providing methods by which these settlers may organize and mutually protect each other from the rapacity of individuals. The lands, as lands, are of but slight value, as they cannot be used for ordinary agricultural purposes, i.e., the cultivation of crops; but their value consists in the scant grasses which they spontaneously produce, and these values can be made available only by the use of the waters necessary for the subsistence of stock, and that necessary for the small amount of irrigable land which should be attached to the several pasturage farms. Thus, practically, all values inhere in the water, and an equitable division of the waters can be made only by a wise system of parcelling the lands; and the people in organized bodies can well be trusted with this right, while individuals could not thus be trusted. These considerations have led to the plan suggested in the bill submitted for the organization of pasturage districts.

When the area to which it is possible to take the water of any given stream is much greater than the stream is competent to serve, if the land titles and water rights are severed, the owner of any tract of land is at the mercy of the owner of the water right. In general the lands greatly exceed the capacities of the streams. Thus the lands have no value without water. If the water rights fall into the hands of irrigating companies and the lands into the hands of individual farmers, the farmers then will be dependent upon the stock companies, and eventually the monopoly of water rights will be an intolerable burden to the people.

The magnitude of the interests involved must not be overlooked. All the present and future agriculture of more than four-tenths of the area of the United States is dependent upon irrigation, and practically all values for agricultural industries inhere, not in the lands, but in the water. Monopoly of land need not be feared. The question for legislators to solve is to devise some practical means by which water rights may be distributed among individual farmers and water monopolies prevented. . . .

The pioneer is fully engaged in the present with its hopes of immediate remuneration for labor. The present development of the country fully occupies him. For this reason every effort put forth to increase the area of the agricultural land by irrigation is welcomed. Every man who turns his attention to this department of industry is considered a public benefactor. But if in the eagerness for present development a land and water system shall grow up in which the practical control of agriculture shall fall into the hands of water companies, evils will result therefrom that generations may not be able to correct, and the very men who are now lauded as benefactors to the country will, in the ungovernable reaction which is sure to come, be denounced as oppressors of the people.

The right to use water should inhere in the land to be irrigated, and water rights should go with land titles.

For the great purposes of irrigation and hydraulic mining the water has no value in its natural channel. In general the water cannot be used for irrigation on the lands immediately contiguous to the streams—i.e., the flood plains or bottom valleys. . . . Thus, to use the water it must be diverted from its natural course often miles or scores of miles from where it is to be used. . . .

[I]t is to be feared that water rights will in many cases be separated from all land rights as the system is now forming. . . . Monopolies of water will be secured, and the whole agriculture of the country will be tributary thereto—a condition of affairs which an American citizen having in view the interests of the largest number of the people cannot contemplate with favor.

remuneration: payment

benefactor: contributor

lauded: praised

denounced: harshly criticized
oppressors: people who take away the rights of others

tributary: dependent on

contemplate: think about

61. Chief Joseph (Inmutooyahlatlat), *"I Will Fight No More Forever": Speech to the U.S. Army* (1877)

For more information see
Chapter 18, Book 7, *Reconstruction and Reform.*

In 1877, the U.S. government ordered the Nez Perce Indians, then living in eastern Oregon's Wallowa valley, to move to a reservation in Idaho. Several bands, including one led by Chief Joseph, refused to move. Meanwhile, several Nez Perce youth, angered by broken treaty promises, attacked and killed 18 Idaho settlers. For three months in the summer and fall of 1877, the U.S. cavalry and infantry pursued Chief Joseph and 800 of his followers, who were headed toward Canada—and safety. They eluded and outfought 2,000 Army soldiers in

13 battles before finally surrendering in a Montana snowstorm, just 40 miles from the Canadian border. Only 418 men, women, and children survived.

On October 5, Chief Joseph, leader of the Nez Perce, rode up to the American soldiers who had chased his people across 1,200 miles of rugged lands in Idaho, Montana, and Wyoming. He surrendered to them with the stirring words, "From where the sun now stands I will fight no more forever."

Tell General Howard I know his heart. What he told me before, I have it in my heart. I am tired of fighting. Our chiefs are killed. Looking Glass is dead. Toohoolhoolzote is dead. The old men are all dead. It is the young men who say, "Yes" or "No." He who led the young men is dead. It is cold, and we have no blankets. The little children are freezing to death. My people, some of them, have run away to the hills, and have no blankets, no food. No one knows where they are—perhaps freezing to death. I want to have time to look for my children, and see how many of them I can find. Maybe I shall find them among the dead. Hear me, my chiefs! I am tired. My heart is sick and sad. From where the sun now stands I will fight no more forever.

For more information see Chapter 18, Book 7, *Reconstruction and Reform*.

62. From Chief Joseph (Inmutooyahlatlat), *Address in Washington* (1879)

The surrender of Chief Joseph ended a decade of warfare between Indians and the U.S. government in the Far West. It meant that virtually all western Indians had been forced to live on government reservations. Under the terms of the surrender, the Nez Perce were promised that they could live on a reservation in Lapwai, Idaho, but instead they were sent to Oklahoma. Chief Joseph traveled to the nation's capital to plead for justice on behalf of his people. On January 14, 1879, he delivered a two-hour speech before an audience of congressmen and diplomats. In his address, Chief Joseph recounted the entire story of the Nez Perce, from the days of their first contact with whites to their exile onto reservations.

. . . [T]here are some things I want to know which no one seems able to explain.

I cannot understand how the government sends a man out to fight us, as it did General Miles, and then breaks his word. Such a government has something wrong about it.

I cannot understand why so many chiefs are allowed to talk so many different ways, and promise so many different things. I have seen the Great Father Chief [president], the next Great Chief [secretary of the Interior], the Commissioner Chief [Hayt], the Law Chief [General Butler], and many other law chiefs [congressmen], and they all say they are my friends, and that I shall have justice. But while their mouths all talk right I do not understand why nothing has been done for my people.

I have heard talk and talk, but nothing is done. Good words do not last long unless they amount to something.

Words do not pay for my dead people. They do not pay for my country, now overrun by white men. They do not protect my father's grave. They do not pay for all my horses and cattle.

Good words will not give me back my children. Good words will not make good the promise of your War Chief General Miles. Good words will not give my people good health and stop them from dying. Good words will not get my people a home where they can live in peace and take care of themselves.

I am tired of talk that comes to nothing.

It makes my heart sick when I remember all the good words and the broken promises.

There has been too much talking by men who had no right to talk. Too many misrepresentations have been made; too many misunderstandings have come up between the white men about the Indians.

If the white man wants to live in peace with the Indian he can live in peace. There need be no trouble. Treat all men alike. Give them the same law. Give them all an even chance to live and grow.

All men were made by the same Great Spirit Chief. They are all brothers. The earth is the mother of all people, and all people should have equal rights upon it.

You might as well expect the rivers to run backward as that any man who was born a free man should be contented when penned up and denied liberty to go where he pleases. If you tie a horse to a stake, do you expect he will grow fat? If you pen an Indian up on a small spot of earth and compel him to stay there, he will not be contented, nor will he grow and prosper.

compel: force

I have asked some of the great white chiefs where they get their authority to say to the Indian that he shall stay in one place, while he sees white men going where they please. They cannot tell me.

I only ask of the government to be treated as all other men are treated. If I cannot go to my own home, let me have a home in some country where my people will not die so fast.

I would like to go to the Bitterroot valley. There my people would be healthy; where they are now, they are dying. Three have died since I left my camp to come to Washington.

When I think of our condition my heart is heavy. I see men of my race treated as outlaws and driven from country to country, or shot down like animals.

I know that my race must change. We cannot hold our own with the white men as we are. We only ask an even chance to live as other men live.

We ask to be recognized as men. We ask that the same law shall work alike on all men. If the Indian breaks the law, punish him by the law. If the white man breaks the law, punish him also.

Let me be a free man—free to travel, free to stop, free to work, free to trade where I choose, free to choose my own teachers, free to follow the religion of my fathers, free to think and talk and act for myself—and I will obey every law, or submit to the penalty.

When the white man treats an Indian as they treat each other, then we will have no more wars. We shall all be alike—brothers of one father and one mother, with one sky above us and one government for all.

Then the Great Spirit Chief who rules above will smile upon this land, and send rain to wash out the bloody spots made by brothers' hands from the face of the earth.

For this time the Indian race are waiting and praying.

I hope that no more groans of wounded men and women will ever go to the ear of the Great Spirit Chief above, and that all people may be one people.

In-mut-too-yah-lat-lat has spoken for his people.

For more information see
Chapters 24 and 25, Book 7, *Reconstruction and Reform.*

63. From Stanley Matthews, opinion in *Yick Wo* v. *Hopkins, Sheriff, etc.* (1886)

This case established the principle that a law that appears to be racially neutral on the surface is unconstitutional if it is applied in a discriminatory manner. A San Francisco law made it a crime to operate a laundry business in any building not made of brick or stone. City officials could, however, grant exceptions to some wooden structures.

San Francisco's officials used the law to blatantly discriminate against people of Chinese descent. City officials licensed 80 wooden laundries run by whites but denied permits to about 200 Chinese laundry operators. In a landmark decision, the U.S. Supreme Court struck down the San Francisco law, ruling that it violated the 14th Amendment and its guarantee of equal protection under the law. A unanimous court ruled that the 14th Amendment's guarantee of equal protection applies "to all persons . . . without regard to any difference of race, of color, or of nationality."

The rights of the petitioners, as affected by the proceedings of which they complain, are not less because they are aliens and subjects of the emperor of China. By the third article of the treaty between this government and that of China, concluded November 17, 1880, it is stipulated: "If Chinese laborers, or Chinese of any other class, now either permanently or temporarily residing in the territory of the United States, meet with ill treatment at the hands of any other person, the government of the United States will exert all its powers to devise measures for their protection, and to secure to them the same rights, privileges, immunities, and exemptions as may be enjoyed by citizens or subjects of the most favored nation, and to which they are entitled by treaty." The fourteenth amendment to the constitution is not confined to the protection of citizens. It says: "Nor shall any state deprive any person of life, liberty, or property without due process of law; nor deny to any person within its jurisdiction the equal protection of the laws." These provisions are universal in their application, to all persons within the territorial jurisdiction, without regard to any differences of race, of color, or of nationality; and the equal protection of the laws is a pledge of the protection of equal laws. . . .

[The] fundamental rights to life, liberty, and the pursuit of happiness, considered as individual possessions, are secured by those maxims of constitutional law which are the monuments showing the victorious progress of the race in securing to men the blessings of civilization under the reign of just and equal laws, so that, in the famous language of the Massachusetts bill of rights, the government of the commonwealth "may be a government of laws and not of men." For the very idea that one man may be compelled to hold his life, or the means of living, or any material right essential to the enjoyment of life, at the mere will of another, seems to be intolerable in any country where freedom prevails, as being the essence of slavery itself. . . .

petitioners: people who file a lawsuit against someone else
proceedings: actions
aliens: foreigners

immunities: protections
exemptions: freedoms from
due process of law: to act fairly, according to established legal procedures

universal: applying to everyone
jurisdiction: area over which an authority has power

requisite: requirement

It appears that both petitioners have complied with every requisite deemed by the law, or by the public officers charged with its administration, necessary for the protection of neighboring property from fire, or as a precaution against injury to the public health. No reason whatever, except the will of the supervisors, is assigned why they should not be permitted to carry on, in the accustomed manner, their harmless and useful occupation, on which they depend for a livelihood; and while this consent of the supervisors is withheld from them, and from 200 others who have also petitioned, all of whom happen to be Chinese subjects, 80 others, not Chinese subjects, are permitted to carry on the same business under similar conditions. The fact of this discrimination is admitted. No reason for it is shown, and the conclusion cannot be resisted that no reason for it exists except hostility to the race and nationality to which the petitioners belong, and which, in the eye of the law, is not justified. The discrimination is therefore illegal, and the public administration which enforces it is a denial of the equal protection of the laws, and a violation of the fourteenth amendment of the constitution. The imprisonment of the petitioners is therefore illegal, and they must be discharged. . . .

For more information see
Chapter 1, Book 8, *An Age of Extremes.*

64. From Andrew Carnegie, *Wealth* (1889)

The industrialist Andrew Carnegie published this essay, sometimes called "The Gospel of Wealth," in 1889. In it, he argued that rich people have a moral duty to help the poor. "The man who dies rich," he declared, "dies disgraced." But he did not believe that wealthy people should simply give their money away. He wanted them to promote progress according to the "principles of scientific charity." The millionaire, he argued, should be a "trustee for his poorer brethren, bringing to their service his superior wisdom, experience, and ability to administer, doing for them better than they would or could do for themselves."

Carnegie set up foundations and eventually donated more than $180 million for museums, concert halls, universities, and 2,811 libraries around the world. He provided library buildings, but expected local communities to staff and furnish the buildings themselves.

The problem of our age is the proper administration of wealth, that the ties of brotherhood may still bind together the rich and poor in harmonious relationship. The conditions of human life have not only been changed, but revolutionized, within the past few hundred years. In former days there was little difference between the dwelling, dress, food, and environment of the chief and those of his retainers. . . . The contrast between the palace of the millionaire and the cottage of the laborer with us to-day measures the change which has come with civilization. This change, however, is not to be deplored, but welcomed as highly beneficial. It is well, say, essential, for the progress of the race that the houses of some should be homes for all that is highest and best in literature and the arts, and for all the refinements of civilization, rather than that none should be so. Much better this great irregularity than universal squalor. Without wealth there can be no Meccenas. . . .

[T]o-day the world obtains commodities of excellent quality at prices which even the preceding generation would have deemed incredible. In the commercial world similar causes have produced similar results, and the race is benefited thereby. The poor enjoy what the rich could not before afford. What were the luxuries have become the necessaries of life. . . .

Objections to the foundations upon which society is based are not in order, because the condition of the race is better with these than it has been with any other which has been tried. . . . No evil, but good, has come to the race from the accumulation of wealth by those who have had the ability and energy to produce it. . . .

We start, then, with a condition of affairs under which the best interests of the race are promoted, but which inevitably gives wealth to the few. . . . What is the proper mode of administering wealth after the laws upon which civilization is founded have thrown it into the hands of the few? . . .

There are but three modes in which surplus wealth can be disposed of. It can be left to the families of the decedents; or it can be bequeathed for public purposes; or, finally, it can be administered by its possessors during their lives. . . .

There remains, then, only one mode of suing great fortunes; but in this we have the true antidote for the temporary unequal distribution of wealth, the reconciliation of the rich and the poor—a reign of harmony, another ideal, differing, indeed, from that of the Communist in requiring only the further evolution of existing conditions, not the total overthrow of our civilization. It is founded upon the most intense Individualism. . . . Under its sway we shall have an ideal State, in which the surplus wealth of the few will become, in the best sense, property of the many, because administering for the common good; and this wealth, which passes through the hands of the few, can be made a much more potent force for the elevation of our race than if distributed in small sums to the people themselves. Even

deplored: considered a very bad thing

squalor: dirtiness, poverty
Meccenas: generous patrons; Maecenas was a Roman statesman and patron of literature
commodities: goods

accumulation: building up

surplus: extra, unneeded
decedents: people who have died
bequeathed: given

suing: asking for and being given
antidote: remedy, cure
reconciliation: act of making equal
evolution: development, refinement

potent: strong, having an impact

unostentatious: not fancy
extravagance: fancy and wasteful

trust funds: savings accounts held on behalf of another

bestowing: giving

alms: small amounts of money given directly to the poor

Peter Cooper . . . Senator Stanford: wealthy men who donated money for community projects

distribution: giving, donating
Individualism: gathering of personal wealth

the poorest can be made to see this, and to agree that great sums gathered by some of their fellow-citizens—spent for public purposes, from which masses reap the principal benefit, are more valuable to them than if scattered among themselves in trifling amounts through the course of many years. . . .

This, then, is held to be the duty of the man of wealth: To set an example of modest, unostentatious living, shunning display or extravagance; to provide moderately for the legitimate wants of those dependent upon him; and, after doing so, to consider all surplus revenues which come to him simply as trust funds, which he is called upon to administer, and strictly bound as a matter of duty to administer in the manner which, in his judgment, is best calculated to produce the most beneficial results for the community—the man of wealth thus becoming the mere trustee and agent for his poorer brethren, bringing to their service his superior wisdom, experience, and ability to administer, doing for them better than they would or could do for themselves. . . .

In bestowing charity, the main consideration should be to help those who will help themselves; to provide part of the means by which those who desire to improve may do so; to give those who desire to rise the aids by which they may rise; to assist, but rarely or never to do all. Neither the individual nor the race is improved by alms giving. Those worthy of assistance, except in rare cases, seldom require assistance. . . .

The rich man is thus almost restricted to following the examples of Peter Cooper, Enoch Pratt of Baltimore, Mr. Pratt of Brooklyn, Senator Stanford, and others, who know that the best means of benefiting the community is to place within its reach the ladders upon which the aspiring can rise—free libraries, parks, and means of recreation, by which men are helped in body and mind; works of art, certain to give pleasure and improve the general condition of the people; in this manner returning their surplus wealth to the mass of their fellows in the forms best calculated to do them lasting good.

Thus is the problem of rich and poor to be solved. The laws of accumulation will be left free, the laws of distribution free. Individualism will continue, but the millionaire will be but a trustee for the poor, intrusted for a season with a great part of the increased wealth of the community, but administering it for the community far better than it could or would have done for itself. The best minds will thus have reached a stage in the development of the race in which it is clearly seen that there is no mode of disposing of surplus wealth creditable to thoughtful and earnest men into whose hands it flows, save by using it year by year for the general good. . . .

Such, in my opinion, is the true gospel concerning wealth, obedience to which is destined some day to solve the problem of the rich and the poor, and to bring "Peace on earth, among men good will."

65. From *Preamble to the Platform of the Populist Party* (1892)

For more information see
Chapters 9 and 14, Book 8, *An Age of Extremes.*

In 1892, the Populist party, an alliance of farmers from the South and the Great Plains, held its first national convention in Omaha, Nebraska. "We seek to restore the government . . . to the hands of 'the plain people,'" the party platform declared. Many farmers felt victimized by falling crop prices. They complained of exploitation by railroads, moneylenders, land speculators, and big businesses.

The Omaha platform proposed many reforms that the country would eventually adopt, including a graduated income tax, direct election of U.S. Senators, and an eight-hour workday. It also supported the secret ballot, the right of workers to organize, and the initiative and recall (mechanism that would allow voters to propose legislation and remove public officials from office). More important than its specific proposals, the Omaha platform envisioned a new role for the federal government. It called for a strong, active government dedicated to ending "oppression, injustice and poverty."

The conditions which surround us best justify our co-operation; we meet in the midst of a nation brought to the verge of moral, political, and material ruin. Corruption dominates the ballot-box, the Legislatures, the Congress, and touches even the ermine of the bench. The people are demoralized; most of the States have been compelled to isolate the voters at the polling places to prevent universal intimidation and bribery. The newspapers are largely subsidized or muzzled, public opinion silenced, business prostrated, homes covered with mortgages, labor impoverished, and the land concentrating in the hands of capitalists. The urban workmen are denied the right to organize for self-protection, imported pauperized labor beats down their wages, a hireling standing army, unrecognized by our laws, is established to shoot them down, and they are rapidly degenerating into European conditions. The fruits of the toil of millions are boldly stolen to build up colossal fortunes for a few, unprecedented in the history of mankind; and the possessors of

material: financial
Corruption: dishonesty
ermine of the bench: judges
isolate: hold apart from others
subsidized: supported financially
intimidation: controlling someone through fear
prostrated: weakened, overcome
mortgages: loans to pay for a house
capitalists: businesspeople
pauperized: made very poor
hireling: person who is paid for a job
degenerating: breaking down
colossal: huge
unprecedented: having never existed before

prolific: producing a great deal

legal-tender currency: official money issued by the government
gold-bearing: backed by gold

demonetized: no longer used as money
abridged: cut short
usurers: people who charge very high interest rates for loans
bankrupt: ruin financially
conspiracy: network of people who agree to act against the best interests of others
forebodes: predicts a negative outcome
despotism: the unchecked exercise of power

sham: fake
tariff: tax
rings: monies obtained through begging or blackmail
trusts: groups of people that control all the companies in an industry
watered stock: shares of a company that are sold for more than they are worth
mammon: riches, improperly loved and worshipped

posterity: future generations

these, in turn, despise the Republic and endanger liberty. From the same prolific womb of governmental injustice we breed the two great classes—tramps and millionaires.

The national power to create money is appropriated to enrich bond-holders; a vast public debt payable in legal-tender currency has been funded into gold-bearing bonds, thereby adding millions to the burdens of the people.

Silver, which has been accepted as coin since the dawn of history, has been demonetized to add to the purchasing power of gold by decreasing the value of all forms of property as well as human labor, and the supply of currency is purposely abridged to fatten usurers, bankrupt enterprise, and enslave industry. A vast conspiracy against mankind has been organized on two continents, and it is rapidly taking possession of the world. If not met and overthrown at once it forebodes terrible social convulsions, or the destruction of civilization, or the establishment of an absolute despotism.

We have witnessed for more than a quarter of a century the struggles of the two great political parties for power and plunder, while grievous wrongs have been inflicted upon the suffering people. We charge that the controlling influences dominating both these parties have permitted the existing dreadful conditions to develop without serious effort to prevent or restrain them. Neither do they now promise us any substantial reform. They have agreed together to ignore, in the coming campaign, every issue but one. They propose to drown the outcries of a plundered people with the uproar of a sham battle over the tariff, so that capitalists, corporations, national banks, rings, trusts, watered stock, the demonetization of silver and the oppressions of the usurers may all be lost sight of. They propose to sacrifice our homes, lives, and children on the altar of mammon; to destroy the multitude in order to secure corruption funds from the millionaires.

Assembled on the anniversary of the birthday of the nation, and filled with the spirit of the grand general and chief who established our independence, we seek to restore the government of the Republic to the hands of the "plain people," with which class it originated. We assert our purposes to be identical with the purposes of the National Constitution; to form a more perfect union and establish justice, insure domestic tranquillity, provide for the common defence, promote the general welfare, and secure the blessings of liberty for ourselves and our posterity.

We declare that this Republic can only endure as a free government while built upon the love of the people for each other and for the nation; that it cannot be pinned together by bayonets; that the Civil War is over, and that every passion and resentment which grew out of it must die with it, and that we must be in fact, as we are in name, one united brotherhood of free men.

Our country finds itself confronted by conditions for which there is no precedent in the history of the world; our annual agricultural productions amount to billions of dollars in value, which must, within a few weeks or months, be exchanged for billions of dollars' worth of commodities consumed in their production; the existing currency supply is wholly inadequate to make this exchange; the results are falling prices, the formation of combines and rings, the impoverishment of the producing class. We pledge ourselves that if given power we will labor to correct these evils by wise and reasonable legislation, in accordance with the terms of our platform.

precedent: previous instance

We believe that the power of government—in other words, of the people—should be expanded (as in the case of the postal service) as rapidly and as far as the good sense of an intelligent people and the teachings of experience shall justify, to the end that oppression, injustice, and poverty shall eventually cease in the land.

While our sympathies as a party of reform are naturally upon the side of every proposition which will tend to make men intelligent, virtuous, and temperate, we nevertheless regard these questions, important as they are, as secondary to the great issues now pressing for solution, and upon which not only our individual prosperity but the very existence of free institutions depend; and we ask all men to first help us to determine whether we are to have a republic to administer before we differ as to the conditions upon which it is to be administered, believing that the forces of reform this day organized will never cease to move forward until every wrong is righted and equal rights and equal privileges securely established for all the men and women of this country.

temperate: moderate, not excessive

66. The Pledge of Allegiance (1892, revised 1923 and 1954)

The "Pledge of Allegiance" first appeared in 1892 in *The Youth's Companion*, a popular children's magazine. It was written to commemorate the 400th anniversary of Columbus's discovery of the New World and to unite Americans during a time of massive immigration. We are not sure whether the pledge was written by James B. Upsham (the magazine's editor), Francis Bellamy (an ordained minister), or a combination of the two men. Upsham said that he was inspired to write the pledge after reading a newspaper editorial criticizing flag-raising ceremonies. The editor said that the ceremonies were no more than "worship of a textile fabric." He was convinced that the pledge children said at the time—"I give my hand and heart to my country, one nation, one language, one flag"— was not stirring enough and that the country needed a more impressive pledge.

The pledge has been changed twice over the years. In 1923, the words "the flag of the United States of America" was substituted for "my flag," and Congress added the phrase "under God" in 1954. There has also been a change in the salute to the flag. Originally, people saluted the flag by raising their right arms upward. But to distinguish their show of respect to the flag from the Nazi salute, Americans began to place their right hands over the hearts.

I pledge allegiance
To the flag of the United States of America
And to the republic for which it stands,
One nation under God,
Indivisible, with liberty and justice for all.

For more information see

Chapter 35, Book 7, *Reconstruction and Reform.*

67. From Booker T. Washington, *Address at the Atlanta Exposition* (1895)

In a 10-minute speech delivered on a hot September afternoon at the Cotton States Exposition in Atlanta, Booker T. Washington urged African Americans to accept social segregation as the price for acquiring education and economic security. He argued that northern industrialists should be urged to invest in the South and that African Americans should share in the economic growth that northern investment would bring. In return, African Americans should abandon, at least temporarily, the quest for full political and civil rights. "In all things purely social," he explained, "we can be as separate as the fingers, yet as the hand in all things essential to mutual progress." In his speech, Washington opposed labor unions and foreign immigration. He argued that these were not in the interests of African Americans.

W.E.B. DuBois, the nation's first black to earn a doctoral degree, condemned Washington for failing to speak out publicly for racial equality. But in secret, Washington fought lynching and financed court tests of laws that upheld segregation and bars to black voting.

Mr. President and Gentlemen of the Board of Directors and Citizens: One-third of the population of the South is of the Negro race. No enterprise seeking the material, civil, or moral welfare of this section can disregard this element of our population and reach the highest success. I but convey to you, Mr. President and directors, the sentiment of the masses of my race when I say that in no way have the value and manhood of the American Negro been more fittingly and generously recognized than by the managers of this magnificent exposition at every stage of its progress. It is a recognition that will do more to cement the friendship of the two races than any occurrence since the dawn of our freedom.

Not only this, but the opportunity here afforded will awaken among us a new era of industrial progress. Ignorant and inexperienced, it is not strange that in the first years of our new life we began at the top instead of at the bottom; that a seat in Congress or the state legislature was more sought than real estate or industrial skill; that the political convention or stump speaking had more attractions than starting a dairy farm or truck garden.

A ship lost at sea for many days suddenly sighted a friendly vessel. From the mast of the unfortunate vessel was seen a signal, "Water, water; we die of thirst!" The answer from the friendly vessel at once came back, "Cast down your bucket where you are." And a third and fourth signal for water was answered, "Cast down your bucket where you are." The captain of the distressed vessel, at last heeding the injunction, cast down his bucket, and it came up full of fresh, sparkling water from the mouth of the Amazon River. To those of my race who depend on bettering their condition in a foreign land or who underestimate the importance of cultivating friendly relations with the Southern white man, who is their next-door neighbor, I would say: "Cast down your bucket where you are"—cast it down in making friends in every manly way of the people of all races by whom we are surrounded.

Cast it down in agriculture, mechanics, in commerce, in domestic service, and in the professions. And in this connection it is well to bear in mind that whatever other sins the South may be called to bear, when it comes to business, pure and simple, it is in the South that the Negro is given a man's chance in the commercial world, and in nothing is this exposition more eloquent than in emphasizing this chance. Our greatest danger is that in the great leap from slavery to freedom we may overlook the fact that the masses of us are to live by the productions of our hands, and fail to keep in mind that we shall prosper in proportion as we learn to dignify and glorify common labor and put brains and skill into the common occupations of life;

enterprise: undertaking

convey: express
sentiment: feeling

stump speaking: traveling around and giving speeches
truck garden: garden for growing vegetables that are put on trucks and sold in the city

181

superficial: unimportant
substantial: important
gew-gaws: worthless things

shall prosper in proportion as we learn to draw the line between the superficial and the substantial, the ornamental gew-gaws of life and the useful. No race can prosper till it learns that there is as much dignity in tilling a field as in writing a poem. It is at the bottom of life we must begin, and not at the top. Nor should we permit our grievances to overshadow our opportunities.

fidelity: faith
treacherous: unreliable, deceitful

To those of the white race who look to the incoming of those of foreign birth and strange tongue and habits for the prosperity of the South, were I permitted I would repeat what I say to my own race, "Cast down your bucket where you are." Cast it down among the eight millions of Negroes whose habits you know, whose fidelity and love you have tested in days when to have proved treacherous meant the ruin of your firesides. Cast down your bucket among these people who have, without strikes and labor wars, tilled your fields, cleared your forests, built your railroads and cities, and brought forth trea-

bowels: depths

sures from the bowels of the earth, and helped make possible this magnificent representation of the progress of the South. Casting down your bucket among my people, helping and encouraging them as you are doing on these grounds, and to education of head, hand,

surplus: extra, unneeded

and heart, you will find that they will buy your surplus land, make blossom the waste places in your fields, and run your factories. While doing this, you can be sure in the future, as in the past, that you and your families will be surrounded by the most patient, faithful, law-abiding, and unresentful people that the world has seen. As we have proved our loyalty to you in the past, in nursing your children, watching by the sick-bed of your mothers and fathers, and often following them with tear-dimmed eyes to their graves, so in the future, in our humble way, we shall stand by you with a devotion that no foreigner can approach, ready to lay down our lives, if need be, in defense of yours, interlacing our industrial, commercial, civil, and religious life with yours in a way that shall make the interests of both races one. In all things that are purely social we can be as separate as the fingers, yet one as the hand in all things essential to mutual progress.

There is no defense or security for any of us except in the highest intelligence and development of all. If anywhere there are efforts tending to curtail the fullest growth of the Negro, let these efforts be turned into stimulating, encouraging, and making him the most useful and intelligent citizen. Effort or means so invested will pay a thousand percent interest. These efforts will be twice blessed—"blessing him that gives and him that takes."

inevitable: cannot be avoided

There is no escape through law of man or God from the inevitable:

The laws of changeless justice bind
Oppressor with oppressed;

And close as sin and suffering joined
We march to fate abreast.

Nearly sixteen millions of hands will aid you in pulling the load upward; or they will pull against you the load downward. We shall constitute one-third and more of the ignorance and crime of the South, or one-third its intelligence and progress; we shall contribute one-third to the business and industrial prosperity of the South, or we shall prove a veritable body of death, stagnating, depressing, retarding every effort to advance the body politic. Gentlemen of the exposition, as we present to you our humble effort at an exhibition of our progress, you must not expect overmuch. Starting thirty years ago with ownership here and there in a few quilts and pumpkins and chickens (gathered from miscellaneous sources), remember the path that has led from these to the inventions and production of agricultural implements, buggies, steam engines, newspapers, books, statuary, carving, paintings, the management of drugstores and banks, has not been trodden without contact with thorns and thistles. While we take pride in what we exhibit as a result of our independent efforts, we do not for a moment forget that our part in this exhibition would fall far short of your expectations but for the constant help that has come to our educational life, not only from the Southern states, but especially from Northern philanthropists, who have made their gifts a constant stream of blessing and encouragement.

The wisest among my race understand that the agitation of questions of social equality is the extreme folly, and that progress in the enjoyment of all the privileges that will come to us must be the result of severe and constant struggle rather than of artificial forcing. No race that has anything to contribute to the markets of the world is long in any degree ostracized. It is important and right that all privileges of the law be ours, but it is vastly more important that we be prepared for the exercises of these privileges. The opportunity to earn a dollar in a factory just now is worth infinitely more that the opportunity to spend a dollar in an opera house.

In conclusion, may I repeat that nothing in thirty years has given us more hope and encouragement, and drawn us so near to you of the white race, as this opportunity offered by the exposition; and here bending, as it were, over the altar that represents the results of the struggles of your race and mine, both starting practically empty-handed three decades ago, I pledge that in your effort to work out the great and intricate problem which God has laid at the doors of the South, you shall have at all times the patient, sympathetic help of my race; only let this be constantly in mind, that, while from representations in these buildings of the product of the field, of forest, of mine,

stagnating: motionless, lacking energy or force

implements: tools
statuary: statues

philanthropists: people who give money to charity

ostracized: left out

intricate: complicated

material: touchable, real

animosities: discord, hostilities

of factory, letters, and art, much good will come, yet far above and beyond material benefits will be that higher good, that, let us pray God, will come, in a blotting out of sectional differences and racial animosities and suspicions, in a determination to administer absolute justice, in a willing obedience among all classes to the mandates of the law. This, this, coupled with our material prosperity, will bring into our beloved South a new heaven and a new earth.

For more information see
Chapter 12, Book 10, *All the People*.

68. From John Marshall Harlan, dissenting opinion in *Plessy* v. *Ferguson* (1896)

In 1896, the Supreme Court declared that racial segregation was acceptable under the Constitution. In *Plessy* v. *Ferguson* the court upheld a Louisiana law that required railroads operating within the state to provide "separate but equal" accommodations for blacks and whites. The law also required people to ride in railroad cars assigned to them by race. The case involved Homer Plessy, who was one-eighth Negro and who had sat in a whites-only railroad car. He was arrested and the U.S. Supreme Court eventually upheld Louisiana's law by a 7-to-1 vote. The majority ruled that the the 13th Amendment, which abolished all vestiges of slavery, and the 14th Amendment, which guarantees "equal protection of the laws," did not prohibit "distinction based on color." This decision provided the legal basis for segregation for nearly six decades, until the Supreme Court rejected the "separate but equal" doctrine in 1954 in the case of *Brown* v. *Board of Education*.

The dissenting vote was cast by John Marshall Harlan, the son of a Kentucky slaveholder. "There is in this country no superior, dominant, ruling class of citizens," he wrote in an angry dissent. "Our Contitution is color-blind. . . ." His grandson and namesake, John Marshall Harlan II, was one of the justices who overturned the Plessy decision and ruled that attempts to segregate public schools were unconstitutional.

judicial tribunal: court of law

pertains: has to do with

I deny that any legislative body or judicial tribunal may have regard to the race of citizens when the civil rights of those citizens are involved. Indeed, such legislation as that here in question is inconsistent not only with that equality of rights which pertains to citizenship, national and state, but with the personal liberty enjoyed by every one within the United States.

The thirteenth amendment does not permit the withholding or the deprivation of any right necessarily inhering in freedom. It not only struck down the institution of slavery as previously existing in the United States, but it prevents the imposition of any burdens or disabilities that constitute badges of slavery or servitude. It decreed universal civil freedom in this country. This court has so adjudged. But, that amendment having been found inadequate to the protection of the rights of those who had been in slavery, it was followed by the fourteenth amendment, which added greatly to the dignity and glory of American citizenship, and to the security of personal liberty, by declaring that "all persons born or naturalized in the United States, and subject to the jurisdiction thereof, are citizens of the United States and of the state wherein they reside," and that "no state shall make or enforce any law which shall abridge the privileges or immunities of citizens of the United States; nor shall any state deprive any person of life, liberty or property without due process of law, nor deny to any person within its jurisdiction the equal protection of the laws." These two amendments, if enforced according to their true intent and meaning, will protect all the civil rights that pertain to freedom and citizenship. Finally, and to the end that no citizen should be denied, on account of his race, the privilege of participating in the political control of his country, it was declared the fifteenth amendment that "the rights of citizens of the United States to vote shall not be denied or abridged by the United States or by any state on account of race, color or previous condition of service."

These notable additions to the fundamental law were welcomed by friends of liberty throughout the world. They removed the race line from our governmental systems. They had, as this court has said, a common purpose, namely, to secure "to a race recently emancipated, a race that through many generations have been held in slavery, all the civil rights that the superior race enjoy." They declared, in legal effect, this court has further said, "that the law in the states shall be the same for the black as for the white; that all persons, whether colored of white, shall stand equal before the laws of the states; and in regard to the colored race, for whose protection the amendment was primarily designed, that no discrimination shall be made against them by law because of their color.". . . .

It was said that the statute of Louisiana does not discriminate against either race, but prescribes a rule applicable alike to white and colored citizens. But this argument does not meet the difficulty. Every one knows that the statute in question had its origin in the purpose, not so much to exclude white persons from railroad cars occupied by blacks, as to exclude colored people from coaches occupied by or assigned to white persons. Railroad corporations of Louisiana

imposition: unfair requirements
decreed: declared

jurisdiction: area over which an authority has power

prescribes: establishes
applicable: relevant, appropriate
statute: law

coaches: railroad cars

guise: disguise, deceptive appearance
compel: force

conveyance: vehicle

did not make discrimination among whites in the matter of commodation for travelers. The thing to accomplish was, under the guise of giving equal accommodation for whites and blacks, to compel the latter to keep to themselves while traveling in railroad passenger coaches. It a white man and a black man choose to occupy the same public conveyance on a public highway, it is their right to do so; and no government, proceeding alone on grounds of race, can prevent it without infringing the personal liberty of each.

It is one thing for railroad carriers to furnish, or to be required by law to furnish, equal accommodations for all whom they are under a legal duty to carry. It is quite another thing for government to forbid citizens of the white and black races from traveling in the same public conveyance, and to punish officers of railroad companies for permitting persons of the two races to occupy the same passenger coach. If a state can prescribe . . . that whites and blacks shall not travel as passengers in the same railroad coach, why may it not so regulate the use of the streets of its cities and towns as to compel white citizens to keep on one side of a street, and black citizens to keep on the other? Why may it not . . . punish whites and blacks who ride together in street cars or in open vehicles on a public road or street? Why may it not require sheriffs to assign whites to one side of a court room, and blacks to the other? And why may it not also prohibit the commingling of the two races in the galleries of legislative halls or in public assemblages convened for the consideration of the political questions of the day? Further . . . why may not the state require the separation in railroad coaches of native and naturalized citizens of the United States, or of Protestants and Roman Catholics? . . .

assemblages: gatherings

The white race deems itself to be the dominant race in this country. And so it is, in prestige, in achievements, in education, in wealth, and in power. So, I doubt not, it will continue to be for all time, if it remains true to its great heritage, and holds fast to the principles of constitutional liberty. But in view of the constitution, in the eye of the law, there is in this country no superior, dominant, ruling class of citizens. In respect of civil rights, all citizens are equal before the law. The humblest is the peer of the most powerful. The law regards man as man, and takes no account of his surroundings or of his color when his civil rights as guaranteed by the supreme law of the land are involved. It is therefore to be regretted that this high tribunal . . . has reached the conclusion that it is competent for a state to regulate the enjoyment of citizens of their civil rights solely upon the basis of race.

tribunal: court

In my opinion, the judgment this day rendered will, in time, prove to be quite as pernicious as the decision made by this tribunal in the

pernicious: harmful in its effects

Dred Scott case. . . . The present decision . . . will not only stimulate aggressions, more or less brutal and irritating, upon the admitted rights of colored citizens, but will encourage the belief that it is possible, by means of state enactments, to defeat the beneficent purposes which the people of the United States had in view when they adopted the recent amendments of the constitution, by one of which the blacks of this country were made citizens of the United States and of the states in which they respectively reside . . . Sixty millions of whites are in no danger from the presence here of eight millions of blacks. The destinies of the two races, in this country, are indissolubly linked together, and the interests of both require that the common government of all shall not permit the seeds of race hate to be planted under the sanction of law. What can more certainly arouse race hate, what more certainly create and perpetuate a feeling of distrust between these races, than state enactments which, in fact, proceed on the ground that colored citizens are so inferior and degraded that they cannot be allowed to sit in public coaches occupied by white citizens? That, as all will admit, is the real meaning of such legislation as was enacted in Louisiana.

beneficent: well intended

indissolubly: unable to break apart

enactments: laws

The sure guaranty of the peace and security of each race is the clear, distinct, unconditional recognition by our governments . . . of every right that inheres in civil freedom, and of the equality before the law of all citizens of the United States, without regard to race. State enactments regulating the enjoyment of civil rights upon the basis of race, and cunningly devised to defeat legitimate results of the [Civil War], under the pretense of recognizing equality of rights, can have no other result than to render permanent peace impossible, and to keep alive a conflict of races, the continuance of which must do harm to all concerned. . . .

inheres: exists naturally

The arbitrary separation of citizens, on the basis of race, while they are on a public highway, is a badge of servitude wholly inconsistent with the civil freedom and the equality before the law established by the constitution. It cannot be justified on any legal grounds. . . . We boast of the freedom enjoyed by our people above all other peoples. But it is difficult to reconcile that boast with a state of the law which, practically, puts the brand of servitude and degradation upon a large class of our fellow citizens,—our equals before the law. The thin disguise of "equal" accommodations for passengers in railroad coaches will not mislead any one, not atone for the wrong this day done. . . .

arbitrary: random, without reason

atone: make up for

I am of opinion that the state of Louisiana is inconsistent with the personal liberty of citizens, white and black, in that state, and hostile to the spirit and letter of the constitution of the United States. If laws of like character should be enacted in the several states of the Union,

sinister: having harmful
intentions

the effect would be in the highest degree mischievous. Slavery, as an institution tolerated by law, would, it is true, have disappeared from our country; but there would remain a power in the states, by sinister legislation, to interfere with the full enjoyment of the blessings of freedom, to regulate civil rights, common to all citizens, upon the basis of race, and to place in a condition of legal inferiority a large body of American citizens, now constituting a part of the political community, called the "People of the United States," for whom, and by whom through representatives, our government is administered. . . .

For more information see
Chapter 29, Book 8, *An Age of Extremes.*

69. William McKinley, *War Message* (1898)

President William McKinley was reluctant to call for war against Spain in 1898. The last President to have served in the Civil War, he said that he had seen too much death at battles such as Antietam to be enthusiastic about war with Spain. "I've been through one war. I have seen the dead piled up, and I do not want to see another." But newspaper reports of Spain's cruelty to Cuban rebels, the sinking of the *U.S.S. Maine* in Cuba's Havana harbor, and the pressure of public opinion forced McKinley into the war that made the United States an international power.

The Spanish-American War marked a turning point in American history. The United States, which had just surpassed Britain to become the world's largest industrial power, also became a world power. It set up a military government on Cuba and made the soldiers' withdrawal contingent on the Cubans accepting the Platt amendment, which gave the United States the right to intervene in Cuba to protect "life, property, and individual liberties." The 144-day war also resulted in the United States taking control of the Phillippines, Puerto Rico, and Guam.

neutral: not favoring one party or the other
precedents: previous instances that are used as a model
internecine: destroying both sides
hostile constraint: use of force to hold back
truce: a temporary stop in a war

The forcible intervention of the United States as a neutral to stop the war, according to the large dictates of humanity and following many historical precedents where neighboring states have interfered to check the hopeless sacrifices of life by internecine conflicts beyond their borders, is justifiable on rational grounds. It involves, however, hostile constraint upon both the parties to the contest, as well to enforce a truce as to guide the eventual settlement.

The grounds for such intervention may be briefly summarized as follows:

First. In the cause of humanity and to put an end to the barbarities, bloodshed, starvation, and horrible miseries now existing there, and which the parties to the conflict are either unable or unwilling to stop or mitigate. It is no answer to say this is all in another country, belonging to another nation, and is therefore none of our business. It is specially our duty, for it is right at our door.

barbarities: savage acts

Second. We owe it to our citizens in Cuba to afford them that protection and indemnity for life and property which no government there can or will afford, and to that end to terminate the conditions that deprive them of legal protection.

indemnity: security against damage, loss, or injury

Third. The right to intervene may be justified by the very serious injury to the commerce, trade, and business of our people and by the wanton destruction of property and devastation of the island.

wanton: careless, excessive

Fourth, and which is of the utmost importance. The present condition of affairs in Cuba is a constant menace to our peace and entails upon this Government an enormous expense. With such a conflict waged for years in an island so near us and with which our people have such trade and business relations; when the lives and liberty of our citizens are in constant danger and their property destroyed and themselves ruined; where our trading vessels are liable to seizure and are seized at our very door by war ships of a foreign nation; the expeditions of filibustering that we are powerless to prevent altogether, and the irritating questions and entanglements thus arising— all these and others that I need not mention, with the resulting strained relations, are a constant menace to our peace and compel us to keep on a semi-war footing with a nation with which we are at peace.

liable: possibly open to enduring
seizure: taking by force
filibustering: military actions of adventurers from foreign countries
entanglements: complications
compel: force

These elements of danger and disorder already pointed out have been strikingly illustrated by a tragic event which has deeply and justly moved the American people. I have already transmitted to Congress the report of the naval court of inquiry on the destruction of the battle ship *Maine* in the harbor of Havana during the night of the 15th of February. The destruction of that noble vessel has filled the national heart with inexpressible horror. Two hundred and fifty-eight brave sailors and marines and two officers of our Navy, reposing in the fancied security of a friendly harbor, have been hurled to death, grief and want brought to their homes and sorrow to the nation.

reposing: resting
fancied: imagined

The naval court of inquiry, which, it is needless to say, commands the unqualified confidence of the Government, was unanimous in its conclusion that the destruction of the *Maine* was caused

unanimous: united

189

by an exterior explosion—that of a submarine mine. It did not assume to place the responsibility. That remains to be fixed.

In any event, the destruction of the *Maine*, by whatever exterior cause, is a patent and impressive proof of a state of things in Cuba that is intolerable. That condition is thus shown to be such that the Spanish Government can not assure safety and security to a vessel of the American Navy in the harbor of Havana on a mission of peace, and rightfully there. . . .

The long trial has proved that the object for which Spain has waged the war can not be attained. The fire of insurrection may flame or may smolder with varying seasons, but it has not been and it is plain that it can not be extinguished by present methods. The only hope of relief and repose from a condition which can no longer be endured is the enforced pacification of Cuba. In the name of humanity, in the name of civilization, in behalf of endangered American interests which give us the right and the duty to speak and to act, the war in Cuba must stop. . . .

attained: gained
insurrection: rebellion

repose: peacefulness
enforced pacification: halting of all acts of aggression, imposed peace

For more information see
Chapters 27–30, Book 8, *An Age of Extremes.*

70. From Theodore Roosevelt, *The Roosevelt Corollary to the Monroe Doctrine* (1904)

In 1904, President Theodore Roosevelt announced a new United States policy toward Latin America. Fearful that European countries might intervene in Latin America to collect debts or defend the property or lives of their citizens, he asserted the right of the United States to exercise "international police power" in Latin America. The Roosevelt Corollary changed the Monroe Doctrine from a policy designed to protect the Americas from European intervention to one justifying U.S. intervention in Latin America.

The Dominican Republic (then known as Santo Domingo) was unable to pay its debts to several European countries. To prevent European intervention, Roosevelt asserted the United States' right to intervene in Latin America to prevent "chronic wrongdoing." In 1905, he persuaded the Dominican Republic to allow the United States to supervise its debt repayment to France, Germany, and Italy. Over the next 20 years, the Roosevelt Corollary provided justification for American intervention in Cuba, Nicaragua, Mexico, Haiti, and the Dominican Republic.

It is not true that the United States feels any land hunger or entertains any projects as regards the other nations of the Western Hemisphere save such as are for their welfare. All that this country desires is to see the neighboring countries stable, orderly, and prosperous. Any country whose people conduct themselves well can count upon our hearty friendship. If a nation shows that it knows how to act with reasonable efficiency and decency in social and political matters, if it keeps order and pays its obligations, it need fear no interference from the United States. Chronic wrongdoing, or an impotence which results in a general loosening of the ties of civilized society, may in America, as elsewhere, ultimately require intervention by some civilized nation, and in the Western Hemisphere the adherence of the United States to the Monroe Doctrine may force the United States, however reluctantly, in flagrant cases of such wrongdoing or impotence, to the exercise of an international police power. If every country washed by the Caribbean Sea would show the progress in stable and just civilization which with the aid of the Platt amendment Cuba has shown since our troops left the island, and which so many of the republics in both Americas are constantly and brilliantly showing, all question of interference by this Nation with their affairs would be at an end. Our interests and those of our southern neighbors are in reality identical. They have great natural riches, and if within their borders the reign of law and justice obtains, prosperity is sure to come to them. While they thus obey the primary laws of civilized society they may rest assured that they will be treated by us in a spirit of cordial and helpful sympathy. We would interfere with them only in the last resort, and then only if it became evident that their inability or unwillingness to do justice at home and abroad had violated the rights of the United States or had invited foreign aggression to the detriment of the entire body of American nations. It is a mere truism to say that every nation, whether in America or anywhere else, which desires to maintain its freedom, its independence, must ultimately realize that the right of such independence can not be separated from the responsibility of making good use of it.

In asserting the Monroe Doctrine, in taking such steps as we have taken in regard to Cuba, Venezuela, and Panama, and in endeavoring to circumscribe the theater of war in the Far East, and to secure the open door in China, we have acted in our own interest as well as in the interest of humanity at large. There are, however, cases in which, while our own interests are not greatly involved, strong appeal is made to our sympathies. . . . But in extreme cases action may be justifiable and proper. What form the action shall take must depend upon the circumstances of the case; that is, upon the degree of the

Chronic: constant
impotence: weakness

adherence: sticking

flagrant: extreme

Platt amendment: act that supported and outlined American involvement in Cuban affairs

obtains: prevails, wins

cordial: gracious

detriment: loss
truism: obviously true statement

circumscribe: draw boundaries around, limit

191

atrocity: outrageous, abusive act

atrocity and upon our power to remedy it. The cases in which we could interfere by force of arms as we interfered to put a stop to intolerable conditions in Cuba are necessarily very few.

From Annual Message, December 5, 1905

It must be understood that under no circumstances will the United States use the Monroe Doctrine as a cloak for territorial aggression. We desire peace with all the world, but perhaps most of all with the other peoples of the American Continent. There are, of course, limits to the wrongs which any self-respecting nation can endure. It is always possible that wrong actions toward this Nation, or toward citizens of this Nation, in some State unable to keep order among its own people, unable to secure justice from outsiders, and unwilling to do justice to those outsiders who treat it well, may result in our having to take action to protect our rights; but such action will not be taken with a view to territorial aggression, and it will be taken at all only with extreme reluctance and when it has become evident that every other resource has been exhausted.

territorial aggression: attempts to invade and control a foreign country or government

Moreover, we must make it evident that we do not intend to permit the Monroe Doctrine to be used by any nation on this Continent as a shield to protect it from the consequences of its own misdeeds against foreign nations. If a republic to the south of us commits a tort against a foreign nation such as an outrage against a citizen of that nation, then the Monroe Doctrine does not force us to interfere to prevent punishment of the tort, save to see that the punishment does not assume the form of territorial occupation in any shape. The case is more difficult when it refers to a contractual obligation. Our own Government has always refused to enforce such contractual obligations on behalf of its citizens by an appeal to arms. It is much to be wished that all foreign governments would take the same view. But they do not; and in consequence we are liable at any time to be brought face to face with disagreeable alternatives. On the one hand, this country would certainly decline to go to war to prevent a foreign government from collecting a just debt; on the other hand, it is very inadvisable to permit any foreign power to take possession, even temporarily, of the custom houses of an American Republic in order to enforce the payment of its obligations; for such temporary occupation might turn into a permanent occupation. The only escape from these alternatives may at any time be that we must ourselves undertake to bring about some arrangement by which so much as possible of a just obligation shall be paid. It is far better that this country should put through such an arrangement, rather than allow any foreign country to undertake it. To do so insures the defaulting

tort: wrongful act

liable: likely

defaulting: falling behind on a payment schedule

republic from having to pay debt of an improper character under duress, while it also insures honest creditors of the republic from being passed by in the interest of dishonest or grasping creditors. Moreover, for the United States to take such a position offers the only possible way of insuring us against a clash with some foreign power. The position is, therefore, in the interest of peace as well as in the interest of justice. It is of benefit to our people; it is of benefit to foreign peoples; and most of all it is really of benefit to the people of the country concerned. . . .

duress: strain

71. From *Declaration of the Conservation Conference* (1908)

> **For more information see**
> Chapter 25, Book 8, *An Age of Extremes.*

Toward the end of his second term, President Theodore Roosevelt held the first national conference on conservation in Washington, D.C. The conference was attended by governors, members of Congress, the cabinet, the justices of the Supreme Court, and national prominent conservationists and scientists. In his opening address, the President called the depletion of the nation's timber and mineral resources "the weightiest problem before the nation." The following declaration, drafted at the end of the conference, called for the federal government to establish a National Conservation Commission to inventory the nation's water, mineral, soil, and forest resources. As a result of the conference, 36 states also established conservation commissions.

As President, Roosevelt added 130 million acres of timberland to federal forest reserves, established more than 50 wildlife sanctuaries, and created five new national parks. He also preserved 18 areas as national monuments, including the Grand Canyon. Roosevelt and his chief forester, Gifford Pinchot, were the first to apply the word "conservation" to environmental policy.

We the Governors of the States and Territories of the United States of America, in Conference assembled, do hereby declare the conviction that the great prosperity of our country rests upon the abundant resources of the land chosen by our forefathers for their homes and where they laid the foundation of this great Nation.

We look upon these resources as a heritage to be made use of in establishing and promoting the comfort, prosperity, and happiness of the American People, but not to be wasted, deteriorated, or needlessly destroyed.

deteriorated: run down

perpetuity: ability to endure

exhaustion: being used up

transcendent: surpassing all others

avenues of commerce: natural roads upon which goods can travel

erosion: wearing down

navigation: the possibility of a ship traveling on a body of water

monopoly: control by a single party

husbanding: careful management

renewal: regrowth

We agree that our country's future is involved in this; that the great natural resources supply the material basis on which our civilization must continue to depend, and on which the perpetuity of the Nation itself rests.

We agree, in the light of facts brought to our knowledge and from information received from sources which we can not doubt, that this material basis is threatened with exhaustion. Even as each succeeding generation from the birth of the Nation has performed its part in promoting the progress and development of the Republic, so do we in this generation recognize it as a high duty to perform our part; and this duty in large degree lies in the adoption of measures for the conservation of the natural wealth of the country.

We declare our firm conviction that this conservation of our natural resources is a subject of transcendent importance, which should engage unremittingly the attention of the Nation, the States, and the People in earnest cooperation. These natural resources include the land on which we live and which yields our food; the living waters which fertilize the soil, supply power, and form great avenues of commerce; the forests which yield the materials for our homes, prevent erosion of the soil, and conserve the navigation and other uses of our streams; and the minerals which form the basis of our industrial life, and supply us with heat, light, and power.

We agree that the land should be so used that erosion and soil-wash shall cease; that there should be reclamation of arid and semi-arid regions by means of irrigation, and of swamp and overflowed regions by means of drainage; that the waters should be so conserved and used as to promote navigation, to enable the arid regions to be reclaimed by irrigation, and to develop power in the interests of the People; that the forests which regulate our rivers, support our industries, and promote the fertility and productiveness of the soil should be preserved and perpetuated; that the minerals found so abundantly beneath the surface should be so used as to prolong their utility; that the beauty, healthfulness, and habitability of our country should be preserved and increased; that the sources of national wealth exist for the benefit of the People, and that monopoly thereof should not be tolerated.

We commend the wise forethought of the President in sounding the note of warning as to the waste and exhaustion of the natural resources of the country, and signify our high appreciation of his action in calling this Conference to consider the same and to seek remedies therefor through cooperation of the Nation and the States. . . .

We urge the continuation and extension of forest policies adapted to secure the husbanding and renewal of our diminishing timber supply, the prevention of soil erosion, the protection of headwaters, and the maintenance of the purity and navigability of our streams. We recognize that the private ownership of forest lands entails responsibilities in the interests of all the People, and we favor the enactment of laws looking to the protection and replacement of privately owned forests.

We recognize in our waters a most valuable asset of the People of the United States, and we recommend the enactment of laws looking to the conservation of water resources for irrigation, water supply, power, and navigation, to the end that navigable and source streams may be brought under complete control and fully utilized for every purpose. We especially urge on the Federal Congress the immediate adoption of a wise, active, and thorough waterway policy, providing for the prompt improvement of our streams and the conservation of their watersheds required for the uses of commerce and the protection of the interests of our People.

We recommend the enactment of laws looking to the prevention of waste in the mining and extraction of coal, oil, gas, and other minerals with a view to their wise conservation for the use of the People, and to the protection of human life in the mines.

Let us conserve the foundations of our prosperity.

Respectfully submitted,

[SIGNATURES]

headwaters: the source of a stream

watersheds: the places where river systems drain

72. From Woodrow Wilson, *First Inaugural Address* (1913)

For more information see
Chapter 34, Book 8, *An Age of Extremes.*

At its best, a Presidential inaugural address can give the country a clear sense of a President's philosophy and goals. In his first inaugural address, Woodrow Wilson voiced the ideals that inspired Progressive-era reformers with eloquence and passion. He was proud of the nation's economic achievements, but he feared that the country had failed "to count the human cost." The costs included the reckless exploitation of natural and human resources and the misuse of government "for private and selfish purposes." As the first Democrat in the White House in sixteen years and the first Southern Democratic President in half a century, he assured the country that a revolution had taken place in the his party's thinking. He pledged to use government as an active instrument of reform. "There can be no equality of opportunity," he said, ". . . if men and women and children are not shielded in their lives . . . from . . . the great industrial and social processes which they cannot alter, control or singly cope with."

In his address, Wilson spelled out his policy agenda. He promised to reduce tariff rates, reform the outdated banking system, and prevent big businesses from suppressing competition. He also wanted to conserve natural resources, make agriculture more efficient, and enable small businesses to borrow money more easily.

My Fellow Citizens:

There has been a change of government. It began two years ago, when the House of Representatives became Democratic by a decisive majority. It has now been completed. The Senate about to assemble will also be Democratic. The offices of President and Vice-President have been put into the hands of Democrats. What does the change mean? That is the question that is uppermost in our minds to-day. That is the question I am going to try to answer, in order, if I may, to interpret the occasion.

It means much more than the mere success of a party. The success of a party means little except when the Nation is using that party for a large and definite purpose. No one can mistake the purpose for which the Nation now seeks to use the Democratic Party. It seeks to use it to interpret a change in its own plans and point of view. Some old things with which we had grown familiar, and which had begun to creep into the very habit of our thought and of our lives, have altered their aspect as we have latterly looked critically upon them, with fresh, awakened eyes; have dropped their disguises and shown themselves alien and sinister. Some new things, as we look frankly upon them, willing to comprehend their real character, have come to assume the aspect of things long believed in and familiar, stuff of our own convictions. We have been refreshed by a new insight into our own life.

We see that in many things that life is very great. It is incomparably great in its material aspects, in its body of wealth, in the diversity and sweep of its energy, in the industries which have been conceived and built up by the genius of individual men and the limitless enterprise of groups of men. It is great, also, very great, in its moral force.

Nowhere else in the world have noble men and women exhibited in more striking forms the beauty and the energy of sympathy and helpfulness and counsel in their efforts to rectify wrong, alleviate suffering, and set the weak in the way of strength and hope. We have built up, moreover, a great system of government, which has stood through a long age as in many respects a model for those who seek to set liberty upon foundations that will endure against fortuitous change, against storm and accident. Our life contains every great thing, and contains it in rich abundance.

aspect: appearance

alien: foreign
sinister: suggesting evil

But the evil has come with the good, and much fine gold has been corroded. With riches has come inexcusable waste. We have squandered a great part of what we might have used, and have not stopped to conserve the exceeding bounty of nature, without which our genius for enterprise would have been worthless and impotent, scorning to be careful, shamefully prodigal as well as admirably efficient. We have been proud of our industrial achievements, but we have not hitherto stopped thoughtfully enough to count the human cost, the cost of lives snuffed out, of energies overtaxed and broken, the fearful physical and spiritual cost to the men and women and children upon whom the dead weight and burden of it all has fallen pitilessly the years through. The groans and agony of it all had not yet reached our ears, the solemn, moving undertone of our life, coming up out of the mines and factories and out of every home where the struggle had its intimate and familiar seat. With the great Government went many deep secret things which we too long delayed to look into and scrutinize with candid, fearless eyes. The great Government we loved has too often been made use of for private and selfish purposes and those who used it had forgotten the people.

At last a vision has been vouchsafed us of our life as a whole. We see the bad with the good, the debased and decadent with the sound and vital. With this vision we approach new affairs. Our duty is to cleanse, to reconsider, to restore, to correct the evil without impairing the good, to purify and humanize every process of our common life without weakening or sentimentalizing it. There has been something crude and heartless and unfeeling in our haste to succeed and be great. Our thought has been "Let every man look out for himself, let every generation look out for itself," while we reared giant machinery which made it impossible that any but those who stood at the levers of control should have a chance to look out for themselves. We had not forgotten our morals. We remembered well enough that we had set up a policy which was meant to serve the humblest as well as the most powerful, with an eye single to the standards of justice and fair play, and remembered it with pride. But we were very heedless and in a hurry to be great.

We have come now to the sober second thought. The scales of heedlessness have fallen from our eyes. We have made up our minds to square every process of our national life again with the standards we so proudly set up at the beginning and have always carried at our hearts. Our work is a work of restoration.

We have itemized with some degree of particularity the things that ought to be altered and here are some of the chief items: A tariff which cuts us off from our proper part in the commerce of the world,

corroded: dissolved, eaten away
squandered: wasted

prodigal: wasteful

scrutinize: look at closely
candid: honest

vouchsafed: granted, given
debased: unwholesome
decadent: in a state of decline or decay

sentimentalizing: looking at with emotion instead of reason

humblest: least important

scales of heedlessness: not seeing something due to not paying enough attention

particularity: detail

currency: cash

credits: loans
capital: money to be invested
leading strings: restraining
device for a young child

water-courses: streams or canals

unregarded: neglected

body politic: state

Sanitary laws: health codes

violates the just principles of taxation, and makes the Government a facile instrument in the hands of private interests; a banking and currency system based upon the necessity of the Government to sell its bonds fifty years ago and perfectly adapted to concentrating cash and restricting credits; an industrial system which, take it on all its sides, financial as well as administrative, holds capital in leading strings, restricts the liberties and limits the opportunities of labor, and exploits without renewing or conserving the natural resources of the country; a body of agricultural activities never yet given the efficiency of great business undertakings or served as it should be through the instrumentality of science taken directly to the farm, or afforded the facilities of credit best suited to its practical needs; water-courses undeveloped, waste places unreclaimed, forests untended, fast disappearing without plan or prospect of renewal, unregarded waste heaps at every mine. We have studied as perhaps no other nation has the most effective means of production, but we have not studied cost or economy as we should either as organizers of industry, as statesmen, or as individuals.

Nor have we studied and perfected the means by which government may be put at the service of humanity, in safeguarding the health of the Nation, the health of its men and its women and its children, as well as their rights in the struggle for existence. This is no sentimental duty. The firm basis of government is justice, not pity. These are matters of justice. There can be no equality or opportunity, the first essential of justice in the body politic, if men and women and children be not shielded in their lives, their very vitality, from the consequences of great industrial and social processes which they can not alter, control, or singly cope with. Society must see to it that it does not itself crush or weaken or damage its own constituent parts. The first duty of law is to keep sound the society it serves. Sanitary laws, pure food laws, and laws determining conditions of labor which individuals are powerless to determine for themselves are intimate parts of the very business of justice and legal efficiency.

These are some of the things we ought to do, and not leave the others undone, the old-fashioned, never-to-be-neglected, fundamental safeguarding of property and of individual right. This is the high enterprise of the new day: To lift everything that concerns our life as a Nation to the light that shines from the hearthfire of every man's conscience and vision of the right. It is inconceivable that we should do this as partisans; it is inconceivable we should do it in ignorance of the facts as they are or in blind haste. We shall restore, not destroy. We shall deal with our economic system as it is and as it may be modified, not as it might be if we had a clean sheet of paper to write upon; and step by step we shall make it what it should be, in the spirit of those who question their own wisdom and seek counsel and knowledge, not shallow self-satisfaction or the excitement of excursions whither they can not tell. Justice, and only justice, shall always be our motto.

And yet it will be no cool process of mere science. The Nation has been deeply stirred, stirred by a solemn passion, stirred by the knowledge of wrong, of ideals lost, of government too often debauched and made an instrument of evil. The feelings with which we face this new age of right and opportunity sweep across our heartstrings like some air out of God's own presence, where justice and mercy are reconciled and the judge and the brother are one. We know our task to be no mere task of politics but a task which shall search us through and through, whether we be able to understand our time and the need of our people, whether we be indeed their spokesmen and interpreters, whether we have the pure heart to comprehend and the rectified will to choose our high course of action.

comprehend: understand
recitified: morally correct

This is not a day of triumph; it is a day of dedication. Here muster, not the forces of party, but the forces of humanity. Men's hearts wait upon us; men's lives hang in the balance; men's hopes call upon us to say what we will do. Who shall live up to the great trust? Who dares fail to try? I summon all honest men, all patriotic, all forward-looking men, to my side. God helping me, I will not fail them, if they will but counsel and sustain me!

73. From Woodrow Wilson, *War Message* (1917)

For more information see
Chapter 35, Book 8, *An Age of Extremes.*

World War I began in Europe on August 4, 1914. By early 1917, the European powers had fought to a standstill, with nearly 5 million dead and another 5 million burrowed in trenches. President Woodrow Wilson had supported American neutrality, and in 1916 he campaigned for reelection with the slogan "He kept us out of war." He had also tried to arrange a negotiated settlement, a "peace without victory." But his efforts failed. In early 1917, Germany resumed a policy of unrestricted submarine warfare against merchant ships, which threatened an American commitment to maintaining open sea lanes across the Atlantic. Then newspapers published the Zimmermann telegram, which revealed a secret German plot to start a war between the United States and Mexico.

When President Wilson asked Congress to declare war in April 1917, he was convinced that by entering the conflict as a combatant the United States would be able to shape a peace settlement. Wilson said that his aim was not to advance narrow American interests but to "make the world safe for democracy"—to establish a world in which all nations could live in lasting peace.

extraordinary: special

I have called the Congress into extraordinary session because there are serious, very serious choices of policy to be made, and made immediately, which it was neither right nor constitutionally permissible that I should assume the responsibility of making.

On the third of February last I officially laid before you the extraordinary announcement of the Imperial German Government that on and after the first day of February it was its purpose to put aside all restraints of law or of humanity and use its submarines to sink every vessel that sought to approach either the ports of Great Britain and Ireland or the western coasts of Europe or any of the ports controlled by the enemies of Germany within the Mediterranean. . . .

subscribed: agreed

I was for a little while unable to believe that such things would in fact be done by any government that had hitherto subscribed to the humane practices of civilized nations. International law had its origin in the attempt to set up some law which would be respected and observed upon the seas, where no nation had right of dominion and where lay the free highways of the world. . . . This minimum of right the German Government has swept aside under the plea of retaliation and necessity and because it had no weapons which it could use at sea except these which it is impossible to employ as it is employing them without throwing to the winds all scruples of humanity or of respect for all understandings that were supposed to underlie the intercourse of the world. I am not now thinking of the loss of property involved, immense and serious as that is, but only of the wanton and wholesale destruction of the lives of non-combatants, men, women, and children, engaged in pursuits which have always, even in the darkest periods of modern history, been deemed innocent and legitimate. Property can be paid for; the lives of peaceful and innocent people cannot be. The present German submarine warfare against commerce is a warfare against mankind.

dominion: domination

plea of retaliation: argument for the right to strike back

scruples: ethical and moral concerns
intercourse: communication
wanton: careless and excessive
non-combatants: people who are not soldiers

legitimate: valid

It is a war against all nations. American ships have been sunk, American lives taken, in ways which it has stirred us very deeply to learn of, but the ships and people of other neutral and friendly nations have been sunk and overwhelmed in the waters in the same way. There has been no discrimination. The challenge is to all mankind. Each nation must decide for itself how it will meet it. The choice we make for ourselves must be made with a moderation of

neutral: not favoring one side or another
discrimination: favor shown to one side or another

counsel and a temperateness of judgement befitting our character and our motives as a nation. We must put excited feeling away. Our motive will not be revenge or the victorious assertion of the physical might of the nation, but only the vindication of right, of human right, of which we are only a single champion. . . .

With a profound sense of the solemn and even tragical character of the step I am taking and of the grave responsibilities which it involves, but in unhesitating obedience to what I deem my constitutional duty, I advise that the Congress declare the recent course of the Imperial German Government to be in fact nothing less than war against the government and people of the United States; that it formally accept the status of belligerent which has thus been thrust upon it; and that it take immediate steps not only to put the country in a more thorough state of defense but also to exert all its power and employ all its resources to bring the Government of the German Empire to terms and end the war. . . .

We have no quarrel with the German people. We have no feeling towards them but one of sympathy and friendship. It was not upon their impulse that their government acted in entering this war. It was not with their previous knowledge or approval. . . .

We are accepting this challenge of hostile purpose because we know that in such a Government, following such methods, we can never have a friend; and that in the presence of its organized power, always lying in wait to accomplish we know not what purpose, there can be no assured security for the democratic Governments of the world. We are now about to accept gauge of battle with this natural foe to liberty and shall, if necessary, spend the whole force of the nation to check and nullify its pretensions and its power. We are glad, now that we see the facts with no veil of false pretense about them, to fight thus for the ultimate peace of the world and for the liberation of its peoples, the German peoples included: for the rights of nations great and small and the privilege of men everywhere to choose their way of life and of obedience. The world must be made safe for democracy. Its peace must be planted upon the tested foundations of political liberty. We have no selfish ends to serve. We desire no conquest, no dominion. We seek no indemnities for ourselves, no material compensation for the sacrifices we shall freely make. We are but one of the champions of the rights of mankind. We shall be satisfied when those rights have been made as secure as the faith and the freedom of nations can make them. . . .

It will be all the easier for us to conduct ourselves as belligerents in a high spirit of right and fairness because we act without animus, not in enmity towards a people or with the desire to bring any injury

moderation of counsel: careful and restrained consideration
temperateness: moderation
vindication: justification

profound: deep
tragical: deeply sorrowful

belligerent: hostile party

exert: exercise

hostile: aggressive, combative

gauge: measure
foe: enemy
nullify: wipe out
pretense: appearance

indemnities: securities against damage, loss, or injury
compensation: payment

belligerents: fighters
animus: feeling of ill will

201

amuck: in a violent frenzy

intimate relations: close diplomatic and business dealings
mutual: shared, held in common

forbearance: capacity to endure

native: inborn

fealty: loyalty

countenance: support or approval
malignant: evil

dominion: rule

or disadvantage upon them, but only in armed opposition to an irresponsible government which has thrown aside all considerations of humanity and of right and is running amuck. We are, let me say again, the sincere friends of the German people, and shall desire nothing so much as the early reestablishment of intimate relations of mutual advantage between us—however hard it may be for them, for the time being, to believe that this is spoken from our hearts. We have borne with their present Government through all these bitter months because of that friendship—exercising a patience and forbearance which would otherwise have been impossible. We shall, happily, still have an opportunity to prove that friendship in our daily attitude and actions towards the millions of men and women of German birth and native sympathy who live amongst us and share our life, and we shall be proud to prove it towards all who are in fact loyal to their neighbors and to the Government in the hour of test. They are, most of them, as true and loyal Americans as if they had never known any other fealty of allegiance. They will be prompt to stand with us in rebuking and restraining the few who may be of a different mind and purpose. If there should be disloyalty, it will be dealt with with a firm hand of stern repression; but, if it lifts its head at all, it will lift it only here and there and without countenance except from a lawless and malignant few.

It is a distressing and oppressive duty, Gentlemen of the Congress, which I have performed in thus addressing you. There are, it may be, many months of fiery trial and sacrifice ahead of us. It is a fearful thing to lead this great peaceful people into war, into the most terrible and disastrous of all wars, civilization itself seeming to be in the balance. But the right is more precious than peace, and we shall fight for the things which we have always carried nearest our hearts—for democracy, for the right of those who submit to authority to have a voice in their own Governments, for the rights and liberties of small nations, for a universal dominion of right by such a concert of free peoples as shall bring peace and safety to all nations and make the world itself at last free. To such a task we can dedicate our lives and our fortunes, everything that we have, with the pride of those who know that the day has come when America is privileged to spend her blood and her might for the principles that gave her birth and happiness and the peace which she has treasured. God helping her, she can do no other.

74. Woodrow Wilson, *"The Fourteen Points"*: *Address to Congress* (1918)

For more information see
Chapter 2, Book 9, *War, Peace, and All That Jazz.*

The Fourteen Points were a set of principles proposed by President Woodrow Wilson in 1918 as the basis for ending World War I and for preserving world peace. Convinced that a harsh peace treaty would be the basis of future wars, Wilson opposed stripping Germany of territory or imposing reparations (huge financial penalties) on the losers. To ensure economic future prosperity, he called for free trade and freedom on the seas. He also recognized the growth of nationalism by calling for the right of all people to national self-determination, the freedom to determine their own form of government. Finally, to preserve peace, President Wilson called for open diplomacy, arms reduction, and an international organization to solve disputes between nations.

Peace forces within Germany agreed to surrender on the basis of the Fourteen Points. In 1918, a brief revolution in Germany forced the Kaiser to step down. Yet despite promises of a just peace, Wilson was unable to win support for his Fourteen Points. The treaty ending World War I imposed a harsh settlement. It required Germany to pay $34 billion in reparations, far more than it could afford. In addition, Germany was stripped of territories where many ethnic Germans lived and had to accept blame for causing the war.

Gentlemen of the Congress:

. . . It will be our wish and purpose that the processes of peace, when they are begun, shall be absolutely open and that they shall involve and permit henceforth no secret understandings of any kind. The day of conquest and aggrandizement is gone by; so is also the day of secret covenants entered into in the interest of particular governments and likely at some unlooked-for moment to upset the peace of the world. It is this happy fact, now clear to the view of every public man whose thoughts do not still linger in an age that is dead and gone, which makes it possible for every nation whose purposes are consistent with justice and the peace of the world to avow now or at any other time the objects it has in view.

We entered this war because violations of right had occurred which touched us to the quick and made the life of our own people impossible unless they were corrected and the world secured once for all against their recurrence. What we demand in this war, therefore, is nothing peculiar to ourselves. It is that the world be made fit

henceforth: from now on
conquest: military victory
aggrandizement: growing more powerful by exploiting others
covenants: agreements

frankly: honestly
territorial waters: the first few miles of the ocean, closest to the shore, that belong to a country

economic barriers: ways that governments control the flow of goods in and out of their borders

national armaments: weapons held by a country
impartial: fair
colonial: involving people or a territory ruled by another, stronger power

evacuation: removal of an occupying force

unhampered: free

acid test: a test that absolutely proves something, beyond doubt

sovereignty: rule

and safe to live in; and particularly that it be made safe for every peace-loving nation which, like our own, wishes to live its own life, determine its own institutions, be assured of justice and fair dealing by the other peoples of the world as against force and selfish aggression. All the peoples of the world are in effect partners in this interest, and for our own part we see very clearly that unless justice be done to others it will not be done to us. The program of the world's peace, therefore, is our program; and that program, the only possible program, as we see it, is this:

I. Open covenants of peace, openly arrived at, after which there shall be no private international understandings of any kind but diplomacy shall proceed always frankly and in the public view.

II. Absolute freedom of navigation upon the seas, outside territorial waters, alike in peace and in war, except as the seas may be closed in whole or in part by international action for the enforcement of international covenants.

III. The removal, so far as possible, of all economic barriers and the establishment of an equality of trade conditions among all the nations consenting to the peace and associating themselves for its maintenance.

IV. Adequate guarantees given and taken that national armaments will be reduced to the lowest point consistent with domestic safety.

V. A free, open-minded, and absolutely impartial adjustment of all colonial claims, based upon a strict observance of the principle that in determining all such questions of sovereignty the interests of the populations concerned must have equal weight with the equitable claims of the government whose title is to be determined.

VI. The evacuation of all Russian territory and such a settlement of all questions affecting Russia as will secure the best and freest coöperation of the other nations of the world in obtaining for her an unhampered and unembarrassed opportunity for the independent determination of her own political development and national policy and assure her of a sincere welcome into the society of free nations under institutions of her own choosing; and, more than a welcome, assistance also of every kind that she may need and may herself desire. The treatment accorded Russia by her sister nations in the months to come will be the acid test of their good will, of their comprehension of her needs as distinguished from their own interests, and of their intelligent and unselfish sympathy.

VII. Belgium, the whole world will agree, must be evacuated and restored, without any attempt to limit the sovereignty which she enjoys in common with all other free nations. No other single act will serve as this will serve to restore confidence among the nations in the laws which they have themselves set and determined for the government of their relations with one another. Without this healing act the whole structure and validity of international law is forever impaired.

VIII. All French territory should be freed and the invaded portions restored, and the wrong done to France by Prussia in 1871 in the matter of Alsace-Lorraine, which has unsettled the peace of the world for nearly fifty years, should be righted, in order that peace may once more be made secure in the interest of all.

IX. A readjustment of the frontiers of Italy should be effected along clearly recognizable lines of nationality.

X. The peoples of Austria-Hungary, whose place among the nations we wish to see safeguarded and assured, should be accorded the freest opportunity of autonomous development.

XI. Rumania, Serbia, and Montenegro should be evacuated; occupied territories restored; Serbia accorded free and secure access to the sea; and the relations of the several Balkan states to one another determined by friendly counsel along historically established lines of allegiance and nationality; and international guarantees of the political and economic independence and territorial integrity of the several Balkan states should be entered into.

XII. The Turkish portions of the present Ottoman Empire should be assured a secure sovereignty, but the other nationalities which are now under Turkish rule should be assured an undoubted security of life and an absolutely unmolested opportunity of autonomous development, and the Dardanelles should be permanently opened as a free passage to the ships and commerce of all nations under international guarantees.

XIII. An independent Polish state should be erected which should include the territories inhabited by indisputably Polish populations, which should be assured a free and secure access to the sea, and whose political and economic independence and territorial integrity should be guaranteed by international covenant.

XIV. A general association of nations must be formed under specific covenants for the purpose of affording mutual guarantees of political independence and territorial integrity to great and small states alike.

In regard to these essential rectifications of wrong and assertions of right we feel ourselves to be intimate partners of all the governments and peoples associated together against the Imperialists. We cannot be separated in interest or divided in purpose. We stand together until the end.

For such arrangements and covenants we are willing to fight and to continue to fight until they are achieved; but only because we wish the right to prevail and desire a just and stable peace such as can be

validity: truth

nationality: national origin

automonous: independent

counsel: advice, diplomacy

integrity: wholeness

unmolested: unbothered

free passage: a waterway through which ships can travel without having to present documents or pay taxes
erected: built
indisputably: unarguably

mutual: affecting both sides equally

rectifications: rightings

Imperialists: governments trying to establish empires

prevail: win

205

provocations: reasons

impairs: harms
distinction of learning: feat of scholarship
pacific: peaceful
enviable: admirable
hostile: unfriendly

presume: try
modification: change

Reichstag: German parliament from 1867 to 1945
creed: set of beliefs

vindication: proving the moral correctness

culminating: at the climax

secured only by removing the chief provocations to war, which this program does not remove. We have no jealousy of German greatness, and there is nothing in this program that impairs it. We grudge her no achievement or distinction of learning or of pacific enterprise such as have made her record very bright and very enviable. We do not wish to injure her or to block in any way her legitimate influence or power. We do not wish to fight her either with arms or with hostile arrangements of trade if she is willing to associate herself with us and the other peace-loving nations of the world in covenants of justice and law and fair dealing. We wish her only to accept a place of equality among the peoples of the world,—the new world in which we now live,—instead of a place of mastery.

Neither do we presume to suggest to her any alteration or modification of her institutions. But it is necessary, we must frankly say, and necessary as a preliminary to any intelligent dealings with her on our part, that we should know whom her spokesmen speak for when they speak to us, whether for the Reichstag majority or for the military party and the men whose creed is imperial domination.

We have spoken now, surely, in terms too concrete to admit of any further doubt or question. An evident principle runs through the whole program I have outlined. It is the principle of justice to all peoples and nationalities, and their right to live on equal terms of liberty and safety with one another, whether they be strong or weak. Unless this principle be made its foundation no part of the structure of international justice can stand. The people of the United States could act upon no other principle; and to the vindication of this principle they are ready to devote their lives, their honor, and everything that they possess. The moral climax of this the culminating and final war for human liberty has come, and they are ready to put their own strength, their own highest purpose, their own integrity and devotion to the test.

For more information see
Chapters 14–17, Book 9, *War, Peace, and All That Jazz.*

75. Herbert Hoover, *"Rugged Individualism": Campaign Speech in New York City* (1928)

In 1928, the Republican Party nominated Herbert Hoover for the Presidency. He had been a world-famous mining engineer and served as Secretary of Commerce under Presidents Harding and Coolidge. In this speech, which closed his successful Presidential campaign, Hoover, a self-made millionaire, expressed his view that the American system was based on "rugged individualism" and "self-reliance." Government, which had assumed unprecedented economic powers during World War I, should, in his view, shrink back to its pre-war size and avoid intervening in business.

During the early days of the Great Depression, Hoover launched the largest public works projects in American history. But he continued to believe that problems of poverty and unemployment were best left to "voluntary organization and community service." He feared that federal relief programs would undermine individual character by making recipients dependent on the government. He did not recognize that the sheer size of the nation's economic problems meant that "rugged individualism" was no longer sufficient to solve them.

After the war, when the Republican party assumed administration of the country, we were faced with the problem of determination of the very nature of our national life. During one hundred and fifty years we have builded up a form of self-government and a social system which is peculiarly our own. It differs essentially from all others in the world. It is the American system. It is just as definite and positive a political and social system as has ever been developed on earth. It is founded upon a particular conception of self-government in which decentralized local responsibility is the very base. Further than this, it is founded upon the conception that only through ordered liberty, freedom, and equal opportunity to the individual will his initiative and enterprise spur on the march of progress. And in our insistence upon equality of opportunity has our system advanced beyond all the world.

During the war we necessarily turned to the government to solve every difficult economic problem. The government having absorbed every energy of our people for war, there was no other solution. For the preservation of the state the Federal Government became a centralized despotism which undertook unprecedented responsibilities, assumed autocratic powers, and took over the business of citizens. To a large degree we regimented our whole people temporarily into a socialistic state. However justified in time of war if continued in peace-time it would destroy not only our American system but with it our progress and freedom as well.

When the war closed, the most vital of all issues both in our own country and throughout the world was whether governments should continue their wartime ownership and operation of many instrumentalities of production and distribution. We were challenged with a peace-time choice between the American system of rugged individualism and a European philosophy of diametrically opposed doctrines—doctrines of paternalism and state socialism.

conception: idea
decentralized: local, small scale

initiative: drive
enterprise: bold undertaking

despotism: unchecked power
unprecedented: never-before attempted
autocratic: dictatorial
regimented: strictly organized
socialistic state: state where power is highly centralized
vital: important
instrumentalities: factories and networks
diametrically opposed doctrines: entirely opposite ways of looking at the world
paternalism: system where a government controls its people the way parents control their young children

207

resolutely: definitely

retarded recuperation:
the economy starting to flourish
again later than it should have
revived: brought back to life

prohibition: banning alcohol
farm relief: helping farmers

tenets: basic beliefs

hydroelectric: generating
electricity by using the power
of falling or rushing water

The acceptance of these ideas would have meant the destruction of self-government through centralization of government. It would have meant the undermining of the individual initiative and enterprise through which our people have grown to unparalleled greatness.

The Republican Party from the beginning resolutely turned its face away from these ideas and these war practices. . . . When the Republican Party came into full power it went at once resolutely back to our fundamental conception of the state and the rights and responsibilities of the individual. Thereby it restored confidence and hope in the American people, it freed and stimulated enterprise, it restored the government to its position as an umpire instead of a player in the economic game. For these reasons the American people have gone forward in progress while the rest of the world has halted, and some countries have even gone backwards. If anyone will study the causes of retarded recuperation in Europe, he will find much of it due to stifling of private initiative on one hand, and overloading of the government with business on the other.

There has been revived in this campaign, however, a series of proposals which, if adopted, would be a long step toward the abandonment of our American system and a surrender to the destructive operation of governmental conduct of commercial business. Because the country is faced with difficulty and doubt over certain national problems—that is prohibition, farm relief, and electrical power—our opponents propose that we must thrust government a long way into the businesses which give rise to these problems. In effect, they abandon the tenets of their own party and turn to state socialism as a solution for the difficulties presented by all three. It is proposed that we shall change from prohibition to the state purchase and sale of liquor. If their agricultural relief program means anything, it means that the government shall directly or indirectly buy and sell and fix prices of agricultural products. And we are to go into the hydroelectric power business. In other words, we are confronted with a huge program of government in business.

There is, therefore, submitted to the American people a question of fundamental principle. That is: shall we depart from the principles of our American political and economic system, upon which we have advanced beyond all the rest of the world, in order to adopt methods based on principles destructive of its very foundations? And I wish to emphasize the seriousness of these proposals. I wish to make my position clear; for this goes to the very roots of American life and progress.

I should like to state to you the effect that this projection of government in business would have upon our system of self-government and our economic system. That effect would reach to the daily life of every man and woman. It would impair the very basis of liberty and freedom not only for those left outside the fold of expanded bureaucracy but for those embraced within it.

impair: harm

Let us first see the effect upon self-government. When the Federal Government undertakes to go into commercial business it must at once set up the organization and administration of that business, and it immediately finds itself in a labyrinth, every alley of which leads to the destruction of self-government.

labyrinth: maze

Commercial business requires a concentration of responsibility. Self-government requires decentralization and many checks and balances to safeguard liberty. Our Government to succeed in business would need to become in effect a despotism. There at once begins the destruction of self-government. . . .

It is a false liberalism that interprets itself into the government operation of commercial business. Every step of bureaucratizing of the business of our country poisons the very roots of liberalism— that is, political equality, free speech, free assembly, free press, and equality of opportunity. It is the road not to more liberty, but to less liberty. Liberalism should be found not striving to spread bureaucracy but striving to set bounds to it. True liberalism seeks all legitimate freedom first in the confident belief that without such freedom the pursuit of all other blessings and benefits is vain. That belief is the foundation of all American progress, political as well as economic.

liberalism: theory of government that favors free trade
bureaucratizing: adding layers of excessive paperwork and official routine

Liberalism is a force truly of the spirit, a force proceeding from the deep realization that economic freedom cannot be sacrificed if political freedom is to be preserved. Even if Governmental conduct of business could give us more efficiency instead of less efficiency, the fundamental objection to it would remain unaltered and unabated. It would destroy political equality. It would increase rather than decrease abuse and corruption. It would stifle initiative and invention. It would undermine the development of leadership. It would cramp and cripple the mental and spiritual energies of our people. It would extinguish equality and opportunity. It would dry up the spirit of liberty and progress. For these reasons primarily it must be resisted. For a hundred and fifty years liberalism has found its true spirit in the American system, not in the European systems.

I do not wish to be misunderstood in this statement. I am defining a general policy. It does not mean that our government is to part with one iota of its national resources without complete protection to the public interest. I have already stated that where the government is engaged in public works for purposes of flood control, of navigation,

iota: tiny bit

irrigation: supplying water to
farmland
commodities: material goods

free-for-all: without rules
devil-take-the-hindmost:
the slowest or dullest people, who
are unprotected, lose

laissez faire: economic system
that has no rules and allows
people to do as they choose

undermining: eating away at

inheritance: something handed
down from parents to children

industrious: good workers

adherence: sticking to

abolition: doing away with

of irrigation, of scientific research or national defense, or in pioneering a new art, it will at times necessarily produce power or commodities as a by-product. But they must be a by-product of the major purpose, not the major purpose itself.

Nor do I wish to be misinterpreted as believing that the United States is free-for-all and devil-take-the-hindmost. The very essence of equality of opportunity and of American individualism is that there shall be no domination by any group or combination in this republic, whether it be business or political. On the contrary, it demands economic justice as well as political and social justice. It is no system of laissez faire.

I feel deeply on this subject because during the war I had some practical experience with governmental operation and control. I have witnessed not only at home but abroad the many failures of government in business. I have seen its tyrannies, its injustices, its destructions of self-government, its undermining of the very instincts which carry our people forward to progress. I have witnessed the lack of advance, the lowered standards of living, the depressed spirits of people working under such a system. My objection is based not upon theory or upon a failure to recognize wrong or abuse, but I know the adoption of such methods would strike at the very roots of American life and would destroy the very basis of American progress.

Our people have the right to know whether we can continue to solve our great problems without abandonment of our American system. I know we can. . . .

And what have been the results of the American system? Our country has become the land of opportunity to those born without inheritance, not merely because of the wealth of its resources and industry but because of this freedom of initiative and enterprise. Russia has natural resources equal to ours. Her people are equally industrious, but she has not had the blessings of one hundred and fifty years of our form of government and our social system.

By adherence to the principles of decentralized self-government, ordered liberty, equal opportunity, and freedom to the individual, our American experiment in human welfare has yielded a degree of well-being unparalleled in all the world. It has come nearer to the abolition of poverty, to the abolition of fear of want, than humanity has ever reached before. Progress of the past seven years is the proof of it. This alone furnishes the answer to our opponents, who ask us to introduce destructive elements into the system by which this has been accomplished. . . .

I have endeavored to present to you that the greatness of America has grown out of a political and social system and a method of control of economic forces distinctly its own—our American system—which has carried this great experiment in human welfare farther than ever before in all history. We are nearer today to the ideal of the abolition of poverty and fear from the lives of men and women than ever before in any land. And I again repeat that the departure from our American system by injecting principles destructive to it which our opponents propose, will jeopardize the very liberty and freedom of our people, and will destroy equality of opportunity not alone to ourselves but to our children. . . .

jeopardize: endanger

76. From Franklin D. Roosevelt, *"The Only Thing We Have to Fear is Fear Itself": First Inaugural Address* (1933)

On a bleak March day, Franklin D. Roosevelt took the oath of office as President and assured the public that "The only thing we have to fear is fear itself." With words of optimism and hope, Roosevelt backed an active role for government in addressing the Great Depression. He pledged "to wage war against the emergency as great as the power that would be given me if we were . . . invaded by a foreign foe."

The Depression demanded action to revive the economy and calm the public's fears. With his infectious optimism and self-assurance, Roosevelt succeeded in restoring people's hopes. In his inaugural address he promised decisive action, and during the first 100 days of his administration he pushed 15 major bills through Congress. The federal government provided insurance to protect bank deposits, federal regulations to protect stock-market investors, jobs programs, and subsidies to farmers.

President Hoover, Mr. Chief Justice, my friends:

This is a day of national consecration, and I am certain that my fellow-Americans expect that on my induction into the Presidency I will address them with a candor and a decision which the present situation of our nation impels.

This is pre-eminently the time to speak the truth, the whole truth, frankly and boldly. Nor need we shrink from honestly facing conditions in our country today. This great nation will endure as it has endured, will revive and will prosper.

consecration: blessing
induction: installation
candor: honesty
impels: demands
pre-eminently: overwhelmingly

211

assert: state

curtailment: lowering

stricken: hit by
plague of locusts: Biblical
disaster
perils: dangers
languishes: wastes away
abdicated: given up
unscrupulous money changers:
selfish bankers; a New Testament
reference
outworn: outgrown
credit: loans
lure: appeal
induce: coax
exhortations: pleas
perish: die
fled: run away from
high seats: important positions
temple of our civilization: banks
and financial institutions; reference to the Temple in Jerusalem
ancient truths: the good way that
it used to be before the money
changers got there
restoration: renewal

So first of all let me assert my firm belief that the only thing we have to fear is fear itself—nameless, unreasoning, unjustified terror which paralyzes needed efforts to convert retreat into advance.

In every dark hour of our national life a leadership of frankness and vigor has met with that understanding and support of the people themselves which is essential to victory. I am convinced that you will again give that support to leadership in these critical days.

In such a spirit on my part and on yours we face our common difficulties. They concern, thank God, only material things. Values have shrunken to fantastic levels; taxes have risen; our ability to pay has fallen, government of all kinds is faced by serious curtailment of income; the means of exchange are frozen in the currents of trade; the withered leaves of industrial enterprise lie on every side; farmers find no markets for their produce; the savings of many years in thousands of families are gone.

More important, a host of unemployed citizens face the grim problem of existence, and an equally great number toil with little return. Only a foolish optimist can deny the dark realities of the moment.

Yet our distress comes from no failure of substance. We are stricken by no plague of locusts. Compared with the perils which our forefathers conquered because they believed and were not afraid, we have still much to be thankful for. Nature still offers her bounty and human efforts have multiplied it. Plenty is at our doorstep, but a generous use of it languishes in the very sight of the supply.

Primarily, this is because the rulers of the exchange of mankind's goods have failed through their own stubbornness and their own incompetence, have admitted their failure and abdicated. Practices of the unscrupulous money changers stand indicted in the court of public opinion, rejected by the hearts and minds of men.

True, they have tried, but their efforts have been cast in the pattern of an outworn tradition. Faced by failure of credit, they have proposed only the lending of more money.

Stripped of the lure of profit by which to induce our people to follow their false leadership, they have resorted to exhortations, pleading tearfully for restored confidence. They know only the rules of a generation of self-seekers.

They have no vision, and when there is no vision the people perish.

The money changers have fled from their high seats in the temple of our civilization. We may now restore that temple to the ancient truths.

The measure of the restoration lies in the extent to which we apply social values more noble than mere monetary profit.

Happiness lies not in the mere possession of money; it lies in the joy of achievement, in the thrill of creative effort.

The joy and moral stimulation of work no longer must be forgotten in the mad chase of evanescent profits. These dark days will be worth all they cost us if they teach us that our true destiny is not to be ministered unto but to minister to ourselves and to our fellow-men.

evanescent: short-term

Recognition of the falsity of material wealth as the standard of success goes hand in hand with the abandonment of the false belief that public office and high political position are to be valued only by the standards of price of place and personal profit; and there must be an end to a conduct in banking and in business which too often has given to a sacred trust the likeness of callous and selfish wrongdoing.

material wealth: money and the physical things that money can buy

callous: unfeeling

Small wonder that confidence languishes, for it thrives only on honesty, on honor, on the sacredness of obligations, on faithful protection, on unselfish performance. Without them it cannot live.

Restoration calls, however, not for changes in ethics alone. This nation asks for action, and action now.

Our greatest primary task is to put people to work. This is no unsolvable problem if we face it wisely and courageously.

It can be accomplished in part by direct recruiting by the government itself, treating the task as we would treat the emergency of a war, but at the same time, through this employment, accomplishing greatly needed projects to stimulate and reorganize the use of our natural resources.

Hand in hand with this, we must frankly recognize the overbalance of population in our industrial centers and, by engaging on a national scale in the redistribution, endeavor to provide a better use of the land for those best fitted for the land.

The task can be helped by definite efforts to raise the values of agricultural products and with this the power to purchase the output of our cities.

It can be helped by preventing realistically the tragedy of the growing loss, through foreclosure, of our small homes and our farms.

foreclosure: when banks repossess (take back) something because the owner cannot pay back a loan

It can be helped by insistence that the Federal, State and local governments act forthwith on the demand that their cost be drastically reduced.

It can be helped by the unifying of relief activities which today are often scattered, uneconomical and unequal. It can be helped by national planning for and supervision of all forms of transportation and of communications and other utilities which have a definitely public character.

There are many ways in which it can be helped, but it can never be helped merely by talking about it. We must act, and act quickly.

Finally, in our progress toward a resumption of work we require two safeguards against a return of the evils of the old order; there must be a strict supervision of all banking and credits and investments; there must be an end to speculation with other people's money, and there must be provision for an adequate but sound currency.

These are the lines of attack. I shall presently urge upon a new Congress in special session detailed measures for their fulfillment, and I shall seek the immediate assistance of the several States. . . .

I am prepared under my constitutional duty to recommend the measures that a stricken nation in the midst of a stricken world may require.

These measures, or such other measures as the Congress may build out of its experience and wisdom, I shall seek, within my constitutional authority, to bring to speedy adoption.

But in the event that the Congress shall fail to take one of these two courses, and in the event that the national emergency is still critical, I shall not **evade** the clear course of duty that will then confront me.

I shall ask the Congress for the one remaining **instrument** to meet the crisis—broad executive power to wage a war against the emergency as great as the power that would be given me if we were in fact invaded by a foreign foe.

For the trust reposed in me I will return the courage and the devotion that befit the time. I can do no less.

We face the **arduous** days that lie before us in the warm courage of national unity; with the clear consciousness of seeking old and precious moral values; with the clean satisfaction that comes from the stern performance of duty by old and young alike.

We aim at the assurance of a rounded and permanent national life.

We do not distrust the future of essential democracy. The people of the United States have not failed. In their need they have registered a **mandate** that they want direct, vigorous action.

They have asked for discipline and direction under leadership. They have made me the present instrument of their wishes. In the spirit of the gift I take it.

In this dedication of a nation we humbly ask the blessing of God. May He protect each and every one of us! May He guide me in the days to come!

evade: escape from

instrument: legal tool

arduous: difficult

mandate: order

77. Emma Lazarus, *The New Colossus* (1935)

For more information see
Chapter 7, Book 8, *An Age of Extremes.*

A gift from France in 1884, the Statue of Liberty was originally meant to symbolize the friendship and commitment to liberty shared by the French and American people. But for millions of immigrants it has been a beacon of freedom and opportunity. Emma Lazarus gave powerful expression to this idea in her poem "The New Colossus." The poem's title refers to the Colossus of Rhodes, a giant bronze statue of the sun god Helios that stood near the harbor of the Greek island of Rhodes. As a young woman who was born to a privileged New York City family, Lazarus wrote poems about love and death that brought her to the attention of Ralph Waldo Emerson and Henry Wadsworth Longfellow. Attacks on Jews in Russia in 1881 and 1882 inspired Lazarus, who was Jewish, to become an ardent defender of Jews fleeing anti-Semitism in Czarist Russia. She wrote "The New Colossus" for an auction that raised money for the statue's pedestal. Lazarus died of cancer at the age of 38, just a year after writing her famous poem.

> Not like the brazen giant of Greek fame,
> With conquering limbs astride from land to land,
> Here at our sea-washed, sunset gates shall stand
> A mighty woman with a torch, whose flame
> Is the imprisoned lightning, and her name
> Mother of Exile. From her beacon-hand
> Glows world-wide welcome; her mild eyes command
> The air-bridged harbor that twin cities frame.
>
> "Keep, ancient lands, your storied pomp!" cries she
> With silent lips. "Give me your tired, your poor,
> Your huddled masses yearning to breathe free,
> The wretched refuse of your teeming shore.
> Send these, the homeless, tempest-tost to me,
> I lift my lamp beside the golden door!"

brazen: made of brass

78. From Harlan F. Stone, dissenting opinion in *Minersville School District* v. *Gobitis* (1940)

In 1935 in Minersville, Pennsylvania, 12-year-old Lillian Gobitis and her younger brother, William, were expelled from school for refusing to salute the flag. As

Jehovah's Witnesses, the two schoolchildren believed that saluting the flag violated biblical law. They felt that the Bible prohibited people from worshiping "graven images." At that time 16 states, including Pennsylvania, had laws that required students to salute the flag. In 1940, the case of Lillian and William Gobitis reached the Supreme Court. By a vote of 8 to 1, the court ruled that the children could be compelled to salute the flag.

Justice Harlan Stone cast the one dissenting vote, and in his written opinion scolded the court for their disregard of the First and Fourteenth Amendments. It is unconstitutional, he wrote, to force citizens to say things that they do not believe and that are forbidden by their religion.

liable: open to

compulsion: demand

convictions: beliefs

genuine: real

sustained: ruled to be correct

sentiment: belief

indoctrinate: teach an unthinking belief

coerce: force
affirmation: a statement of belief

Two youths, now fifteen and sixteen years of age, are by the judgment of this Court held liable to expulsion from the public schools and to denial of all publicly supported educational privileges because of their refusal to yield to the compulsion of a law which commands their participation in a school ceremony contrary to their religious convictions. They and their father are citizens and have not exhibited by any action or statement of opinion, any disloyalty to the Government of the United States. They are ready and willing to obey all its laws which do not conflict with what they sincerely believe to be the higher commandments of God. It is not doubted that these convictions are religious, that they are genuine, or that the refusal to yield to the compulsion of the law is in good faith and with all sincerity. It would be a denial of their faith as well as the teachings of most religions to say that children of their age could not have religious convictions.

The law which is thus sustained is unique in the history of Anglo-American legislation. It does more than suppress freedom of speech and more than prohibit the free exercise of religion, which . . . are forbidden by the First Amendment and are violations of the liberty guaranteed by the Fourteenth. For by this law the state seeks to coerce these children to express a sentiment which, as they interpret it, they do not entertain, and which violates their deepest religious convictions. . . . Since the state, in competition with parents, may through teaching in the public schools indoctrinate the minds of the young, it is said that in aid of its undertaking to inspire loyalty and devotion to constituted authority and the flag which symbolizes it, it may coerce the pupil to make affirmation contrary to his belief and violation of his religious faith. And, finally, it is said that since the Minersville School Board and others are of the opinion that the country will be better served by conformity than by the observance of religious liberty which the Constitution prescribes, the courts are not free to pass judgment on the Board's choice. . . .

conformity: everyone being the same

The guarantees of civil liberty are but guarantees of freedom of the human mind and spirit and of reasonable freedom and opportunity to express them. They presuppose the right of the individual to hold such opinions as he will and to give them reasonably free expression, and his freedom, and that of the state as well, to teach and persuade others by the communication of ideas. The very essence of the liberty which they guarantee is the freedom of the individual from compulsion as to what he shall think and what he shall say, at least where the compulsion is to bear false witness to his religion. If these guarantees are to have any meaning they must, I think, be deemed to withhold from the state any authority to compel belief of the expression of it where that expression violates religious convictions, whatever may be the legislative view of the desirability of such compulsion.

presuppose: assume

History teaches us that there have been but few infringements of personal liberty by the state which have not been justified, as they are here, in the name of righteousness and the public good, and few which have not been directed, as they are now, at politically helpless minorities. The framers were not unaware that under the system which they created most governmental curtailments of personal liberty would have the support of a legislative judgment that the public interest would be better served by its curtailment than by its constitutional protection. I cannot conceive that in prescribing, as limitations upon the powers of government, the freedom of the mind and spirit secured by the explicit guaranties of freedom of speech and religion, they intended . . . that the compulsory expression of belief which violates religious convictions would better serve the public interest than their protection. The Constitution may well elicit expressions of loyalty to it and to the government which it created, but it does not command such expressions or otherwise give any indication that compulsory expressions of loyalty play any such part in our scheme of government as to override the constitutional protection of freedom of speech and religion. And while such expressions of loyalty, when voluntarily given, may promote national unity, it is quite another matter to say that their compulsory expression by children in violation of their own and their parents' religious convictions can be regarded as playing so important a part in our national unity as to leave school boards free to exact it despite the constitutional guarantee of freedom of religion. The very terms of the Bill of Rights preclude, it seems to me, any reconciliation of such

infringements: violations of

minorities: people who differ from the majority

curtailments: control
prescribing: claiming

compulsory: mandatory

elicit: bring out

preclude: rule out

compulsions with the constitutional guarantees by a legislative declaration that they are more important to the public welfare than the Bill of Rights. . . .

The Constitution expresses more than the conviction of the people that democratic processes must be preserved at all costs. It is also an expression of faith and a command that freedom of mind and spirit must be preserved, which government must obey, if it is to adhere to that justice and moderation without which no free government can exist. For this reason it would seem that legislation which operates to repress the religious freedom of small minorities, which is admittedly within the scope of the protection of the Bill of Rights, must at least be subject to the same judicial scrutiny as legislation which we have recently held to infringe the constitutional liberty of religious and racial minorities. . . .

adhere: stick to

repress: hold back

scrutiny: hard look

For more information see
Chapters 29 and 30, Book 9, *War, Peace, and All That Jazz.*

79. Franklin D. Roosevelt, *Message Asking for War Against Japan* (1941)

On Sunday morning, December 7, 1941, Japanese carrier-based aircraft staged a surprise attack on the U.S. naval fleet at Pearl Harbor, Hawaii. Airplanes launched from half a dozen aircraft carriers sank or heavily damaged 18 U.S. naval vessels, destroyed more than 180 U.S. aircraft, and killed 2,403 Americans. The next day President Roosevelt called for the United States to declare war on Japan. Relations between the United States and Japan had deteriorated after Japan invaded China in 1937. When Japan established military bases in Southeast Asia in 1940 and 1941, the United States responded by freezing Japanese bank accounts and prohibiting the export of scrap iron, oil, and aviation fuel to Japan. In a last-ditch effort to avoid war, the United States and Japan held negotiations in Washington, D.C., in November 1941. But while the diplomats met, the Japanese were preparing their surprise attack.

Japan attacked Pearl Harbor because a crippled U.S. Pacific fleet would allow them to seize rubber plantations in French Indochina and British Malaya and oil fields in the Dutch East Indies. It would also help Japan achieve victory over China, which it had been fighting for four years.

infamy: notoriety

Yesterday, December 7, 1941—a date which will live in infamy—the United States of America was suddenly and deliberately attacked by naval and air forces of the Empire of Japan.

The United States was at peace with that nation and, at the solicitation of Japan, was still in conversation with its Government and its Emperor looking toward the maintenance of peace in the Pacific. Indeed, one hour after Japanese air squadrons had commenced bombing in Oahu, the Japanese Ambassador to the United States and his colleague delivered to the Secretary of State a formal reply to a recent American message. While this reply stated that it seemed useless to continue the existing diplomatic negotiations, it contained no threat or hint of war or armed attack.

It will be recorded that the distance of Hawaii from Japan makes it obvious that the attack was deliberately planned many days or even weeks ago. During the intervening time the Japanese Government has deliberately sought to deceive the United States by false statements and expressions of hope for continued peace.

The attack yesterday on the Hawaiian Islands has caused severe damage to American naval and military forces. Very many American lives have been lost. In addition American ships have been reported torpedoed on the high seas between San Francisco and Honolulu.

Yesterday the Japanese Government also launched an attack against Malaya. Last night Japanese forces attacked Hong Kong. Last night Japanese forces attacked Guam. Last night Japanese forces attacked Philippine Islands. Last night the Japanese attacked Wake Island. This morning the Japanese attacked Midway Island.

Japan has, therefore, undertaken a surprise offensive extending throughout the Pacific area. The facts of yesterday speak for themselves. The people of the United States have already formed their opinions and well understand the implications to the very life and safety of our nation.

As Commander-in-Chief of the Army and Navy, I have directed that all measures be taken for our defense.

Always will we remember the character of the onslaught against us.

No matter how long it may take us to overcome this premeditated invasion, the American people in their righteous might will win through to absolute victory.

I believe I interpret the will of the Congress and of the people when I assert that we will not only defend ourselves to the uttermost but will make very certain that this form of treachery shall never endanger us again.

Hostilities exist. There is no blinking at the fact that our people, our territory and our interests are in grave danger.

With confidence in our armed forces—with the unbonded determination of our people—we will gain the inevitable triumph—so help us God.

solicitation: request

commenced: begun

onslaught: attack

treachery: betrayal

Hostilities: war

dastardly: cowardly

I ask that the Congress declare that since the unprovoked and dastardly attack by Japan on Sunday, December seventh, a state of war has existed between the United States and the Japanese Empire.

For more information see
Chapters 29 and 30, Book 9, *War, Peace, and All That Jazz.*

80. Franklin D. Roosevelt, *Declaration of War on Germany and Italy* (1941)

Four days after the Japanese attack on Pearl Harbor, Germany and Italy declared war on the United States. Roosevelt immediately asked Congress to declare war on them in return, pledging to mobilize the nation's resources to defeat "the forces of savagery and barbarism."

To the Congress of the United States:

On the morning of Dec. 11 the Government of Germany, pursuing its course of world conquest, declared war against the United States.

The long-known and the long-expected has thus taken place. The forces endeavoring to enslave the entire world now are moving toward this hemisphere.

Never before has there been a greater challenge to life, liberty and civilization.

Delay invites great danger. Rapid and united effort by all of the peoples of the world who are determined to remain free will insure a world victory of the forces of justice and of righteousness over the forces of savagery and of barbarism.

Italy also has declared war against the United States.

I therefore request the Congress to recognize a state of war between the United States and Germany, and between the United States and Italy.

FRANKLIN D. ROOSEVELT

Declaring that a state of war exists between the Government of Germany and the government and the people of the United States and making provision to prosecute the same.

prosecute the same: fight the war

Whereas the Government of Germany has formally declared war against the government and the people of the United States of America:

Therefore, be it

Resolved by the Senate and House of Representatives of the United States of America in Congress assembled, that the state of war between the United States and the Government of Germany which has thus been thrust upon the United States is hereby formally declared; and the President is hereby authorized and directed to employ the entire naval and military forces of the United States and the resources of the government to carry on war against the Government of Germany; and, to bring the conflict to a successful termination, all of the resources of the country are hereby pledged by the Congress of the United States.

81. Franklin D. Roosevelt, *"The Four Freedoms": Message to Congress* (1941)

For more information see Chapter 24, Book 9, *War, Peace, and All That Jazz.*

In 1941, in his annual State of the Union message, President Franklin D. Roosevelt called for "a world founded on four essential freedoms. Freedom of speech and expression, freedom of worship, freedom from want, and freedom from fear." The United States would not enter World War II for another 11 months. But in his speech, the President contrasted American values with those of Nazi Germany, which emphasized racial purity and military conquest. Roosevelt used his State of the Union address to urge support for nations such as Britain that were fighting to preserve democratic values. He requested a "lend-lease" program to supply Britain with war equipment to fight Germany. After hearing Roosevelt's address, the country's foremost illustrator, Norman Rockwell, began to paint images of the President's Four Freedoms. These images became powerful national symbols during World War II.

To the Congress of the United States:

I address you, the Members of the Seventy-Seventh Congress, at a moment unprecedented in the history of the Union. I use the word "unprecedented," because at no previous time has American security been as seriously threatened from without as it is today. . . .

unprecedented: something that has not happened before

It is true that prior to 1914 the United States often had been disturbed by events in other Continents. We had even engaged in two wars with European nations and in a number of undeclared wars in the West Indies, in the Mediterranean and in the Pacific for the maintenance of American rights and for the principles of peaceful commerce. In no case, however, had a serious threat been raised against our national safety or our independence.

convey: express

What I seek to convey is the historic truth that the United States as a nation has at all times maintained opposition to any attempt to lock us in behind an ancient Chinese wall while the procession of civilization went past. Today, thinking of our children and their children, we oppose enforced isolation for ourselves or for any part of the Americas.

Even when the World War broke out in 1914, it seemed to contain only small threat of danger to our own American future. But, as time went on, the American people began to visualize what the downfall of democratic nations might mean to our own democracy.

Peace of Versailles: The 1919 treaty that ended World War I

pacification: making peace with an enemy by giving up more than is wise

tyranny: rule by a single, all-powerful leader

We need not over-emphasize imperfections in the Peace of Versailles. We need not harp on failure of the democracies to deal with problems of world deconstruction. We should remember that the Peace of 1919 was far less unjust than the kind of "pacification" which began even before Munich, and which is being carried on under the new order of tyranny that seeks to spread over every continent today. The American people have unalterably set their faces against that tyranny.

propaganda: information, often untrue, spread to make people believe something

Every realist knows that the democratic way of life is at this moment being directly assailed in every part of the world—assailed either by arms, or by secret spreading of poisonous propaganda by those who seek to destroy unity and promote discord in nations still at peace. During sixteen months this assault has blotted out the whole pattern of democratic life in an appalling number of independent nations, great and small. The assailants are still on the march, threatening other nations, great and small.

Therefore, as your President, performing my constitutional duty to "give to the Congress information of the state of the Union," I find it necessary to report that the future and the safety of our country and of our democracy are overwhelmingly involved in events far beyond our borders.

gallantly: heroically

Armed defense of democratic existence is now being gallantly waged in four continents. If that defense fails, all the population and all the resources of Europe, Asia, Africa and Australasia will be dominated by the conquerors. The total of those populations and their resources greatly exceeds the sum total of the population and resources of the whole of the Western Hemisphere—many times over.

In times like these it is immature—and incidentally untrue—for anybody to brag that an unprepared America, single-handed, and with one hand tied behind its back, can hold off the whole world. . . .

Our national policy is this.

First, by an impressive expression of the public will and without regard to partisanship, we are committed to all-inclusive national defense.

partisanship: party politics inside the country

Second, by an impressive expression of the public will and without regard to partisanship, we are committed to full support of all those resolute peoples, everywhere, who are resisting aggression and are thereby keeping war away from our Hemisphere. By this support, we express our determination that the democratic cause shall prevail; and we strengthen the defense and security of our own nation.

Third, by an impressive expression of the public will and without regard to partisanship we are committed to the proposition that principles of mortality and considerations for our own security will never permit us to acquiesce in a peace dictated by aggressors and sponsored by appeasers. We know that enduring peace cannot be bought at the cost of other people's freedom.

mortality: death
acquiesce: go along with

In the recent national election there was no substantial difference between the two great parties in respect to that national policy. No issue was fought out on this line before the American electorate. Today, it is abundantly evident that American citizens everywhere are demanding and supporting speedy and complete action in recognition of obvious danger. Therefore, the immediate need is a swift and driving increase in our armament production. . . .

Our most useful and immediate role is to act as an arsenal for them as well as for ourselves. They do not need man power. They do need billions of dollars worth of the weapons of defense. . . .

armament: weapons
arsenal: weapons supplier and storehouse

Let us say to the democracies: "We Americans are vitally concerned in your defense of freedom. We are putting forth our energies, our resources and our organizing powers to give you the strength to regain and maintain a free world. We shall send you, in ever-increasing numbers, ships, planes, tanks, guns. This is our purpose and our pledge." . . . .

As men do not live by bread alone, they do not fight by armaments alone. Those who man our defenses, and those behind them who build our defenses, must have the stamina and courage which come from an unshakable belief in the manner of life which they are defending. The mighty action which we are calling for cannot be based on a disregard of all things worth fighting for.

stamina: long-term strength

The Nation takes great satisfaction and much strength from the things which have been done to make its people conscious of their individual stake in the preservation of democratic life in America. Those things have toughened the fibre of our people, have renewed their faith and strengthened their devotion to the institutions we make ready to protect. Certainly this is no time to stop thinking about the social and economic problems which are the root cause of the social revolution which is today a supreme factor in the world.

fibre: basic character

There is nothing mysterious about the foundations of a healthy and strong democracy. The basic things expected by our people of

turmoil: confusion

social economy: parts of the economic life of the country that affect people's well-being

their political and economic systems are simple. They are: equality of opportunity for youth and for others; jobs for those who can work; security for those who need it; the ending of special privilege for the few; the preservation of civil liberties for all; the enjoyment of the fruits of scientific progress in a wider and constantly rising standard of living.

These are the simple and basic things that must never be lost sight of in the turmoil and unbelievable complexity of our modern world. The inner and abiding strength of our economic and political systems is dependent upon the degree to which they fulfill these expectations.

Many subjects connected with our social economy call for immediate improvement. As examples: We should bring more citizens under the coverage of old age pensions and unemployment insurance. We should widen the opportunities for adequate medical care. We should plan a better system by which persons deserving or needing gainful employment may obtain it.

I have called for personal sacrifice. I am assured of the willingness of almost all Americans to respond to that call. . . .

In the future days, which we seek to make secure, we look forward to a world founded upon four essential human freedoms.

The first is freedom of speech and expression—everywhere in the world.

The second is freedom of every person to worship God in his own way—everywhere in the world.

The third is freedom from want—which, translated into world terms, means economic understandings which will secure to every nation a healthy peace time life for its inhabitants—everywhere in the world.

The fourth is freedom from fear—which, translated into world terms, means a worldwide reduction of armaments to such a point and in such a thorough fashion that no nation will be in a position to commit an act of physical aggression against any neighbor—anywhere in the world.

millennium: time of perfect happiness, far in the future
antithesis: opposite

That is no vision of a distant millennium. It is a definite basis for a kind of world attainable in our own time and generation. That kind of world is the very antithesis of the so-called new order of tyranny which the dictators seek to create with the crash of a bomb.

To that new order we oppose the greater conception—the moral order. A good society is able to face schemes of world domination and foreign revolutions alike without fear.

Since the beginning of our American history we have been engaged in change—in a perpetual peaceful revolution—a revolution which goes on steadily, quietly adjusting itself to changing conditions—without the concentration camp or the quick-lime in the ditch. The world order which we seek is the cooperation of free countries, working together in a friendly, civilized society.

This nation has placed its destiny in the hands and heads and hearts of its millions of free men and women; and its faith in freedom under the guidance of God. Freedom means the supremacy of human rights everywhere. Our support goes to those who struggle to gain those rights or keep them. Our strength is in our unity of purpose.

To that high concept there can be no end save victory.

quick-lime: substance that eats away and dissolves organic matter

supremacy: overall importance

82. From Robert Jackson, Opinion in *West Virginia State Board of Education* v. *Barnette*, 1943

In 1942 the board of education of West Virginia adopted a resolution that required students to stand, salute the flag, and recite the Pledge of Allegiance. The board's resolution justified the rule by quoting directly from the Supreme Court's 1940 decision in *Minersville* v. *Gobitis*. Students who refused to salute the flag were to be expelled from school. Their parents could then be arrested for allowing their children to be "delinquent" from school.

A group of parents sued the board of education, and the U.S. Supreme Court decided to review the case and to take a new look at their decision in *Minersville*. A majority of the court (6 to 3) decided that their decision in the Minersville case had been wrong. In Justice Robert H. Jackson's opinion, issued on Flag Day, he wrote that Americans could not be forced to demonstrate their allegiance to "what shall be orthodox in politics, nationalism, religion, or other matters of opinion." This was true for the young as well as for adults. Justice Jackson stated that educators must not "teach youth to discount important principles of our government as platitudes."

There is no doubt that, in connection with the pledges, the flag salute is a form of utterance. Symbolism is a primitive but effective way of communicating ideas. The use of an emblem or flag to symbolize some system, idea, institution, or personality, is a short cut from mind to mind. Causes and nations, political parties, lodges and ecclesiastical groups seek to knit the loyalty of their followings to a flag or banner, a color or design. The State announces rank, function, and

utterance: speech

ecclesiastical: church

maces: scepters

raiment: clothing
convey: express

sustain: uphold

vicissitudes: ups and downs

coerce: force
Nationalism: strong pride in one's country
phenomenon: unusual event or trend
dynasty: a powerful family that exerts influence on society for generations
severity: harshness
provocation: cause

futility: pointlessness
coherence: sharing of one belief or feeling
Inquisition: Catholic Church's attempt to uncover and remove heretics, instituted in Spain in 1479
totalitarian: dictatorial, having complete power
unanimity: shared condition

authority through crowns and maces, uniforms and black robes; the church speaks through the Cross, the Crucifix, the altar and shrine, and clerical raiment. Symbols of State often convey political ideas just as religious symbols come to convey theological ones. Associated with many of these symbols are appropriate gestures of acceptance or respect: a salute, a bowed or bared head, a bended knee. A person gets from a symbol the meaning he puts into it, and what is one man's comfort and inspiration is another's jest and scorn. . . .

[T]he compulsory flag salute and pledge requires affirmation of a belief and an attitude of mind.

. . . To sustain the compulsory flag salute we are required to say that Bill of Rights which guards the individual's right to speak his own mind, left it open to public authorities to compel him to utter what is not in his mind. . . .

The very purpose of a Bill of Rights was to withdraw certain subjects from the vicissitudes of political controversy, to place them beyond the reach of majorities and officials and to establish them as legal principles to be applied by the courts. One's right to life, liberty, and property, to free speech, a free press, freedom of worship and assembly, and other fundamental rights may not be submitted to vote; they depend on the outcome of no elections. . . .

Struggles to coerce uniformity of sentiment in support of some end thought essential to their time and country have been waged by many good as well as by evil men. Nationalism is a relatively recent phenomenon but at other times and places the ends have been racial or territorial security, support of a dynasty or regime, and particular plans for saving souls. As first and moderate methods to attain unity have failed, those bent on its accomplishment must resort to an ever-increasing severity. As governmental pressure toward unity becomes greater, so strife becomes more bitter as to whose unity it shall be. Probably no deeper division of our people could proceed from any provocation than from finding it necessary to choose what doctrine and whose program public educational officials shall compel youth to unite in embracing. Ultimate futility of such attempts to compel coherence is the lesson of every such effort from the Roman drive to stamp out Christianity as a disturber of its pagan unity, the Inquisition, as a means to religious and dynastic unity, the Siberian exiles as a means to Russian unity, down to the fast failing efforts of our present totalitarian enemies. Those who begin coercive elimination of dissent soon find themselves exterminating dissenters. Compulsory unification of opinion achieves only the unanimity of the graveyard.

It seems trite but necessary to say that the First Amendment to our Constitution was designed to avoid these ends by avoiding these beginnings. There is no mysticism in the American concept of the State or the nature or origin of its authority. We set up government by consent of the governed, and the Bill of Rights denies those in power any legal opportunity to coerce that consent. Authority here is to be controlled by public opinion, not public opinion by authority.

The case is made difficult not because the principles of its decision are obscure but because the flag involved is our own. Nevertheless, we apply the limitations of the Constitution with no fear that freedom to be intellectually and spiritually diverse or even contrary will disintegrate the social organization. To believe that patriotism will not flourish if patriotic ceremonies are voluntary and spontaneous instead of a compulsory routine is to make an unflattering estimate of the appeal of our institutions to free minds. . . . [F]reedom to differ is not limited to things that do not matter much. That would be a mere shadow of freedom. The test of its substance is the right to differ as to things that touch the heart of the existing order.

If there is a fixed star in our constitutional constellation, it is that no official, high or petty, can prescribe what shall be orthodox in politics, nationalism, religion, or other matters of opinion or force citizens to confess by word or act their faith therein. . . .

We think the action of the local authorities in compelling the flag salute and pledge transcends constitutional limitations on their power and invades the sphere of intellect and spirit which it is the purpose of the First Amendment to our Constitution to reserve from all official control.

trite: obvious

mysticism: dreamy rather than logical

orthodox: entirely acceptable, correct

transcends: rises above

83. Learned Hand, *"The Spirit of Liberty": Address on "I Am an American Day"* (1944)

For more than fifty years, Learned Hand served as a federal judge, most of the time on the U.S. Court of Appeals for the Second Circuit in New York. Three Presidents considered nominating Hand for the Supreme Court. Hand gained public acclaim for a speech on "The Spirit of Liberty." He delivered this address in 1944 in New York City's Central Park, where 1.5 million people gathered for an event billed as "I Am an American Day." Hand directed his remarks especially to 150,000 newly naturalized citizens.

Hand told his listeners that immigrants came to America in search of liberty. The essence of liberty, he said, was not found in constitutions, laws, or courthouses, but "in the hearts of men and women." What then, he asked, is the spirit of liberty? "The spirit of liberty is the spirit that is not too sure it is right." What Hand meant is that Americans needed to avoid prejudice and remain open-minded. Hand was an early opponent of Hitler and a critic of anti-Semitism, and as a judge, he defended freedom of expression and civil liberties.

We have gathered here to affirm a faith, a faith in a common purpose, a common conviction, a common devotion. Some of us have chosen America as the land of our adoption; the rest have come from those who did the same. For this reason we have some right to consider ourselves a picked group, a group of those who had the courage to break from the past and brave the dangers and the loneliness of a strange land. What was the object that nerved us, or those who went before us, to this choice? We sought liberty; freedom from oppression, freedom from want, freedom to be ourselves. This we then sought; this we now believe that we are by way of winning. What do we mean when we say that first of all we seek liberty? I often wonder whether we do not rest our hopes too much upon constitutions, upon laws and upon courts. These are false hopes; believe me, these are false hopes. Liberty lies in the hearts of men and women; when it dies there, no constitution, no law, no court can save it; no constitution, no law, no court can even do much to help it. While it lies there it needs no constitution, no law, no court to save it. And what is this liberty which must lie in the hearts of men and women? It is not the ruthless, the unbridled will; it is not freedom to do as one likes. That is the denial of liberty, and leads straight to its overthrow. A society in which men recognize no check upon their freedom soon becomes a society where freedom is the possession of only a savage few; as we have learned to our sorrow.

ruthless: without pity

What this is the spirit of liberty? I cannot define it; I can only tell you my own faith. The spirit of liberty is the spirit which is not too sure that it is right; the spirit of liberty is the spirit which seeks to understand the minds of other men and women; the spirit of liberty is the spirit which weights their interests alongside its own without bias; the spirit of liberty remembers that not even a sparrow falls to earth unheeded; the spirit of liberty is the spirit of Him who, near two thousand years ago, taught mankind that lesson it has never learned, but has never quite forgotten; that there may be a kingdom where the least shall be heard and considered side by side with the greatest. And now in that spirit, that spirit of an America which has never been, and which may never be; nay, which never will be except as the conscience and courage of Americans create it; yet in the spirit of that America which lies hidden in some form in the aspirations of us all; in the spirit of that America for which our young men are at this moment fighting and dying; in that spirit of liberty and of America I ask you to rise and with me pledge our faith in the glorious destiny of our beloved country.

aspirations: hopes

84. From Harry S. Truman, *"The Truman Doctrine": Message to Congress* (1947)

For more information see
Chapter 4, in Book 10, *All the People.*

The Truman Doctrine committed the United States to providing aid to countries resisting communist aggression or conspiracy. In February 1947, Britain informed the United States that it could no longer afford to provide aid to Greece and Turkey. The situation seemed urgent. The Greek monarchy was threatened by guerrilla warfare and the Soviet Union was seeking to control the Dardanelles in Turkey, a water route from the Black Sea to the Mediterranean. The U.S. government feared that the loss of Greece and Turkey to communism would open western Europe and Africa to Soviet influence. It also worried that if the Soviet Union gained control over the eastern Mediterranean, it could stop the flow of Middle Eastern oil.

President Truman responded decisively. He asked Congress for $400 million in economic and military aid for Greece and Turkey. This was an unprecedented amount of foreign aid during peacetime. He also declared that it was the policy of the United States "to support free peoples who are resisting attempted subjugation by armed minorities or by outside pressures." The Truman Doctrine committed the United States to containing the influence of the Soviet Union and combating the spread of communism.

The gravity of the situation which confronts the world today necessitates my appearance before a joint session of the Congress. The foreign policy and the national security of this country are involved.

One aspect of the present situation, which I wish to present to you at this time for your consideration and decision, concerns Greece and Turkey. . . .

gravity: seriousness

implications: consequences

coercion: force

totalitarian: dictatorial, having unchecked power

intimidation: controlling people through fear

subjugation: holding down

I am fully aware of the broad implications involved if the United States extends assistance to Greece and Turkey, and I shall discuss these implications with you at this time.

One of the primary objectives of the foreign policy of the United States is the creation of conditions in which we and other nations will be able to work out a way of life free from coercion. This was a fundamental issue in the war with Germany and Japan. Our victory was won over countries which sought to impose their will, and their way of life, upon other nations.

To ensure the peaceful development of nations, free from coercion, the United States has taken a leading part in establishing the United Nations. The United Nations is designed to make possible lasting freedom and independence for all its members. We shall not realize our objectives, however, unless we are willing to help free peoples to maintain their free institutions and their national integrity against aggressive movements that seek to impose on them totalitarian regimes. This is no more than a frank recognition that totalitarian regimes imposed on free peoples, by direct or indirect aggression, undermine the foundations of international peace and hence the security of the United States.

The peoples of a number of countries of the world have recently had totalitarian regimes forced upon them against their will. The Government of the United States has made frequent protests against coercion and intimidation, in violation of the Yalta Agreement, in Poland, Rumania and Bulgaria. I must also state that in a number of other countries there have been similar developments.

At the present moment in world history nearly every nation must choose between alternative ways of life. The choice is too often not a free one.

One way of life is based upon the will of the majority, and is distinguished by free institutions, representative government, free elections, guarantees of individual liberty, freedom of speech and religion, and freedom from political oppression.

The second way of life is based upon the will of the minority forcibly imposed upon the majority. It relies upon terror and oppression, a controlled press and radio, fixed elections, and the suppression of personal freedoms.

I believe that it must be the policy of the United States to support free peoples who are resisting attempted subjugation by armed minorities or by outside pressures.

I believe that we must assist free peoples to work out their own destinies in their own way.

I believe that our help should be primarily through economic and financial aid which is essential to economic stability and orderly political processes.

The world is not static, and the status quo is not scared. But we cannot allow changes in the status quo in violation of the charter of the United Nations by such methods as coercion, or by such subterfuges as political infiltration. In helping free and independent nations to maintain their freedom, the United States will be giving effect to the principles of the charter of the United Nations. . . .

The seeds of totalitarian regimes are nurtured by misery and want. They spread and grow in the evil soil of poverty and strife. They reach their full growth when the hope of a people for a better life has died. We must keep that hope alive. The free peoples of the world look to us for support in maintaining their freedoms.

If we falter in our leadership, we may endanger the peace of the world—and we shall surely endanger the welfare of this nation.

Great responsibilities have been placed upon us by the swift movement of events. I am confident that the Congress will face these responsibilities squarely.

It is part of my responsibility as Commander-in-Chief of the armed forces to see to it that our country is able to defend itself against any possible aggressor. Accordingly, I have directed the Atomic Energy Commission to continue its work on all forms of atomic weapons, including the so-called hydrogen or super-bomb. Like all other work in the field of atomic weapons, it is being and will be carried forward on a basis consistent with the over-all objectives of our program for peace and security.

This we shall continue to do until a satisfactory plan for international control of atomic energy is achieved. We shall also continue to examine all those factors that affect our program for peace and this country's security.

The activities necessary to carry out our program of technical aid will be diverse in character and will have to be performed by a number of different government agencies and private instrumentalities. It will be necessary to utilize not only the resources of international agencies and the United States Government, but also the facilities and the experience of the private business and non-profit organizations that have long been active in this work. . . .

In the economically underdeveloped areas of the world today there are new creative energies. We look forward to the time when these countries will be stronger and more independent than they are now, and yet more closely bound to us and to other nations by ties of friendship and commerce, and by kindred ideals. On the other hand,

static: motionless
status quo: current state of affairs
subterfuges: disguised methods
political infiltration: sending spies into an enemy group

falter: fail

kindred: similar, compatible

hostile: opposed

unless we aid the newly awakened spirit in these peoples to find the course of fruitful development, they may fall under the control of those whose philosophy is hostile to human freedom, thereby prolonging the unsettled state of the world and postponing the achievement of permanent peace.

Before the peoples of these areas we hold out the promise of a better future through the democratic way of life. It is vital that we move quickly to bring the meaning of that promise home to them in their daily lives.

For more information see
Chapter 7, Book 10, *All the People*.

85. Harry S. Truman, *Statement on the Atomic Bomb* (1950)

In 1945, Harry S. Truman faced one of the most difficult decisions a President has ever had to make. Franklin D. Roosevelt's death in April 1945 had made Truman President. Nazi Germany had been defeated, and now the new chief executive had to decide how best to end the war with Japan. "I have to decide Japanese strategy," he wrote in his diary, "—shall we invade Japan proper or shall we bomb and blockade." Truman was told that Japan was prepared to fight to the end rather than surrender.

Some officials believed that U.S. bombing raids, which had already killed hundreds of thousands of people, would defeat Japan. Others felt that the United States would have to invade Japan, at the cost of tens of thousands of casualties. Then, less than two weeks after becoming President, Truman was informed about a secret American project to develop an atomic bomb. On July 16, 1945, Truman learned that the weapon, with the power of thousands of tons of dynamite, had been successfully tested.

The United States and Britain gave Japan an ultimatum: surrender or face total destruction. When the Japanese government failed to respond, Truman authorized the use of the bomb. When asked to give his formal approval, he wrote without hesitation: "Suggestion approved. Release when ready."

It is part of my resposibility as Commander-in-Chief of the armed forces to see to it that our country is able to defend itself against any possible aggressor. Accordingly, I have directed the Atomic Energy Commission to continue its work on all forms of atomic weapons, including the so-called hydrogen or super-bomb. Like all other work in the field of atomic weapons, it is being and will be carried forward on a basis consistent with the over-all objectives of our program for peace and security.

This we shall continue to do until a satisfactory plan for international control of atomic energy is achieved. We shall also continue to examine all those factors that affect our program for peace and this country's security.

The activities necessary to carry out our program of technical aid will be diverse in character and will have to be performed by a number of different government agencies and private instrumentalities. It will be necessary to utilize not only the resources of international agencies and the United States Government, but also the facilities and the experience of the private business and nonprofit organizations that have long been active in this work. . . .

In the economically underdeveloped areas of the world today there are new creative energies. We look forward to the time when these countries will be stronger and more independent than they are now, and yet more closely bound to us and to other nations by ties of friendship and commerce, and by kindred ideals. On the other hand, unless we aid the newly awakened spirit in these peoples to find the course of fruitful development, they may fall under the control of those whose philosophy is hostile to human freedom, thereby prolonging the unsettled state of the world and postponing the achievement of permanent peace.

kindred: similar

hostile: opposed

Before the peoples of these areas we hold out the promise of a better future through the democratic way of life. It is vital that we move quickly to bring the meaning of that promise home to them in their daily lives.

86. Margaret Chase Smith, *Declaration of Conscience* (1950)

For more information see
Chapter 8, Book 10, *All the People*.

Margaret Chase Smith was known as "the conscience of the Senate" and gained a reputation for courage and independence when she became the first member of Congress to condemn the anti-communist witch hunt led by Senator Joseph McCarthy of Wisconsin. In a fifteen-minute speech on the Senate floor on June 1, 1950, Smith denounced McCarthy for destroying reputations with his reckless charges about communists and "fellow travelers" in government. She never mentioned the anti-communist crusader by name, but there was no doubt about whom she referred to. She told the Senate that it was time to stop conducting "character assassination" behind "the shield of congressional immunity." She then read a "Declaration of Conscience" signed by six fellow Republicans. "The nation sorely needs a Republican victory," she declared, "but I don't want to see the Republican Party ride to political victory on the four horsemen of calumny [misrepresentation]—fear, ignorance, bigotry, and smear." McCarthy threatened to destroy Smith's political career, but she was so highly regarded that Maine voters easily reelected her to the Senate.

"Mr. President," I said, and then I began:

I would like to speak briefly and simply about a serious national condition. It is a national feeling of fear and frustration that could result in national suicide and the end of everything that we Americans hold dear. It is a condition that comes from the lack of effective leadership in either the Legislative Branch or the Executive Branch of our Government.

That leadership is so lacking that serious and responsible proposals are being made that national advisory commissions be appointed to provide such critically needed leadership.

I speak as briefly as possible because too much harm has already been done with irresponsible words of bitterness and selfish political opportunism. I speak as simply as possible because the issue is too great to be obscured by eloquence. I speak simply and briefly in the hope that my words will be taken to heart.

I speak as a Republican. I speak as a woman. I speak as a United States Senator. I speak as an American.

The United States Senate has long enjoyed worldwide respect as the greatest deliberative body in the world. But recently that deliberative character has too often been debased to the level of a forum of hate and character assassination sheltered by the shield of congressional immunity.

It is ironical that we Senators can in debate in the Senate directly or indirectly, by any form of words, impute to any American who is not a Senator any conduct or motive unworthy or unbecoming an American—and without that non-Senator American having any legal redress against us—yet if we say the same thing in the Senate about our colleagues we can be stopped on the grounds of being out of order.

It is strange that we can verbally attack anyone else without restraint and with full protection and yet we hold ourselves above the same type of criticism here on the Senate Floor. Surely the United

opportunism: grasping for opportunities in an unprincipled way
obscured: hidden, confused
eloquence: verbal elegance
deliberative: decision-making
debased: brought down
forum: place
character assassination: destroying someone's reputation
congressional immunity: special legal protection given to members of Congress
ironical: incongruous
impute: attribute
unworthy: not good enough
unbecoming: inappropriate
redress: protection, compensation
verbally: with words

234

States Senate is big enough to take self-criticism and self-appraisal. Surely we should be able to take the same kind of character attacks that we "dish out" to outsiders.

I think that it is high time for the United States Senate and its members to do some soul-searching—for us to weigh our consciences—on the manner in which we are performing our duty to the people of America—on the manner in which we are using or abusing our individual powers and privileges.

I think that it is high time that we remembered that we have sworn to uphold and defend the Constitution. I think that it is high time that we remembered that the Constitution, as amended, speaks not only of the freedom of speech but also of trial by jury instead of trial by accusation.

Whether it be a criminal prosecution in court or a character prosecution in the Senate, there is little practical distinction when the life of a person has been ruined.

Those of us who shout the loudest about Americanism in making character assassinations are all too frequently those who, by our own words and acts, ignore some of the basic principles of Americanism:

The right to criticize;

The right to hold unpopular beliefs;

The right to protest;

The right of independent thought.

The exercise of these rights should not cost one single American citizen his reputation or his right to a livelihood nor should he be in danger of losing his reputation or livelihood merely because he happens to know someone who holds unpopular beliefs. Who of us doesn't? Otherwise none of us could call our souls our own. Otherwise thought control would have set in.

The American people are sick and tired of being afraid to speak their minds lest they be politically smeared as "Communists" or "Fascists" by their opponents. Freedom of speech is not what it used to be in America. It has been so abused by some that it is not exercised by others.

Communists or Fascists: extremists of the political left or right

The American people are sick and tired of seeing innocent people smeared and guilty people whitewashed. But there have been enough proved cases . . . to cause nationwide distrust and strong suspicion that there may be something to the unproved, sensational accusations.

whitewashed: have their guilt covered by a facade of innocence
sensational: shocking

As a Republican, I say to my colleagues on this side of the aisle that the Republican Party faces a challenge today that is not unlike the challenge that it faced back in Lincoln's day. The Republican

unrelentingly: ceaselessly

tentacles: claws

mania: crazed tendency

prudence: good sense

complacency: overconfidence

displace: replace
integrity: honesty

Calumny: false statement intended to harm someone
Bigotry: prejudice
Smear: false and harmful statements

Party so successfully met that challenge that it emerged from the Civil War as the champion of a united nation—in addition to being a Party that unrelentingly fought loose spending and loose programs.

Today our country is being psychologically divided by the confusion and the suspicions that are bred in the United States Senate to spread like cancerous tentacles of "know nothing, suspect everything" attitudes. Today we have a Democratic Administration that has developed a mania for loose spending and loose programs. History is repeating itself—and the Republican Party again has the opportunity to emerge as the champion of unity and prudence.

The record of the present Democratic Administration has provided us with sufficient campaign issues without the necessity of resorting to political smears. America is rapidly losing its position as leader of the world simply because the Democratic Administration has pitifully failed to provide effective leadership.

The Democratic Administration has completely confused the American people by its daily contradictory grave warnings and optimistic assurances—that show the people that our Democratic Administration has no idea of where it is going.

The Democratic Administration has greatly lost the confidence of the American people by its complacency to the threat of communism here at home and the leak of vital secrets to Russia through key officials of the Democratic Administration. There are enough proved cases to make this point without diluting our criticism with unproved charges.

Surely these are sufficient reasons to make it clear to the American people that it is time for a change and that a Republican victory is necessary to the security of this country. Surely it is clear that this nation will continue to suffer as long as it is governed by the present ineffective Democratic Administration.

Yet to displace it with a Republican regime embracing a philosophy that lacks political integrity or intellectual honesty would prove equally disastrous to this nation. The nation sorely needs a Republican victory. But I don't want to see the Republican Party ride to political victory on the Four Horsemen of Calumny—Fear, Ignorance, Bigotry, and Smear.

I doubt if the Republican Party could—simply because I don't believe the American people will uphold any political party that puts political exploitation above national interest. Surely we Republicans aren't that desperate for victory.

I don't want to see the Republican Party win that way. While it might be a fleeting victory for the Republican Party, it would be a more lasting defeat for the American people. Surely it would ultimately be suicide for the Republican Party and the two-party system that has protected our American liberties from the dictatorship of a one party-system.

As members of the Minority Party, we do not have the primary authority to formulate the policy of our Government. But we do have the responsibility of rendering constructive criticism, of clarifying issues, of allaying fears by acting as responsible citizens.

As a woman, I wonder how the mothers, wives, sisters, and daughters feel about the way in which members of their families have been politically mangled in Senate debate—and I use the word "debate" advisedly.

As a United States Senator, I am not proud of the way in which the Senate has been made a publicity platform for irresponsible sensationalism. I am not proud of the reckless abandon in which unproved charges have been hurled from this side of the aisle. I am not proud of the obviously staged, undignified countercharges that have been attempted in retaliation from the other side of the aisle.

I don't like the way the Senate has been made a rendezvous for vilification, for selfish political gain at the sacrifice of individual reputations and national unity. I am not proud of the way we smear outsiders from the Floor of the Senate and hide behind the cloak of congressional immunity and still place ourselves beyond criticism on the Floor of the Senate.

As an American, I am shocked at the way Republicans and Democrats alike are playing directly into the Communist design of "confuse, divide, and conquer." As an American, I don't want a Democratic Administration "whitewash" or "cover-up" any more than I want a Republican smear or witch hunt.

As an American, I condemn a Republican "Fascist" just as much as I condemn a Democrat "Communist." I condemn a Democrat "Fascist" just as much as I condemn a Republican "Communist." They are equally dangerous to you and me and to our country. As an American, I want to see our nation recapture the strength and unity it once had when we fought the enemy instead of ourselves. . . .

constructive: helpful
allaying: relieving, lessening

mangled: beaten up

reckless abandon: careless passion
countercharges: accusations made in response to opponents' accusations
retaliation: revenge
rendezvous: meeting place
vilification: name-calling

87. From Dwight D. Eisenhower, *Farewell Address to the American People* (1961)

Throughout American history Presidents have used their farewell addresses to look back on their experience in office and offer the public practical advice. In his farewell address, President Dwight D. Eisenhower said that a high level of military spending and the establishment of a large arms industry in peacetime as a result of the Cold War were something "new in the American experience." In the most famous words of his presidency, he warned that the country "must guard against the acquisition of unwarranted influence . . . by the military-industrial complex." President Eisenhower believed that the United States had to "maintain balance" between defense spending and the needs of a healthy economy. During his second term, Congress, the press, and the armed services had pressured the President to increase defense spending. But even after the Soviet Union launched *Sputnik,* the first satellite to orbit the earth, he refused to let defense spending upset the federal budget.

President Eisenhower also issued a warning in his speech about the importance of preserving the environment. He said that Americans "must avoid the impulse to live only for today, plundering for our own ease and convenience the precious resources of tomorrow."

My fellow Americans:

Three days from now, after half a century in the service of our country, I shall lay down the responsibilities of office as, in traditional and solemn ceremony, the authority of the Presidency is vested in my successor. . . .

We now stand ten years past the midpoint of a century that has witnessed four major wars among great nations. Three of them involved our own country. Despite these **holocausts** America is today the strongest, the most influential and most productive nation in the world. Understandably proud of this pre-eminence we yet realize that America's leadership and prestige depend, not merely upon our unmatched **material** progress, riches and military strength, but on how we use our power in the interests of world peace and human betterment.

Throughout America's adventure in free government, our basic purposes have been to keep the peace; to foster progress in human achievement, and to enhance liberty, dignity and **integrity** among people and among nations. To strive for less would be unworthy of a free and religious people. Any failure traceable to arrogance, or our lack of **comprehension** or readiness to sacrifice would inflict upon us **grievous** hurt both at home and abroad.

Progress toward these noble goals is persistently threatened by the conflict now **engulfing** the world. It commands our whole attention, absorbs our very beings. We face a hostile **ideology**—global in scope, **atheistic** in character, ruthless in purpose, and **insidious** in method. Unhappily the danger it poses promises to be of indefinite duration. To meet it successfully, there is called for, not so much

holocausts: mass destructions

material: physical, tangible

integrity: honesty

comprehension: understanding
grievous: severe
engulfing: overwhelming
ideology: belief system
atheistic: having the belief that there is no divine power
insidious: working or spreading harmfully and indirectly

the emotional and transitory sacrifices of crisis, but rather those which enable us to carry forward steadily, surely, and without complaint the burdens of a prolonged and complex struggle—with liberty the stake. Only thus shall we remain, despite every provocation, on our charted course toward permanent peace and human betterment. . . .

A vital element in keeping the peace is our military establishment. Our arms must be mighty, ready for instant action, so that no potential aggressor may be tempted to risk his own destruction.

Our military organization today bears little relation to that known by any of my predecessors in peacetime, or indeed by the fighting men of World War II or Korea.

Until the latest of our world conflicts, the United States had no armaments industry. American makers of plowshares could, with time and as required, make swords as well. But now we can no longer risk emergency improvisation of national defense; we have been compelled to create a permanent armaments industry of vast proportions. Added to this, three and a half million men and women are directly engaged in the defense establishment. We annually spend on military security more than the net income of all United States corporations.

This conjunction of an immense military establishment and a large arms industry is new in the American experience. The total influence—economic, political, even spiritual—is felt in every city, every statehouse, every office of the federal government. We recognize the imperative need for this development. Yet we must not fail to comprehend its grave implications. Our toil, resources, and livelihood are all involved; so is the very structure of our society.

In the councils of government, we must guard against the acquisition of unwarranted influence, whether sought or unsought, by the military-industrial complex. The potential for the disastrous rise of misplaced power exists and will persist.

We must never let the weight of this combination endanger our liberties or democratic processes. We should take nothing for granted. Only an alert and knowledgeable citizenry can compel the proper meshing of the huge industrial and military machinery of defense with our peaceful methods and goals, so that security and liberty may prosper together.

Akin to, and largely responsible for the sweeping changes in our industrial-military posture, has been the technological revolution during recent decades.

In this revolution, research has become central; it also becomes more formalized, complex, and costly. A steadily increasing share is conducted for, by, or at the direction of, the federal government. . . .

transitory: short-term

provocation: incitement

"plowshares...swords": an allusion to the Bible, which urges that people become more peaceful, exchanging their weapons for tools. Here, tools can be turned back into weapons if necessary
improvisation: last-minute adaptation
defense establishment: businesses that make goods or provide services for the armed forces
conjunction: connection between
imperative: important and urgent

acquisition: gain
unwarranted: cannot be justified

compel: force

239

allocations: money awarded for a specific project

elite: a handful of powerful or privileged people

plundering: stealing

mortgage: take a loan
material assets: property
insolvent: financially unbalanced, with more debt than credit
phantom: ghost

confederation: alliance

The prospect of domination of the nation's scholars by federal employment, project allocations, and the power of money is ever present—and is gravely to be regarded.

Yet, in holding scientific research and discovery in respect, as we should, we must also be alert to the equal and opposite danger that public policy could itself become the captive of a scientific-technological elite.

It is the task of statesmanship to mold, to balance, and to integrate these and other forces, new and old, within the principles of our democratic system—ever aiming toward the supreme goals of our free society.

Another factor in maintaining balance involves the element of time. As we peer into society's future, we—you and I, and our government—must avoid the impulse to live only for today, plundering, for our own ease and convenience, the precious resources of tomorrow. We cannot mortgage the material assets of our grandchildren without risking the loss also of their political and spiritual heritage. We want democracy to survive for all generations to come, not to become the insolvent phantom of tomorrow.

Down the long lane of the history yet to be written America knows that this world of ours, ever growing smaller, must avoid becoming a community of dreadful fear and hate, and be, instead, a proud confederation of mutual trust and respect.

Such a confederation must be one of equals. The weakest must come to the conference table with the same confidence as do we, protected as we are by our moral, economic, and military strength. That table, though scarred by many past frustrations, cannot be abandoned for the certain agony of the battlefield.

Disarmament, with mutual honor and confidence, is a continuing imperative. Together we must learn how to compose differences, not with arms, but with intellect and decent purpose. Because this need is so sharp and apparent I confess that I lay down my official responsibilities in this field with a definite sense of disappointment. As one who has witnessed the horror and the lingering sadness of war—as one who knows that another war could utterly destroy this civilization which has been so slowly and painfully built over thousands of years—I wish I could say tonight that a lasting peace is in sight.

Happily, I can say that war has been avoided. Steady progress toward our ultimate goal has been made. But, so much remains to be done. As a private citizen, I shall never cease to do what little I can to help the world advance along that road. . . .

88. John F. Kennedy, *"Ask Not What Your Country Can Do for You": Inaugural Address* (1961)

For more information see
Chapter 17, Book 10, *All the People.*

John F. Kennedy was the first President born in the 20th century and the youngest man ever elected to the presidency. During the 1960 presidential campaign, Kennedy promised to "get the country moving again." He called for greater federal aid for education, medical care for the elderly, support for public housing, and aggressive steps to fight poverty. In his inaugural address, however, he largely ignored domestic issues and concentrated on foreign policy, especially the need to contain communist expansion. "Let every nation know," the new President declared, that the United States "shall pay any price . . . to assure the survival and success of liberty." Even though his address focused on foreign affairs, his stirring language—"Ask not what your country can do for you—ask what you can do for your country"—inspired idealism and hope, especially among young Americans.

Vice-President Johnson, Mr. Speaker, Mr. Chief Justice, President Eisenhower, Vice-President Nixon, President Truman, Reverend Clergy, Fellow Citizens:

We observe today not a victory of party but a celebration of freedom—symbolizing an end as well as a beginning—signifying renewal as well as change. For I have sworn before you and Almighty God the same solemn oath our forebearers prescribed nearly a century and three-quarters ago.

forebearers: ancestors

The world is very different now. For man holds in his mortal hands the power to abolish all forms of human life. And yet the same revolutionary beliefs for which our forebearers fought are still at issue around the globe—the belief that the rights of man come not from the generosity of the state but from the hand of God.

We dare not forget today that we are the heirs of that first revolution. Let the word go forth from this time and place, to friend and foe alike, that the torch has been passed to a new generation of Americans—born in this century, tempered by war, disciplined by a hard and bitter peace, proud of our ancient heritage—and unwilling to witness or permit the slow undoing of those human rights to which this nation has always been committed, and to which we are committed today at home and around the world.

tempered: made more moderate

asunder: apart

Let every nation know, whether it wishes us well or ill, that we shall pay any price, bear any burden, meet any hardship, support any friend, oppose any foe to assure the survival and the success of liberty.

This much we pledge—and more.

To those old allies whose cultural and spiritual origins we share, we pledge the loyalty of faithful friends. United, there is little we cannot do in a host of co-operative ventures. Divided, there is little we can do—for we dare not meet a powerful challenge at odds and split asunder.

To those new states whom we welcome to the ranks of the free, we pledge our word that one form of colonial control shall not have passed away merely to be replaced by a far more iron tyranny. We shall not always expect to find them supporting our view. But we shall always hope to find them strongly supporting their own freedom—and to remember that, in the past, those who foolishly sought power by riding the back of the tiger ended up inside.

riding the back of the tiger: doing things that are flashy and exciting but dangerous and unwise

To those people in the huts and villages of half the globe struggling to break the bonds of mass misery, we pledge our best efforts to help them help themselves, for whatever period is required—not because the Communists may be doing it, not because we seek their votes, but because it is right. If a free society cannot help the many who are poor, it cannot save the few who are rich.

To our sister republics south of our border, we offer a special pledge—to convert our good words into good deeds—in a new alliance for progress—to assist free men and free governments in casting off the chains of poverty. But this peaceful revolution of hope cannot become the prey of hostile powers. Let all our neighbors know that we shall join with them to oppose aggression or subversion anywhere in the Americas. And let every other power know that this hemisphere intends to remain the master of its own house.

subversion: attempts to destroy quietly or from the inside

instruments: weapons
instruments: tools
invective: angry words
engulf: surround and overwhelm
humanity: people

To that world assembly of sovereign states, the United Nations, our last best hope in an age where the instruments of war have far outpaced the instruments of peace, we renew our pledge of support—to prevent it from becoming merely a forum for invective—to strengthen its shield of the new and the weak—and to enlarge the area in which its writ may run.

Finally, to those nations who would make themselves our adversary, we offer not a pledge but a request: that both sides begin anew the quest for peace, before the dark powers of destruction unleashed by science engulf all humanity in planned or accidental self-destruction.

We dare not tempt them with weakness. For only when our arms are sufficient beyond doubt can we be certain beyond doubt that they will never be employed.

But neither can two great and powerful groups of nations take comfort from our present course—both sides overburdened by the cost of modern weapons, both rightly alarmed by the steady spread of the deadly atom, yet both racing to alter that uncertain balance of terror that stays the hand of mankind's final war.

So let us begin anew—remembering on both sides that civility is not a sign of weakness, and sincerity is always subject to proof. Let us never negotiate out of fear. But let us never fear to negotiate.

civility: politeness

Let both sides explore what problems unite us instead of belaboring those problems which divide us.

belaboring: making a big deal out of

Let both sides, for the first time, formulate serious and precise proposals for the inspection and control of arms—and bring the absolute power to destroy other nations under the absolute control of all nations.

Let both sides seek to invoke the wonders of science instead of its terrors. Together let us explore the stars, conquer the deserts, eradicate disease, tap the ocean depths, and encourage the arts and commerce.

invoke: call forth
eradicate: destroy

Let both sides unite to heed in all corners of the earth the command of Isaiah—to "undo the heavy burdens . . . [and] let the oppressed go free."

And if a beachhead of co-operation may push back the jungle of suspicion, let both sides join in creating a new endeavor, not a new balance of power, but a new world of law, where the strong are just and the weak secure and the peace preserved.

beachhead: a position opening the way for further development

All this will not be finished in the first one hundred days. Nor will it be finished in the first one thousand days, nor in the life of this administration, nor even perhaps in our lifetime on this planet. But let us begin.

In your hands, my fellow citizens, more than mine, will rest the final success or failure of our course. Since this country was founded, each generation of Americans has been summoned to give testimony to its national loyalty. The graves of young Americans who answered the call to service surround the globe.

Now the trumpet summons us again—not as a call to bear arms, though arms we need—not as a call to battle, though embattled we are—but a call to bear the burden of a long twilight struggle, year in and year out, "rejoicing in hope, patient in tribulation"—a struggle against the common enemies of man: tyranny, poverty, disease, and war itself.

tribulation: times of difficulty
tyranny: rule by a single, all-powerful leader

243

Can we forge against these enemies a grand and global alliance, North and South, East and West, that can assure a more fruitful life for all mankind? Will you join in that historic effort?

In the long history of the world, only a few generations have been granted the role of defending freedom in its hour of maximum danger. I do not shrink from this responsibility—I welcome it. I do not believe that any of us would exchange places with any other people or any other generation. The energy, the faith, the devotion which we bring to this endeavor will light our country and all who serve it—and the glow from that fire can truly light the world.

And so, my fellow Americans: ask not what your country can do for you—ask what you can do for your country.

My fellow citizens of the world: ask not what America will do for you, but what together we can do for the freedom of man.

Finally, whether you are citizens of America or citizens of the world, ask of us here the same high standards of strength and sacrifice which we ask of you. With a good conscience our only sure reward, with history the final judge of our deeds, let us go forth to lead the land we love, asking His blessing and His help, but knowing that here on earth God's work must truly be our own.

89. Martin Luther King, Jr., *"I Have a Dream"*: *Address at the March on Washington* (1963)

In 1941, A. Philip Randolph, the president of the Brotherhood of Sleeping Car Porters, proposed a march on Washington to protest segregation in the armed forces and discrimination in government employment and defense industries. Randolph called off the march when President Franklin D. Roosevelt issued an executive order creating the Fair Employment Practices Committee with the power to end discrimination in war industries. In 1962, Randolph renewed his call for a march on Washington. He believed that a massive march might provide the pressure necessary to convince Congress to pass legislation that would guarantee all Americans "access to public accommodations, decent housing, adequate and integrated education, and the right to vote." At that time, African Americans earned just half as much on average as white Americans and were a third as likely to attend college. Fewer than 100 black Americans held elected office.

On August 28, 1963, over 200,000 people gathered around the Washington Monument and marched 8/10ths of a mile to the Lincoln Memorial. They carried signs reading: "Jobs! Justice! Peace!" and sang the civil rights anthem, "We Shall Overcome." Ten speakers addressed the crowd, but the event's highlight was an address by the Rev. Dr. Martin Luther King, Jr. After he finished his prepared text, he launched into his legendary closing words: "I have a dream that one day this nation will rise up and live out the true meaning of its creed . . . that all men are created equal."

In his speech, King appealed to our country's noblest principles, and showed how the nation's mistreatment of African Americans contradicted our ideals of justice and equality. He presented an inspiring vision of an America undivided by barriers of social caste, color, gender, religion, or region. King's eloquent plea for a color-blind America created momentum for passage of the 1964 Civil Rights Act, which outlawed white-only restaurants and hotels.

I am happy to join with you today in what will go down in history as the greatest demonstration for freedom in the history of our nation.

Fivescore years ago, a great American, in whose symbolic shadow we stand today, signed the Emancipation Proclamation. This momentous decree came as a great beacon light of hope to millions of Negro slaves who had been seared in the flames of withering injustice. It came as a joyous daybreak to end the long night of their captivity.

momentous: historically important

But one hundred years later, the Negro still is not free; one hundred years later, the life of the Negro is still sadly crippled by the manacles of segregation and the chains of discrimination; one hundred years later, the Negro lives on a lonely island of poverty in the midst of a vast ocean of material prosperity; one hundred years later, the Negro is still languished in the corners of American society and finds himself in exile in his own land.

manacles: chains

languished: survived in a weakened, impoverished, undignified state

So we've come here today to dramatize a shameful condition. In a sense we've come to our nation's capital to cash a check. When the architects of our republic wrote the magnificent words of the Constitution and the Declaration of Independence, they were signing a promissory note to which every American was to fall heir. This note was the promise that all men, yes, black men as well as white men, would be guaranteed the unalienable rights of life, liberty, and the pursuit of happiness.

promissory note: promise to pay back

unalienable: cannot be separated from

It is obvious today that America has defaulted on this promissory note in so far as her citizens of color are concerned. Instead of honoring this sacred obligation, America has given the Negro people a bad check; a check which has come back marked "insufficient funds." We refuse to believe that there are insufficient funds in the great

vaults: banks

hallowed: sacred

tranquilizing: calming
gradualism: doing things slowly, one at a time
desolate: lifeless, gloomy, deserted

degenerate: break down

militancy: political activism

inextricably: inseparably

vaults of opportunity of this nation. And so we've come to cash this check, a check that will give us upon demand the riches of freedom and the security of justice.

We have also come to this hallowed spot to remind America of the fierce urgency of now. This is no time to engage in the luxury of cooling off or to take the tranquilizing drug of gradualism. Now is the time to make real the promises of democracy; now is the time to rise from the dark and desolate valley of segregation to the sunlit path of racial justice; now is the time to lift our nation from the quicksands of racial injustice to the solid rock of brotherhood; now is the time to make justice a reality for all God's children. It would be fatal for the nation to overlook the urgency of the moment. This sweltering summer of the Negro's legitimate discontent will not pass until there is an invigorating autumn of freedom and equality.

Nineteen sixty-three is not an end, but a beginning. And those who hope that the Negro needed to blow off steam and will now be content, will have a rude awakening if the nation returns to business as usual.

There will be neither rest nor tranquility in America until the Negro is granted his citizenship rights. The whirlwinds of revolt will continue to shake the foundations of our nation until the bright day of justice emerges.

But there is something that I must say to my people who stand on the warm threshold which leads into the palace of justice. In the process of gaining our rightful place we must not be guilty of wrongful deeds.

Let us not seek to satisfy our thirst for freedom by drinking from the cup of bitterness and hatred. We must forever conduct our struggle on the high plane of dignity and discipline. We must not allow our creative protest to degenerate into physical violence. Again and again we must rise to the majestic heights of meeting physical force with soul force.

The marvelous new militancy which has engulfed the Negro community must not lead us to a distrust of all white people, for many of our white brothers, as evidenced by their presence here today, have come to realize that their destiny is tied up with our destiny and they have come to realize that their freedom is inextricably bound to our freedom. This offense we share mounted to storm the battlements of injustice must be carried forth by a biracial army. We cannot walk alone.

And as we walk, we must make the pledge that we shall always march ahead. We cannot turn back. There are those who are asking the devotees of civil rights, "When will you be satisfied?" We can never be satisfied as long as the Negro is the victim of the unspeakable horrors of police brutality.

We can never be satisfied as long as our bodies, heavy with fatigue of travel, cannot gain lodging in the motels of the highways and the hotels of the cities. We cannot be satisfied as long as the Negro's basic mobility is from a smaller ghetto to a larger one.

mobility: ability to move

We can never be satisfied as long as our children are stripped of their selfhood and robbed of their dignity by signs stating "for whites only." We cannot be satisfied as long as a Negro in Mississippi cannot vote and a Negro in New York believes he has nothing for which to vote. No, we are not satisfied, and we will not be satisfied until justice rolls down like waters and righteousness like a mighty stream.

I am not unmindful that some of you have come here out of excessive trials and tribulation. Some of you have come fresh from narrow jail cells. Some of you have come from areas where your quest for freedom left you battered by the storms of persecution and staggered by the winds of police brutality. You have been the veterans of creative suffering. Continue to work with the faith that unearned suffering is redemptive.

tribulation: time of trouble

redemptive: brings its own reward

Go back to Mississippi; go back to Alabama; go back to South Carolina; go back to Georgia; go back to Louisiana; go back to the slums and ghettos of the northern cities, knowing that somehow this situation can, and will be changed. Let us not wallow in the valley of despair.

So I say to you, my friends, that even though we must face the difficulties of today and tomorrow, I still have a dream. It is a dream deeply rooted in the American dream that one day this nation will rise up and live out the true meaning of its creed—we hold these truths to be self evident, that all men are created equal.

I have a dream that one day on the red hills of Georgia, sons of former slaves and sons of former slave-owners will be able to sit down together at the table of brotherhood.

I have a dream that one day, even the state of Mississippi, a state sweltering with the heat of injustice, sweltering with the heat of oppression, will be transformed into an oasis of freedom and justice.

oasis: green and welcoming refuge in a desert

I have a dream my four little children will one day live in a nation where they will not be judged by the color of their skin but by content of their character. I have a dream today!

interposition: some southern states' attempt to use state's rights strategies against desegregation in the 1960s

I have a dream that one day, down in Alabama, with its vicious racists, with its governor having his lips dripping with the words of interposition and nullification, that one day, right there in Alabama, little black boys and black girls will be able to join hands with little

nullification: states' rights strategy used unsuccessfully by southern states in 1832-33

every valley shall be exalted...:
a phrase from the Bible's description of the coming of God

hew: cut

prodigious: impressive

curvaceous: rounded

hamlet: small village

Gentiles: non-Jews

white boys and white girls as sisters and brothers. I have a dream today!

I have a dream that one day every valley shall be exalted, every hill and mountain shall be made low, the rough places shall be made plain, and the crooked places shall be made straight and the glory of the Lord will be revealed and all flesh shall see it together.

This is our hope. This is the faith that I go back to the South with.

With this faith we will be able to hew out of the mountain of despair a stone of hope. With this faith we will be able to transform the jangling discords of our nation into a beautiful symphony of brotherhood.

With this faith we will be able to work together, to pray together, to struggle together, to go to jail together, to stand up for freedom together, knowing that we will be free one day. This will be the day when all of God's children will be able to sing with new meaning—"my country 'tis of thee; sweet land of liberty; of thee I sing; land where my fathers died, land of the pilgrim's pride; from every mountain side, let freedom ring"—and if America is to be a great nation, this must become true.

So let freedom ring from the prodigious hilltops of New Hampshire.

Let freedom ring from the mighty mountains of New York.

Let freedom ring from the heightening Alleghenies of Pennsylvania.

Let freedom ring from the snow-capped Rockies of Colorado.

Let freedom ring from the curvaceous slopes of California.

But not only that.

Let freedom ring from Stone Mountain of Georgia.

Let freedom ring from Lookout Mountain of Tennessee.

Let freedom ring from every hill and molehill of Mississippi, from every mountainside, let freedom ring.

And when we allow freedom to ring, when we let it ring from every village and hamlet, from every state and city, we will be able to speed up that day when of all of God's children—black men and white men, Jews and Gentiles, Catholics and Protestants—will be able to join hands and to sing in the words of the old Negro spiritual, "Free at last, free at last; thank God Almighty, we are free at last."

90. From Martin Luther King, Jr., *"Why We Can't Wait": Letter from Birmingham City Jail* (1963)

King's "Letter from Birmingham City Jail" is a classic statement of his vision of racial equality and of his philosophy of nonviolent civil disobedience. In 1963, King launched massive demonstrations to protest job discrimination and segregated lunch counters, restrooms, and department stores in Birmingham, Alabama. In defiance of a Supreme Court ruling, Birmingham had closed its 38 public playgrounds, 8 swimming pools, and 4 golf courses rather than integrate them. Day after day, well-dressed and carefully groomed men, women, and children peacefully marched against segregation. Many were beaten with nightsticks, attacked by snarling dogs, and sprayed with high-pressure fire hoses. Hundreds were jailed for demonstrating without a permit. King himself was one of those arrested. While in jail, he received a newspaper article in which eight white Alabama clergymen asked African Americans to wait patiently for equal rights. The clergymen described King as an extremist and claimed that the best way to achieve equal rights was through negotiations, not protest.

In his jail cell, King drafted a reply on the margins of the newspaper and toilet paper. In his letter, he responded to the clergymen point-by-point. He said that African Americans had waited—"for more than 340 years"—for equal rights. He warned that if the country failed to respond to peaceful protests, then millions of African Americans would turn to violence. Through acts of civil disobedience, King wanted to awaken the American conscience to the gross injustice of racial discrimination. In 1964, King received the Nobel Peace Prize for his efforts to end segregation.

My dear Fellow Clergymen,

While confined here in the Birmingham city jail, I came across your recent statement calling our present activities "unwise and untimely." Seldom, if ever, do I pause to answer criticism of my work and ideas. If I sought to answer all of the criticisms that cross my desk, my secretaries would be engaged in little else in the course of the day, and I would have no time for constructive work. But since I feel that you are men of genuine good will and your criticisms are sincerely set forth, I would like to answer your statement in what I hope will be patient and reasonable terms.

direct-action program: physical non-violent protest that involved people actively rather than passively

gainsaying: denying

notorious: widely and unfavorably known

moratorium: stop

unmindful: unaware

I think I should give the reason for my being in Birmingham, since you have been influenced by the argument of "outsiders coming in." I have the honor of serving as president of the Southern Christian Leadership Conference, an organization operating in every southern state, with headquarters in Atlanta, Georgia. We have some eighty-five affiliate organizations all across the South—one being the Alabama Christian Movement for Human Rights. Whenever necessary and possible we share staff, educational and financial resources with our affiliates. Several months ago our local affiliate here in Birmingham invited us to be on call to engage in a nonviolent direct-action program if such were deemed necessary. We readily consented. . . .

In any nonviolent campaign there are four basic steps: (1) collection of the facts to determine whether injustices are alive, (2) negotiation, (3) self-purification, and (4) direct action. We have gone through all of these steps in Birmingham. There can be no gainsaying of the fact that racial injustice engulfs this community.

Birmingham is probably the most thoroughly segregated city in the United States. Its ugly record of police brutality is known in every section of this country. Its injust treatment of Negroes in the courts is a notorious reality. There have been more unsolved bombings of Negro homes and churches in Birmingham than any city in this nation. These are the hard, brutal and unbelievable facts. On the basis of these conditions Negro leaders sought to negotiate with the city fathers. But the political leaders consistently refused to engage in good faith negotiation.

Then came the opportunity last September to talk with some of the leaders of the economic community. In these negotiating sessions certain promises were made by the merchants—such as the promise to remove the humiliating racial signs from the stores. On the basis of these promises Rev. Shuttlesworth and the leaders of the Alabama Christian Movement for Human Rights agreed to call a moratorium on any type of demonstrations. As the weeks and months unfolded we realized that we were the victims of a broken promise. The signs remained. Like so many experiences of the past we were confronted with blasted hopes, and the dark shadow of a deep disappointment settled upon us. So we had no alternative except that of preparing for direct action, whereby we would present our very bodies as a means of laying our case before the conscience of the local and national community. We were not unmindful of the difficulties involved. So we decided to go through a process of self-purification. We started having workshops on nonviolence and repeatedly asked ourselves the questions, "Are you able to accept blows without retaliating?" "Are you able to endure the ordeals of jail?".... | **retaliating:** striking back

You may well ask, "Why direct action? Why sit-ins, marches, etc.? Isn't negotiation a better path?" You are exactly right in your call for negotiation. Indeed, this is the purpose of direct action. Nonviolent direct action seeks to create such a crisis and establish such creative tension that a community that has constantly refused to negotiate is forced to confront the issue. It seeks so to dramatize the issue that it can no longer be ignored. I just referred to the creation of tension as a part of the work of the nonviolent resister. This may sound rather shocking. But I must confess that I am not afraid of the word tension. I have earnestly worked and preached against violent tension, but there is a type of constructive nonviolent tension that is necessary for growth. Just as Socrates felt that it was necessary to create a tension in the mind so that individuals could rise from the bondage of myths and half-truths to the unfettered realm of creative analysis and objective appraisal, we must see the need of having nonviolent gadflies to create the kind of tension in society that will help men to rise from the dark depths of prejudice and racism to the majestic heights of understanding and brotherhood. So the purpose of the direct action is to create a situation so crisis-packed that it will inevitably open the door to negotiation. We, therefore, concur with you in your call for negotiation. Too long has our beloved Southland been bogged down in the tragic attempt to live in monologue rather than dialogue....

Socrates: 5th century Greek philosopher who was a pioneer in ethics
bondage: slavery
unfettered: free
appraisal: judgment
gadflies: people who raise questions and make others think about the way things are
concur: agree

My friends, I must say to you that we have not made a single gain in civil rights without determined legal and nonviolent pressure. History is the long and tragic story of the fact that privileged groups seldom give up their privileges voluntarily. Individuals may see the moral light and voluntarily give up their unjust posture; but as Reinhold Niebuhr has reminded us, groups are more immoral than individuals.

Reinhold Niebuhr: religious leader from Detroit who became a political activist

We know through painful experience that freedom is never voluntarily given by the oppressor; it must be demanded by the oppressed. Frankly, I have never yet engaged in a direct action movement that was "well-timed," according to the timetable of those who have not suffered unduly from the disease of segregation. For years now I have heard the words "Wait!" It rings in the ear of every Negro with a piercing familiarity. This "Wait" has almost always meant "Never." It has been a tranquilizing thalidomide, relieving the emotional stress for a moment, only to give birth to an ill-formed infant of frustration. We must come to see with the distinguished jurist of yesterday that "justice too long delayed is justice denied." We have

thalidomide: a perscription drug that caused some women to give birth to malformed children

impunity: freedom from
punishment

concoct: create in an artificial way
pathos: feeling of sadness

harried: hassled
degenerating: destructive
resentments: feelings of being
insulted or abused
abyss: great pit
cup of endurance runs over:
from the Bible, where the cup that
runs over is full of joy; here it is
full of bitterness
corroding despair: feeling of
being eaten away inside by anger
and sorrow
diligently: in a committed,
disciplined way
paradoxical: seemingly
contradictory

waited for more than 340 years for our constitutional and God-given rights. The nations of Asia and Africa are moving with jetlike speed toward the goal of political independence, and we still creep at horse and buggy pace toward the gaining of a cup of coffee at a lunch counter. I guess it is easy for those who have never felt the stinging darts of segregation to say, "Wait." But when you have seen vicious mobs lynch your mothers and fathers at will and drown your sisters and brothers at whim; when you have seen hate-filled policemen curse, kick, brutalize and even kill your black brothers and sisters with impunity; when you see the vast majority of your twenty million Negro brothers smothering in an airtight cage of poverty in the midst of an affluent society; when you suddenly find your tongue twisted and your speech stammering as you seek to explain to your six-year-old daughter why she can't go to the public amusement park that has just been advertised on television, and see tears welling up in her little eyes when she is told that Funtown is closed to colored children, and see the depressing clouds of inferiority begin to form in her little mental sky, and see her begin to distort her little personality by unconsciously developing a bitterness toward white people; when you have to concoct an answer for a five-year-old son asking in agonizing pathos: "Daddy, why do white people treat colored people so mean?"; when you take a cross-country drive and find it necessary to sleep night after night in the uncomfortable corners of your automobile because no motel will accept you; when you are humiliated day in and day out by nagging signs reading "white" and "colored"; when your first name becomes "nigger" and your middle name becomes "boy" (however old you are) and your last name becomes "John," and when your wife and mother are never given the respected title "Mrs."; when you are harried by day and haunted by night by the fact that you are a Negro, living constantly at tiptoe stance never quite knowing what to expect next, and plagued with inner fears and outer resentments; when you are forever fighting a degenerating sense of "nobodiness"; then you will understand why we find it difficult to wait. There comes a time when the cup of endurance runs over, and men are no longer willing to be plunged into an abyss of injustice where they experience the blackness of corroding despair. I hope, sirs, you can understand our legitimate and unavoidable impatience.

You express a great deal of anxiety over our willingness to break laws. This is certainly a legitimate concern. Since we so diligently urge people to obey the Supreme Court's decision of 1954 outlawing segregation in the public schools, it is rather strange and paradoxical to find us consciously breaking laws. One may well ask, "How can you advocate breaking some laws and obeying others?" The answer is found in the fact that there are two types of laws: there are *just* and there are *unjust* laws. I would agree with Saint Augustine that "An unjust law is no law at all."

Now what is the difference between the two? How does one determine when a law is just or unjust? A just law is a man-made code that squares with the moral law or the law of God. An unjust law is a code that is out of harmony with the moral law. To put it in the terms of Saint Thomas Aquinas, an unjust law is a human law that is not rooted in eternal and natural law. Any law that uplifts human personality is just. Any law that degrades human personality is unjust. All segregation statutes are unjust because segregation distorts the soul and damages the personality. It gives the segregator a false sense of superiority, and the segregated a false sense of inferiority. . . . So I can urge men to disobey segregation ordinances because they are morally wrong. . . .

ordinances: laws

I hope you can see the distinction I am trying to point out. In no sense do I advocate evading or defying the law as the rabid segregationist would do. This would lead to anarchy. One who breaks an unjust law must do it *openly, lovingly* (not hatefully as the white mothers did in New Orleans when they were seen on television screaming, "nigger, nigger, nigger"), and with a willingness to accept the penalty. I submit that an individual who breaks a law that conscience tells him is unjust, and willingly accepts the penalty by staying in jail to arouse the conscience of the community over its injustice, is in reality expressing the very highest respect for law. . . .

rabid: raging

I must confess that over the last few years I have been gravely disappointed with the white moderate. I have almost reached the regrettable conclusion that the Negro's great stumbling block in the stride toward freedom is not the White Citizen's Counciler or the Ku Klux Klanner, but the white moderate who is more devoted to "order" than to justice; who prefers a negative peace which is the absence of tension to a positive peace which is the presence of justice; who constantly says, "I agree with you in the goal you seek, but I can't agree with your methods of direct action"; who paternalistically feels that he can set the timetable for another man's freedom; who lives by the myth of time and who constantly advised the Negro to wait until a "more convenient season." Shallow understanding from people of good will is more frustrating than absolute misunderstanding from people of ill will. Lukewarm acceptance is much more bewildering than outright rejection. . . .

White Citizen's Counciler: member of a racist group that supported segregation
Ku Klux Klanner: member of a racist group known for its hatred of African Americans
paternalistically: in an inappropriately fatherly way

bewildering: highly confusing

You spoke of our activity in Birmingham as extreme. At first I was rather disappointed that fellow clergymen would see my nonviolent efforts as those of the extremist. I started thinking about the fact that I stand in the middle of two opposing forces in the Negro community. One is a force of complacency made up of Negroes who, as a result of

complacency: overconfidence

253

A HISTORY OF US

black nationalist: someone who believes that blacks should have their own nation
Elijah Muhammad (1897-1975): founder of the Black Muslim movement
repudiated: turned their backs on
latent: present, but not showing

ominous: threatening

channelized: directed, focused

Amos: Old Testament prophet

Paul: St. Paul, who was converted to Christianity and who converted many others
Martin Luther (1483-1546): Protestant reformer who emphasized faith above all else
John Bunyan (1628-1688): author of *Pilgrim's Progress*, a story with a strong moral message

Calvary: the scene of Christ's crucifixion

long years of oppression, have been so completely drained of self-respect and a sense of "somebodiness" that they have adjusted to segregation, and, of a few Negroes in the middle class who, because of a degree of academic and economic security, and because at points they profit by segregation, have unconsciously become insensitive to the problems of the masses. The other force is one of bitterness and hatred, and comes perilously close to advocating violence. It is expressed in the various black nationalist groups that are springing up over the nation, the largest and best known being Elijah Muhammad's Muslim movement. This movement is nourished by the contemporary frustration over the continued existence of racial discrimination. It is made up of people who have lost faith in America, who have absolutely repudiated Christianity, and who have concluded that the white man is an incurable "devil." I have tried to stand between these two forces, saying that we need not follow the "do-nothingism" of the complacent or the hatred and despair of the black nationalist. There is the more excellent way of love and nonviolent protest. . . . The Negro has many pent-up resentments and latent frustrations. He has to get them out. So let him march sometime; let him have his prayer pilgrimages to the city hall; understand why he must have sit-ins and freedom rides. If his repressed emotions do not come out in these nonviolent ways, they will come out in ominous expressions of violence. This is not a threat; it is a fact of history. So I have not said to my people "get rid of your discontent." But I have tried to say that this normal and healthy discontent can be channelized through the creative outlet of nonviolent direct action. . . .

But as I continued to think about the matter I gradually gained a bit of satisfaction from being considered an extremist. Was not Jesus an extremist in love—"Love your enemies, bless them that curse you, pray for them that despitefully use you." Was not Amos an extremist for justice—"Let justice roll down like waters and righteousness like a mighty stream." Was not Paul an extremist for the gospel of Jesus Christ—"I bear in my body the marks of the Lord Jesus." Was not Martin Luther an extremist—"Here I stand; I can do none other so help me God." Was not John Bunyan an extremist—"I will stay in jail to the end of my days before I make a butchery of my conscience." Was not Abraham Lincoln an extremist—"This nation cannot survive half slave and half free." Was not Thomas Jefferson an extremist— "We hold these truths to be self-evident, that all men are created equal." So the question is not whether we will be extremist but what kind of extremist will we be. Will we be extremists for hate or will we be extremists for love? Will we be extremists for the preservation of injustice—or will we be extremists for the cause of justice? In that dramatic scene on Calvary's hill, three men were crucified for the same crime—the crime of extremism. Two were extremists for immorality, and thusly fell below their environment. The other, Jesus Christ, was an extremist for love, truth and goodness, and thereby rose above his environment. So, after all, maybe the South, the nation and the world are in dire need of creative extremists. . . .

dire: desperate

In spite of my shattered dreams of the past, I came to Birmingham with the hope that the white religious leadership of this community would see the justice of our cause, and with deep moral concern, serve as the channel through which our just grievances would get to the power structure. I had hoped that each of you would understand. But again I have been disappointed. I have heard numerous religious leaders of the South call upon their worshipers to comply with a desegregation decision because it is the *law*, but I have longed to hear white ministers say, "Follow this decree because integration is morally *right* and the Negro is your brother." In the midst of blatant injustices inflicted upon the Negro, I have watched white churches stand on the sideline and merely mouth pious irrelevancies and sanctimonious trivialities. In the midst of a mighty struggle to rid our nation of racial and economic injustice, I have heard so many ministers say, "Those are social issues with which the gospel has no real concern," and I have watched so many churches commit themselves to a completely otherworldly religion which made a strange distinction between body and soul, the sacred and the secular. . . .

comply with: obey

blatant: obvious

pious irrelevancies: empty but religious-sounding words
sanctimonious trivialities: self-righteous and unimportant chatter

secular: worldly, not spiritual

[E]ven if the church does not come to the aid of justice, I have no despair about the future. I have no fear about the outcome of our struggle in Birmingham, even if our motives are presently misunderstood. We will reach the goal of freedom in Birmingham and all over the nation, because the goal of America is freedom. Abused and scorned though we may be, our destiny is tied up with the destiny of America. Before the Pilgrims landed at Plymouth we were here. Before the pen of Jefferson etched across the pages of history the majestic words of the Declaration of Independence, we were here. For more than two centuries our foreparents labored in this country without wages; they made cotton king; and they built the homes of their masters in the midst of brutal injustice and shameful humiliation—and yet out of a bottomless vitality they continued to thrive and develop. If the inexpressible cruelties of slavery could not stop us, the opposition we now face will surely fail. We will win our freedom because the sacred heritage of our nation and the eternal will of God are embodied in our echoing demands. . . .

foreparents: ancestors

vitality: life force

I hope this letter finds you strong in the faith. I also hope that circumstances will soon make it possible for me to meet each of you, not as an integrationist or a civil rights leader, but as a fellow clergyman and a Christian brother. Let us all hope that the dark clouds of

scintillating: sparkling

racial prejudice will soon pass away and the deep fog of misunderstanding will be lifted from our fear-drenched communities and in some not too distant tomorrow the radiant stars of love and brotherhood will shine over our great nation with all of their scintillating beauty.

    Yours for the cause of Peace and Brotherhood,
    Martin Luther King, Jr.

For more information see
Chapter 24, Book 10, *All the People*.

91. From the *Civil Rights Act of 1964* (1964)

In 1963, extremists firebombed 35 African-American homes and churches. President John F. Kennedy responded to the violence, and to the growing civil rights movement, by proposing a strong civil rights bill that would require the desegregation of public facilities and outlaw discrimination in employment. To pressure Congress to act on the measure, civil rights leaders organized a massive march on Washington. In August 1963, 200,000 Americans gathered around the Washington Monument and marched to the Lincoln Memorial. The marchers carried signs reading "Effective Civil Rights Laws—Now! Integrated Schools—Now! Decent Housing—Now!" Rev. Dr. Martin Luther King, Jr.'s "I Have a Dream" speech was the highlight of the march.

    It took more than a year before Congress passed the Civil Rights Act into law. The act prohibited discrimination in employment and public facilities such as hotels and restaurants, and it established the Equal Employment Opportunity Commission to prevent discrimination in employment on the basis of race, religion, or sex. In a effort to delay passage, opponents proposed more than 500 amendments to the act and staged a lengthy filibuster, or speech-making marathon, but the Senate eventually passed the bill and it became law.

An Act

jurisdiction: authority
injunctive relief: a court order forbidding something
public accommodations: hotels, restaurants, and other public places or services

    To enforce the constitutional right to vote, to confer jurisdiction upon the district courts of the United States to provide injunctive relief against discrimination in public accommodations, to authorize the Attorney General to institute suits to protect constitutional rights in public facilities and public education, to extend the Commission on Civil Rights, to prevent discrimination in federally assisted programs, to establish a Commission on Equal Employment Opportunity, and for other purposes. . . .

Title I—Voting Rights

. . . (2) No person acting under color of law shall—

(A) in determining whether any individual is qualified under State law or laws to vote in any Federal election, apply any standard, practice, or procedure different from the standards, practices, or procedures applied under such law or laws to other individuals within the same county, parish, or similar political subdivision who have been found by State officials to be qualified to vote. . . .

Title II—Injunctive relief against discrimination in places of Public Accommodation

. . . (a) All persons shall be entitled to the full and equal enjoyment of the goods, services, facilities, and privileges, advantages, and accommodations of any place of public accommodation, as defined in this section, without discrimination or segregation on the ground of race, color, religion, or national origin. . . .

Title VII—Equal Employment Opportunity

Sec. 703 (a) It shall be an unlawful employment practice for an employer-(1) to fail or refuse to hire or to discharge any individual, or otherwise to discriminate against any individual with respect to his compensation, terms, conditions, or privileges of employment, because of such individual's race, color, religion, sex, or national origin. . . .

92. From the *Voting Rights Act of 1965* (1965)

For more information see
Chapter 24, Book 10, *All the People.*

The Civil Rights Act of 1964 prohibited discrimination in employment and public accommodations (such as hotels). But many African Americans were denied an equally fundamental right, the right to vote, because they were required to take unnecessarily difficult literacy tests.

Before the act passed, the most effective barriers to voting were state laws requiring prospective voters to read and interpret sections of the state constitution. In Alabama, voters had to provide written answers to a 20-page test on the U.S. Constitution and state and local government. Questions included: "Where do presidential electors cast ballots for president?" and "Name the rights a person has after he has been indicted by a grand jury."

The Voting Rights Act of 1965 prohibited literacy tests and sent federal examiners to seven southern states to register voters. Within a year, 450,000 African Americans in the South were added to the voting rolls.

Be it enacted by the Senate and House of Representatives of the United States of America in Congress assembled, That this Act shall be known as the "Voting Rights Act of 1965."

SEC. 2. No voting qualification or prerequisite to voting, or standard, practice, or procedure shall be imposed or applied by any State or political subdivision to deny or abridge the right of any citizen of the United States to vote on account of race or color. . . .

SEC. 4. (a) To assure that the right of citizens of the United States to vote is not denied or abridged on account of race or color, no citizen shall be denied the right to vote in any Federal, State, or local election because of his failure to comply with any test or device in any State. . . .

(c) The phrase "test or device" shall mean any requirement that a person as a prerequisite for voting or registration for voting (1) demonstrate the ability to read, write, understand, or interpret any matter, (2) demonstrate any educational achievement or his knowledge of any particular subject, (3) possess good moral character, or (4) prove his qualifications by the voucher of registered voters or members of any other class. . . .

(e) (1) Congress hereby declares that to secure the rights under the fourteenth amendment of persons educated in American-flag schools in which the predominant classroom language was other than English, it is necessary to prohibit the States from conditioning the right to vote of such persons on ability to read, write, understand, or interpret any matter in the English language.

(2) No person who demonstrates that he has successfully completed the sixth primary grade in a public school in, or a private school accredited by, any State or territory, the District of Columbia, or the Commonwealth of Puerto Rico in which the predominant classroom language was other than English, shall be denied the right to vote in any Federal, State, or local election because of his inability to read, write, understand, or interpret any matter in the English language. . . .

(b) Any person whom the examiner finds, in accordance with instructions received under section 9(b), to have the qualifications prescribed by State law not inconsistent with the Constitution and laws of the United States shall promptly be placed on a list of eligible voters. . . .

prerequisite: requirement

abridge: cut short

voucher: evidence

predominant: majority

accredited: given official authorization

Sec. 10. (a) The Congress finds that the requirement of the payment of a poll tax as a precondition to voting (i) precludes persons of limited means from voting or imposes unreasonable financial hardship upon such persons as a precondition to their exercise of the franchise, (ii) does not bear a reasonable relationship to any legitimate State interest in the conduct of elections, and (iii) in some areas has the purpose or effect of denying persons the right to vote because of race or color. Upon the basis of these findings, Congress declares that the constitutional right of citizens to vote is denied or abridged in some areas by the requirement of the payment of a poll tax as a precondition to voting. . . .

precondition: requirement

93. From Hugo L. Black, Opinion in *New York Times Co.* v. *United States* (1971)

For more information see
Chapters 18, 24, 27–28, and 35-36, Book 10, *All the People*.

In 1971, *The New York Times* and *The Washington Post* obtained copies of a 7,000-page secret history of the U.S. involvement in Vietnam prepared by the Department of Defense. They began to publish excerpts, which showed that the U.S. government had misled the public about the war's likely costs and duration. The Nixon administration claimed in court that releasing the document would hurt the American war effort in Vietnam, cost American lives, threaten U.S. peace efforts, and compromise relations with other countries. The court ruled 6 to 3 that the government could not block publication of the papers, despite the fact that they were classified "Top Secret" and the nation was at war.

A majority of the justices held that the publication of the Pentagon Papers as the document was called, did not threaten national security. Two justices (Hugh Black and William Douglas) went further and held that the First Amendment (guaranteeing freedom of the press) does not allow the government to restrain the press prior to publication. In his opinion, Justice Hugo Black wrote that the First Amendment protected the press "so that it could bare the secrets of government and inform the people." "In revealing the workings of government that led to the Vietnam War," he said, newspapers "nobly did precisely that which the Founders hoped and trusted they would do."

In the First Amendment the Founding Fathers gave the free press the protection it must have to fulfill its essential role in our democracy. The press was to serve the governed, not the governors. The Gov-

censure: criticize

unrestrained: free
deception: dishonesty
paramount: first

shot and shell: weapons

ernment's power to censor the press was abolished so that the press would remain forever free to censure the government. The press was protected so that it could bare the secrets of government and inform the people. Only a free and unrestrained press can effectively expose deception in government. And paramount among the responsibilities of a free press is the duty to prevent any part of the government from deceiving the people and sending them off to to distant lands to die of foreign fevers and foreign shot and shell. In my view, far from deserving condemnation for their courageous reporting, the *New York Times,* the *Washington Post,* and other newspapers should be commended for serving the purpose that the Founding Fathers saw so clearly. In revealing the workings of government that led to the Vietnam war, the newspapers nobly did precisely that which the Founders hoped and trusted they would do.

For more information see
Chapter 38, Book 10, *All the People.*

94. From Ronald Reagan, *Speech at Moscow State University* (1988)

During a visit to the Soviet Union in 1988, President Ronald Reagan, a lifelong anti-communist, met with students at Moscow State University and delivered a stirring plea for democracy and individual rights. He told the students that a nation must permit a high degree of freedom—"freedom of thought, freedom of information, freedom of communication"—in order to thrive.

As he addressed the students, President Reagan stood underneath a bust of Lenin, the leader of the Russian Revolution, and in front of a mural filled with revolutionary flags. "Standing here before a mural of your revolution, I want to talk about a very different revolution that is . . . quietly sweeping the globe, without bloodshed or conflict," Reagan said. "It's been called the . . . information revolution." In the future, he declared, economic growth and technological innovation would depend on the inventiveness and daring of individuals.

During his speech, the President presented a short course in American history, describing the Declaration of Independence, the U.S. Constitution, trial by jury, and freedom of worship and speech. "Freedom," he said, "is the right to question and change the established way of doing things." The students responded enthusiastically. No one knew that four decades of Cold War tension were virtually at an end. Nor did anyone suspected that the Soviet Union itself, which Reagan had called the "evil empire" during the early days of his administration, would disintegrate in 1991.

Standing here before a mural of your revolution, I want to talk about a very different revolution that is taking place right now, quietly sweeping the globe, without bloodshed or conflict. Its effects are peaceful, but they will fundamentally after our world, shatter old assumptions, and reshape our lives.

It's easy to underestimate because it's not accompanied by banners or fanfare. It has been called the technological or information revolution, and as its emblem, one might take the tiny silicon chip—no bigger than a fingerprint. One of these chips has more computing power than a roomful of old-style computers.

As part of an exchange program, we now have an exhibition touring your country that shows how information technology is transforming our lives—replacing manual labor with robots, forecasting weather for farmers, or mapping the genetic code of DNA for medical researchers. These microcomputers today aid the design of everything from houses to cars to spacecraft—they even design better and faster computers. They can translate English into Russian or enable the blind to read—or help Michael Jackson produce on one synthesizer the sounds of a whole orchestra. Linked by a network of satellites and fiber-optic cables, one individual with a desktop computer and a telephone commands resources unavailable to the largest governments just a few years ago.

Like a chrysalis, we're emerging from the economy of the Industrial Revolution—an economy confined to and limited by the Earth's physical resources—into . . . an era in which there are no bounds on human imagination and the freedom to create is the most precious natural resource.

Think of that little computer chip. Its value isn't in the sand from which it is made, but in the microscopic architecture designed into it by ingenious human minds. Or take the example of the satellite relaying this broadcast around the world, which replaces thousands of tons of copper mined from the Earth and molded into wire. In the new economy, human invention increasingly makes physical resources obsolete. We're breaking through the material conditions of existence to a world where man creates his own destiny. Even as we explore the most advanced reaches of science, we're returning to the age-old wisdom of our culture, a wisdom contained in the book of Genesis in the Bible: In the beginning was the spirit, and it was from this spirit that the material abundance of creation issued forth.

But progress is not foreordained. The key is freedom—freedom of thought, freedom of information, freedom of communication. The renowned scientist, scholar, and founding father of this University, Mikhail Lomonosov, knew that. "It is common knowledge," he said, "that the achievements of science are considerable and rapid,

mural: a painting on a wall

fiber-optic cables: fine, flexible glass rods that can be used for high-speed communication

material: physical

foreordained: arranged in advanced by a divine force

261

entrepreneurs: people who start businesses, often taking risks to do so

riot: apparent chaos

particularly once the yoke of slavery is cast off and replaced by the freedom of philosophy.". . .

The explorers of the modern era are the entrepreneurs, men with vision, with the courage to take risks and faith enough to brave the unknown. These entrepreneurs and their small enterprises are responsible for almost all the economic growth in the United States. They are the prime movers of the technological revolution. In fact, one of the largest personal computer firms in the United States was started by two college students, no older than you, in the garage behind their home.

Some people, even in my own country, look at the riot of experiment that is the free market and see only waste. What of all the entrepreneurs that fail? Well, many do, particularly the successful ones. Often several times. And if you ask them the secret of their success, they'll tell you, it's all that they learned in their struggles along the way—yes, it's what they learned from failing. Like an athlete in competition, or a scholar in pursuit of the truth, experience is the greatest teacher.

And that's why it's so hard for government planners, no matter how sophisticated, to ever substitute for millions of individuals working night and day to make their dreams come true. . . .

We Americans make no secret of our belief in freedom. In fact, it's something of a national pastime. Every four years the American people choose a new president, and 1988 is one of those years. At one point there were 13 major candidates running in the two major parties, not to mention all the others, including the Socialist and Libertarian candidates—all trying to get my job.

About 1,000 local television stations, 8,500 radio stations, and 1,700 daily newspapers, each one an independent, private enterprise, fiercely independent of the government, report on the candidates, grill them in interviews, and bring them together for debates. In the end, the people vote—they decide who will be the next president.

But freedom doesn't begin or end with elections. Go to any American town, to take just an example, and you'll see dozens of churches, representing many different beliefs—in many places synagogues and mosques—and you'll see families of every conceivable nationality, worshipping together.

Go into any schoolroom, and there you will see children being taught the Declaration of Independence, that they are endowed by their Creator with certain inalienable rights—among them life, liberty, and the pursuit of happiness—that no government can justly deny—the guarantees in their Constitution for freedom of speech, freedom of assembly, and freedom of religion.

Go into any courtroom and there will preside an independent judge, beholden to no government power. There every defendant has the right to a trial by a jury of his peers, usually 12 men and women—common citizens, they are the ones, the only ones, who weigh the evidence and decide on guilt or innocence. In that court, the accused is innocent until proven guilty, and the world of a policeman, or any official, has no greater legal standing than the word of the accused.

Go to any university campus, and there you'll find an open, sometimes heated discussion of the problems in American society and what can be done to correct them. Turn on the television, and you'll see the legislature conducting the business of government right there before the camera, debating and voting on the legislation that will become the law of the land. March in any demonstration, and there are many of them—the people's right of assembly is guaranteed in the Constitution and protected by the police. Go into any union hall, where the members know their right to strike is protected by law. . . .

But freedom is even more than this: Freedom is the right to question, and change the established way of doing things. It is the continuing revolution of the marketplace. It is the understanding that allows us to recognize shortcomings and seek solutions. It is the right to put forth an idea, scoffed at by the experts, and watch it catch fire among the people. It is the right to follow your dream, to stick to your conscience, even if you're the only one in a sea of doubters.

Freedom is the recognition that no single person, no single authority or government has a monopoly on the truth, but that every individual life is infinitely precious, that every one of us put on this earth has been put here for a reason and has something to offer. . . .

Democracy is less a system of government than it is a system to keep government limited, unintrusive: A system of constraints on power to keep politics and government secondary to the important things in life, the true sources of value found only in family and faith.

But I hope you know I go on about these things not simply to extol the virtues of my own country, but to speak to the true greatness of the heart and soul of your land. Who, after all, needs to tell the land of Dostoevsky about the quest for truth, the home of Kandinsky and Scriabin about imagination, the rich and noble culture of the Uzbek man of letters, Alisher Navio, about beauty and heart?

The great culture of your diverse land speaks with a glowing passion to all humanity. Let me cite one of the most eloquent contemporary passages on human freedom. It comes, not from the literature of America, but from this country, from one of the greatest

beholden: obligated

monopoly: exclusive right to

unintrusive: not interfering or imposing

extol: praise

Kandinsky: Wassily Kandinsky (1866-1944), Russian painter
Scriabin: Aleksandr Scriabin 1872-1915), Russian composer

263

emblem: symbol

cudgel: club

writers of the twentieth century, Boris Pasternak, in the novel *Dr. Zhivago*. He writes, "I think that if the beast who sleeps in man could be held down by threats—any kind of threat, whether of jail or of retribution after death—then the highest emblem of humanity would be the lion tamer in the circus with his whip, not the prophet who sacrificed himself. But this is just the point—what has for centuries raised man above the beast is not the cudgel, but an inward music—the irresistible power of unarmed truth."

The irresistible power of unarmed truth. Today the world looks expectantly to signs of change, steps toward greater freedom in the Soviet Union. . . .

Your generation is living in one of the most exciting, hopeful times in Soviet history. It is a time when the first breath of freedom stirs the air and the heart beats to the accelerated rhythm of hope, when the accumulated spiritual energies of a long silence yearn to break free.

Gogol: Nikolay Gogol (1809-1852), Russian novelist and playwright
troika: a Russian carriage driven by a team of three horses

I am reminded of the famous passage near the end of Gogol's *Dead Souls*. Comparing his nation to a speeding troika, Gogol asks what will be its destination. But he writes, "There was no answer save the bell pouring forth marvelous sound."

Tolstoy: Leo Tolstoy (1828-1910), Russian novelist, author of *War and Peace*
reconciliation: making up after a disagreement

We do not know what the conclusion of this journey will be, but we're hopeful that the promise of reform will be fulfilled. In this Moscow spring, this May 1988, we may be allowed that hope—that freedom, like the fresh green sapling planted over Tolstoy's grave, will blossom forth at last in the rich fertile soil of your people and culture. We may be allowed to hope that the marvelous sound of a new openness will keep rising through, ringing through, leading to a new world of reconciliation, friendship, and peace. . . .

abolitionist Person who believed slavery was wrong and tried to stop it in the United States

acquit To declare not guilty

administration The group of officials that makes up the executive branch, including the President

advocate Person who supports a cause

agrarian Related to farming

alien Person who lives in a country but is not a citizen of that country

allies People or countries united for a specific purpose. During World War II, the countries that united to fight Germany.

almanac Informational book updated regularly

amendment Change or addition to the U.S. Constitution

amnesty Pardon for offenses against a government

anarchist Person who rebels against any authority, government, or established power

annex To add on to a nation's territory

antebellum Before the Civil War

Antifederalist Person who believed in strong state government during the early history of the United States

anti-Semitism Hatred and prejudice against Jews

appeal Request for a higher court to review a case

appeasement Act of giving in to keep peace

apprentice Person learning a trade

arbitrary power Power used without considering principles, especially ethical principles

arbitration Settlement of a dispute by someone chosen to hear both sides and then make a decision

archipelago Chain of islands

aristocracy People who have inherited wealth and social position; also government by those people

armada Spanish word used to describe a great fleet of armed ships

armistice Temporary peace agreement

Articles of Confederation The first constitution of the United States; ratified in 1781 and replaced in 1789 by the constitution we have now

assassin A murderer, especially someone who kills a public figure for political reasons

assembly Meeting of people united for a common purpose

assembly line Row of factory workers and machines along which work is passed

autocracy Government by a single authority with unlimited power

baby boom An increase in the U.S. birth rate that began after World War II and continued into the 1950s

ban An official order forbidding something

bicameral legislature Two-part system of representation, as in the U.S. Congress

bigotry Intolerance, prejudice

Bill of Rights First ten amendments to the Constitution

black codes Laws passed by Southern states after the Civil War to limit the rights of former slaves

blitzkrieg German word used to describe sudden warfare intended to surprise the enemy and win a quick victory

blockade Obstacles set up to prevent normal traffic from entering or leaving an area

blue laws Rules banning work and trade on Sundays

blue-collar Relating to people who perform manual labor

Bolsheviks Russian political group that formed the Communist Party

bondage Lack of freedom; slavery

bootlegger Person who illegally made, transported, or sold liquor during Prohibition

boycott To refuse to deal with a nation, company, or organization in order to show disapproval or force a change

breadlines Lines for free food during the Great Depression

broadside Poster featuring news

Cabinet Officially chosen group of advisers to the President

canal Waterway built for transportation

candidate Someone running for political office

capital Money for funding a business or other venture

capital punishment Execution of a criminal by the state

capitalism The economic system in which individuals or companies, rather than government, own most factories and businesses, and in which laborers produce products for a wage

carpetbaggers Derogatory name used by Southerners to label people from the North who went to the South during Reconstruction

census Official count of people

centennial Hundredth anniversary

charter Written set of rules or principles established by a new organization

chronology List of events in the order that they occurred

citizen Someone who is entitled to all the rights and freedoms given by a government

civil disobedience Opposing a law as a matter of principle by refusing to obey it

Civil Rights Act of 1964 Law prohibiting discrimination in public places and employment

civil rights Rights guaranteed to all citizens by the Constitution and acts of Congress

civilian Anyone who is not an active member of the military

civilization Relatively advanced stage of social development

clan Group of families

coalition Union of groups with a common objective

collective bargaining Negotiation between organized workers and an employer

colony Land controlled by a distant or foreign nation

commission Written order giving certain powers, duties, or rights

Committee of Correspondence A group of American Patriots who worked to unite the colonies against Britain

commodity Something that can be bought and sold

commune Group of people living together who share money and responsibilities

communism Government where the state owns most of the land and property and shares them with the citizens

compact Agreement

Compromise of 1850 Plan to deal with differences between slave states and free states

concentration camp Place where Nazis imprisoned, tortured, and killed people during World War II

confederation Alliance of states

congress Group of representatives who come together for discussion, voting, and action

conquistador Conqueror

conservative Someone who tends to want to keep things as they are and to oppose change

constituents People who are represented by an elected official

Constitution The document that outlines the plan of government in the United States

consumers People who buy goods and services for personal needs

containment Policy to stop the spread of communism

continent One of the seven largest bodies of land in the world

contraband Property of the enemy seized during wartime; during the Civil War, slaves freed by the Union army

corporation Business owned by stockholders who hold shares in it

counterculture Culture with values that are very different from those of established society

craft union Labor union organized by shared skills, not by industry

crusade Expedition or war motivated by religious beliefs

culture Social organization and way of life of a group of people

currency Paper bills and coins in circulation within an economy

de facto segregation Segregation in the North and elsewhere caused by social conditions and attitudes rather than law

de jure segregation Segregation imposed by law

Declaration of Independence Statement declaring American colonial independence from Britain, signed on July 4, 1776

delegate Person authorized to speak and act for others

demagogue Charismatic leader who manipulates people with half-truths, false promises, and scare tactics

democracy Government of the people

deport Forced to leave a country

depression Time of economic decline, including high unemployment and falling prices

desert Run away from duty

despotism Complete power over others

dictator Ruler with complete authority and no accountability; an autocrat

direct democracy A system in which everyone votes directly on important issues

discrimination Showing favor toward or prejudice against people because they belong to a particular group

dove Someone who takes an anti-war position

draft System of choosing people who must serve in the armed forces

due process of law The set of rules for bringing a person accused of a crime to trial

economy Management and flow of resources and money in a community

emancipation Granting of freedom

Emancipation Proclamation Document written and signed by President Abraham Lincoln that freed all slaves living in Confederate states during the Civil War

embargo Ban on commerce and trade

emigrant Person who leaves one country to settle in another

empire Group of cities, states, or territories under the rule of one person

entrepreneur Person who takes financial risks to gain large profits

equality Having the same rights, privileges, and rank

escalate Increase, particularly in relation to war

establishment Group of respected, well-known leaders who form a ruling class

executive branch The branch of government that carries out the laws; in the U.S. the President is its head

exile To banish someone from his or her home or country

exports Goods sent to another country

exposition Exhibition, often a large, public one

faction Division of a larger group made up of people who share common views

farm economy System in which people grow their own food, taking care of their own needs and rarely use money

fascist Person who believes in rigid one-party dictatorship

Federalists People who believed in strong central government during the early history of the United States

federation A form of government that divides power between a central government and state governments

feminists People who believe that women deserve the same rights and opportunities as men

feudalism A form of society in which laborers work for a master; in return the master protects them from enemies and gives them enough land to support themselves

First Continental Congress The meeting of colonial leaders held in Philadelphia in 1774

flappers Young women of the 1920s who dressed in a bold new style

fleet Ships under one command

fort A permanent army post

forty-niners People who moved to California during the gold rush of 1849

Fourteen Points President Woodrow Wilson's plan for world peace after World War I

franchise The right to vote

free enterprise An economic system allowing private industry to operate with little government control

free trade Business between nations that is carried out without major restrictions

Freedmen's Bureau An organization set up by Congress to help ex-slaves

freedom rides Bus rides taken by black and white students who together challenged segregation in the South in the early 1960s

Free-Soilers A group of Northerners who wanted to keep slavery from spreading into Western lands in the mid-nineteenth century

Fugitive Slave Act A law passed in 1850 that made it illegal to help runaway slaves

fundamentalism Belief that the Bible is literally true and should be strictly followed

Gadsden Purchase The purchase by the United States of the southern parts of Arizona and New Mexico

generation gap Lack of understanding and communication between older and younger people, especially in the 1960s

genocide Deliberate murder of an entire nation or ethnic group or the destruction of its culture

ghetto A city neighborhood where poor people live crowded together, usually in bad conditions

Gilded Age The period between 1870 and 1900

Great Awakening Christian religious revival in the American colonies during the 1730s and 1740s

greenback Paper money established during the Civil War, named for its color

guerrilla A soldier who fights by using surprise tactics to bring down the enemy

habeas corpus, writ of A court order requiring proof that a prisoner is being justly held

haciendas Large ranches in Spanish-speaking areas where cattle and crops were raised

hawks People who advocate war or the use of force against other nations

hemisphere The northern and southern or eastern and western halves of the globe

Hessians German troops hired by the British during the American Revolution

hierarchy A social system organized by rank

hippies Young people of the 1960s who rebelled against traditional values

the Holocaust The slaughter of Jews by Nazis during World War II

Homestead Act A law passed in 1862 that offered settlers 160 acres of land in return for living and farming there for at least five years

Hoovervilles Settlements of makeshift houses built by homeless people during the Great Depression

hostage Someone held prisoner as a bargaining chip in a conflict

House of Burgesses The group responsible for making laws in colonial Virginia

hunter-gatherers People in tribes who move often to find animals and plants to eat

illiteracy The inability to read and write

immigrants People who move to a new country or region

impeach To charge a public official with crimes or misconduct

imperialism Expanding a nation by taking other lands

import Bring in from another country

inauguration Ceremony that ushers a new President into office

indentured servant Someone who worked for four to seven years as a servant for the master who paid his or her passage to America

indict Charge with a crime

Industrial Revolution System of organizing work using machines and factories that changed the way goods were produced and the way people lived

industrial unions Labor unions organized not by skill but by industry

industrialization The process of going from an agricultural system to one based on factories and machines

infidels Nonbelievers in a dominant religion, according to the believers

inflation The process by which the prices of goods and services increase

integration Bringing together different racial and ethnic groups

international law A set of rules to govern nations' relations with each other

internment Confinement, especially in wartime

investor A person who funds a business hoping to make a profit

isolationism The belief that one nation should not interfere in the affairs of another nation

isthmus A narrow strip of land with water on each side connecting two larger bodies of land

Jim Crow A system of laws beginning in the late 1800s that segregated blacks and forced them to use separate and inferior facilities

jingoism Loud and mindless nationalism

judicial branch The part of a government that decides whether laws have been broken

judicial review The power of the U.S. Supreme Court to decide if laws are constitutional

jury A group chosen to make a judgment, especially in a court of law

Kansas-Nebraska Act A law passed by Congress in 1854 that allowed settlers in Kansas and Nebraska to choose whether to allow slavery there

Ku Klux Klan An organization formed in the South in 1866 that used lynching and violence to intimidate and control blacks and others

labor unions Associations of workers formed to promote and protect the rights of members

League of Nations An organization proposed by President Woodrow Wilson after World War I to unite nations in working for peace and security

legislative branch The branch of government that makes the laws; in the United States it is composed of the Senate and the House of Representatives

legislature A law-making body

liberal Someone who favors reforms or change

literacy Ability to read and write

lobby Attempt to influence lawmakers

Loyalists American colonists who remained loyal to Britain during the American Revolution, also called Tories

lynching Kidnapping and execution of a person by a mob

Magna Carta A groundbreaking agreement signed by King John in 1215 that guaranteed some basic rights to the people of England

majority Group, party, or faction with the largest number of votes

Manifest Destiny Belief held by many Americans in the nineteenth and twentieth centuries that it was God's will that the United States expand its borders

market economy A system in which people earn wages and provide for their needs by buying goods and services

martial law Rule by military authorities

martyr Someone who chooses to die rather than give up a religious belief or political principle

masses A large number of ordinary people

Mayflower Compact An influential document, signed in 1620, that established the rules of Pilgrim society

merchant Person who buys and sells goods

mesas Flat-topped hills

Mexican War Fought from 1846 to 1848, it ended with the United States gaining California and New Mexico

migrate Move

militias Armies made up of people who are not professional soldiers

Minutemen Farmers in colonial America who trained to fight the British

missionary Member of a religious group who tries to persuade others to adopt his or her religion

mission Local headquarters of a religious group that provides services to local people as it tries to convert them

Missouri Compromise Agreement that allowed slavery in Missouri and made it illegal in Maine and most of the rest of the Louisiana Purchase lands

monarchy Government headed by a single ruler, especially a king or queen

monopoly Complete control of an industry, product, or service by a single company

Monroe Doctrine Warning issued by President James Monroe in 1823 that European armies should keep out of the Americas

muckraker Journalist who wrote articles exposing injustice and corruption

mutiny Rebellion against authority, especially of sailors or soldiers against their officers

national debt Total debt of the federal government

nationalism Strong feeling of pride in one's country

Native Americans The first peoples of North America; including Eskimos and Indians

nativism The practice of favoring native-born citizens over immigrants

naturalization The process that grants citizenship to immigrants

Nazis The German political party led by Adolf Hitler

neutral Not favoring one side or another

nomadic Wandering from place to place

nonconformist Person who follows his or her own beliefs instead of what may be traditional or popular

nonviolent resistance Peaceful protest that avoids the use of physical force

Northwest Ordinance An law passed in 1787 that set out rules for how new territories should govern themselves and how they could eventually become states

nullification A state's refusal to recognize or uphold a federal law

oath A pledge to tell the truth or keep promises

offensive An attack, especially by armed forces

orator An effective public speaker

ordinance Law or regulation

pacifism Opposition to the use of force under any circumstance

parallel Imaginary line on the globe that runs in the same direction as the Equator

pardon Official forgiveness for a crime

parliament A legislature

Patriots Americans who wanted to be free of British rule, sometimes called Whigs

patronage The practice by elected officials of appointing friends and supporters to government jobs

peninsula A piece of land almost entirely surrounded by water

pension Retirement pay or old-age insurance

perjury Lying under oath

petition A written, formal statement requesting something

philanthropist A person who works to help others, often by giving money to charitable causes

pilgrim A person who makes a journey for religious purposes

Pilgrim English colonist who arrived in Plymouth in 1620 on the *Mayflower*

pioneer Person who is among the first to settle in an unpopulated area

plantation Very large farm

plateau Flat area, often in a high place or on top of mountains

plea Request or appeal

pogrom Organized massacre of helpless people, particularly of Jews in Eastern Europe

political activist Person who works to change government policies

political asylum Protection the government of one country gives to a political refugee from another country

political bias Attitude for or against a political issue, party, or person before hearing specific arguments

political boss Leader of a political machine

political left People who want to change the current social and political system or power structure

political machine Unofficial city organization designed to keep a particular party or group in power

political party A group of people who share similar political ideas and try to elect candidates to public office

political right People who want to preserve the current social and political system or power structure

poll tax Tax that has been found to be unconstitutional that people in some states used to have to pay before they were allowed to vote

popular sovereignty Belief that people can and should govern themselves

preamble Introduction

precedent Act or decision that is used as a model in later cases

prejudice Dislike of another ethnic group, gender, race, or religion based on stereotypes and ignorance

premier A head of government

presidio Fort, in Spanish

privateers Privately owned, armed ships hired by a government

progressive Person who thinks that life can be improved by government reforms

progressivism Political and social reform movement of the late 1800s and early 1900s that included socialism, the labor movement, municipal reform, prohibition, and other movements

Prohibition Constitution amendment in force between 1920 and 1933 that outlawed the manufacture, transportation, sale, and possession of alcoholic beverages

proletariat Members of the working class

propaganda Spreading ideas or rumors to influence public opinion

proportional representation Political system in which the number of representatives for an area depends on the number of people who live there

protectionism Policy of favoring taxes and quotas on imports and exports to protect local economies

pueblos Indian villages built of sundried clay mud

Puritans Protestants who wanted to reform the Church of England, many of whom came to New England

Quakers A Christian group, officially called the Society of Friends, who believe in respecting the rights of other people and oppose war

quota Limit on the number of people from an ethnic, religious, or other group who will be allowed into a nation, institution, or organization

racketeer Someone involved in organized illegal activities

radical Someone who favors extreme changes in existing laws or conditions

rancheros Owners of big ranches in Mexican America

range A series of adjacent mountains; also, open land for grazing cattle

ratify To formally approve a suggested action

rationing Limiting goods during times of scarcity

raw material Natural product used in manufacturing

Rebels Name for Confederate soldiers during the Civil War

recession A period of reduced business activity

Reconstruction The period from 1865 to 1877 when the federal government controled the former Confederate states

redcoats Nickname for British soldiers during the Revolutionary War

reds Nickname for communists or people thought to be communists

reformer Someone who wants to make the world better by improving social conditions

refugees People who flee their homes during a time of armed conflict or natural disaster

reparations Payments made for damages suffered

repeal Do away with a law

representative democracy System in which people elect representatives to make laws on their behalf; the form of government in the United States

representatives People chosen to speak or act for others

republic System in which people elect representatives to govern them according to law

reservation Public land set aside for special use, especially land set aside for Indian peoples after European Americans took over Indian land

revenues Income, especially from city, state, or national taxes

revolution Overthrow of a government

right-wing Politically very conservative

riots Violent disturbances of the peace

sachem Native American chief or leader

scab Slang for a person hired to replace a striking worker

scalawags Southerners who cooperated with the North during Reconstruction

Scopes trial Tennessee trial in 1925 that challenged the law against teaching evolution in schools

secede Formally withdraw from a political organization

secessionist Antebellum Southerner who wanted the South to withdraw from the Union

segregation The practice of separating one racial, ethnic, or religious group from another, especially in public places

self-determination The right of citizens to choose the form of government under which they will live

Separatists Seventeenth century English Protestants who wanted to separate themselves from the Church of England

settlement house Institution offering social and educational services to immigrants and poor people

sexist Tending to discriminate against one gender in favor of the other

shaman An Indian religious leader

share A piece of ownership of a corporation

sharecroppers People who live and raise crops on land that belongs to other people

siege The surrounding of a city or a fort by an army trying to capture it

sit-down strike Workplace protest against management by workers who refuse both to work or to leave

sit-in Organized demonstration by protesters who sat down in segregated establishments and refused to leave

Social Security Act 1935 legislation that created a social welfare system funded by employee and worker contributions; includes old-age pensions, survivor's benefits for victims of industrial accidents, and unemployment insurance

socialism Government ownership of factories and services with wages determined by workers' needs

Sons of Liberty Group that stirred up riots against the British before and during the Revolutionary War

sovereign A royal ruler, such as a king, queen, or emperor

soviets Councils of workers, soldiers, and peasants in the Soviet Union

speakeasy Illegal saloon that flourished during Prohibition

speculation Financial risks taken in order to make a large profit

Stamp Tax 1765 tax that required American colonists to buy a British stamp for every piece of paper they used

states' rights Theory that each state has the right to nullify acts of the federal government

stereotyping Making assumptions about a real person based on prejudices about the group to which he or she seems to belong

stock exchange Trading center where shares of stock are bought and sold

stock market The business of buying and selling stocks

strait Narrow waterway connecting two larger bodies of water

strike Work stoppage to protest low wages or bad working conditions

strikebreaker In a labor disagreement, someone who interferes with workers' protest against management

subject Person who owes allegiance to a monarchy

subsidy A grant of money, land, or something else of value

suburb A residential community on the outskirts of a city

suffrage Right to vote

suit Legal proceeding

surrender To give up

sweatshop Factory where employees work long hours in poor conditions for low wages

system of checks and balances System of government in which the power of each of the branches of government is limited by that of the others

tariff Tax on imports or exports

tax Money that citizens and businesses are required to contribute to pay for the cost of government and the services it provides

technology Use of scientific ideas for practical purposes

temperance movement Campaign against alcohol consumption

tenement Run-down, overcrowded, low-rent apartment

territory Area within the United States that had not yet qualified for statehood

theocracy Government by church officials in the name of God

Third Reich Germany under Adolf Hitler, 1933 to 1945

Tory In eighteenth-century England, member of the conservative political party that upheld British rule of the colonies; in eighteenth-century America, colonist who remained loyal to England

totalitarian Form of dictatorship that has total control over all aspects of life and that suppresses all political or cultural opposition

Trail of Tears The forced march of 15,000 Cherokees from the Southeast to reservations in the West from 1837 to 1838

transcontinental railroad A railroad completed in 1869 that spanned North America

treaty Formal agreement between nations

trial Examination of the facts of a legal case

triangular trade Trade between the Americas, Europe, and Africa in the 1700s

tribe Small community held together by common ancestry, ethnicity, or politics

truce Agreement to stop fighting

trust Form of monopoly where many different companies in one industry are all owned and run by the same people

tyranny Absolute power, especially when it is unjustly or cruelly used

U-boats German submarines

Underground Railroad Network offering help to slaves as they escaped from South to North

unicameral legislature Government that has a single legislative house

Union The United States of America as a political unit, especially during the Civil War; the North and its forces in the Civil War

United Nations An international organization formed in 1945 to promote peace, security, and economic development among nations

urban Of a city

utopia An ideal place; a perfect society

vaqueros Spanish American cowboys

verdict The official decision of a jury in a legal case

veteran People who served in and survived a war

veto Refusal to approve

Vietcong Guerrilla members of the South Vietnamese communist movement

Wall Street Main financial center of the United States, in New York City

Whig In eighteenth-century England, member of an English political party that generally believed the colonists should be allowed to govern themselves; in eighteenth-century America, Patriot

white-collar job Office job

wilderness Undeveloped land

Yank Name for a Union soldier

yellow journalism Sensational but generally untrue stories published in newspapers to attract readers

yeoman A farmer who cultivated his own small farm

Document Sources

This book reproduces excerpts from some of the most important documents in American history. The following list contains information on where to find the complete documents.

DAH *Documents of American History.* Henry Steele Commager and Milton Cantor, eds. 10th ed. Englewood Cliffs, N.J.: Prentice Hall, 1988.

KD *100 Key Documents in American Democracy.* Peter B. Levy, ed. Westport, Conn.: Greenwood Press, 1994.

PH *The Patriot's Handbook.* George Grant, comp. Kansas City, Mo.: Andrews and McMeel, 1996.

1. Howard, A. E. Dick. *Magna Carta: Text and Commentary.* Charlottesville: University of Virginia Press, 1997.

2. Casas, Bartolemé de las. *A Short Account of the Destruction of the Indies.* Edited and translated by Nigel Griffiths. New York: Penguin, 1992.

3. Sagahún, Bernardino de. *Florentine Codex: A General History of the Things of New Spain.* Salt Lake City: University of Utah Press, 1950-1983.

4. PH, pp. 21-22.

5. DAH, vol. 1, pp. 28-29.

6. *Letters of a Nation: A Collection of Extraordinary American Letters.* Andrew Carroll, ed. New York: Broadway Books, 1999.

7. DAH, vol. 1, pp. 37-38.

8. Schwoerer, Lois G. *The Declaration of Rights, 1869.* Baltimore, Md.: The Johns Hopkins University Press, 1981, pp. 295-298.

9. Saunders, Richard [Benjamin Franklin]. *Poor Richard: The Almanacks for the years 1733-1758.* New York: Paddington Press, 1976.

10. DAH, vol. 1, pp. 57-59.

11. KD, pp. 35-38.

12. Davis, Robert P., et al. *Virginia Presbyterians in American Life: Hanover Presbytery (1755-1950).* Richmond, Va.: Hanover Presbytery, 1982.

13. KD, pp. 40-47.

14. History of US, Book 3, *From Colonies to Country,* pp. 190-192.

15. KD, pp. 47-50.

16. DAH, vol. 1, pp. 111-115.

17. Jefferson, Thomas. *Notes on the State of Virginia.* New York: Penguin, 1999.

18. St. John de Crevecoeur, J. Hector. *Letters from an American Farmer.* Edited with an introduction and notes by Susan Manning. New York: Oxford University Press, 1997.

19. History of US, Book 3, *From Colonies to Country,* p. 200.

20. History of US, Book 3, *From Colonies to Country,* pp. 194-198.

21. PH, pp. 166-172.

22. KD, pp. 57-61.

23. PH, pp. 199-202.

24 and 25. Washington, George. *The Papers of George Washington,* vol. 6. Mark Mastromarino, ed. Charlottesville: University Press of Virginia, 1996.

26. PH, pp. 202-206.

27. KD, pp. 73-77.

28. Washington, H. A. *The Writings of Thomas Jefferson,* vol. 8. Washington, D.C.: Taylor & Maury, 1853.

29. Marbury v. Madison, 5 U.S. 137

30. *The Wisdom of the Native Americans.* Kent Nerburn, ed. San Rafael, Calif: New World Library, 1999.

31. KD, pp. 82-85.

32. McCulloch v. Maryland, 17 U.S. 316

33. PH, pp. 267-269.

34. KD, pp. 94-96.

35. KD, pp. 119-121.

37. DAH, vol. 1, pp. 262-268.

38. Tocqueville, Alexis de. *Democracy in America.* New York: Vintage, 1990.

39. Emerson, Ralph Waldo. *Self-Reliance and Other Essays.* New York: Dover, 1993.

40. O'Sullivan, John L. "Editorial on Manifest Destiny." *The New York Morning News,* vol. 2 (August,1845).

41. KD, pp. 102-103.

42. PH, pp. 359-360.

43. DAH, vol. 1, pp. 315-317.

44.Thoreau, Henry David. *Civil Disobedience and Other Essays.* Amherst, N.Y.: Prometheus, 1998.

45. Calhoun, John C. *The Works of John C. Calhoun,* vol. 4. New York: D. Appleton & Company, 1865.

46. Truth, Sojourner, with Olive Gilbert. *Narrative of Sojourner Truth: A Bondswoman of Olden Time, with a History of her Labors and Correspondence drawn from her Book of Life.* With an introduction by Jeffrey C. Stewart. New York: Oxford University Press, 1991.

47. Douglass, Frederick. *The Oxford Frederick Douglass Reader.* Edited by William L. Andrews. New York: Oxford University Press, 1996.

48. DAH, vol. 1, pp. 339-345.

49. PH, pp. 299-302.

50. DAH, vol. 1, pp. 347-349.

51. KD, pp. 148-150.

52. DAH, vol. 1, pp. 410-411.

53. PH, p. 331.

54. KD, pp. 161-164.

55. DAH, vol. 1, pp. 442-443.

57. DAH, vol. 1, p. 447.

58. Stanton, Elizabeth Cady, Susan B. Anthony, and Matilda Joslyn Gage. *History of Woman Suffrage,* vol. 2. New York: Arno Press, 1969.

59. KD, pp. 215-218.

60. DAH, vol. 1, pp. 552-554.

61. *Wisdom of the Great Chiefs: The Classic Speeches of Red Jacket, Chief Joseph, and Chief Seattle.* Kent Nerburn, ed. San Rafael, Calif.: New World Library, 1994.

62. *Wisdom of the Great Chiefs: The Classic Speeches of Red Jacket, Chief Joseph, and Chief Seattle.* Kent Nerburn, ed. San Rafael, Calif.: New World Library, 1994.

63. Yick Wo v. Hopkins, 118 U.S. 356

64. Carnegie, Andrew. *The Gospel of Wealth.* Bedford, Mass.: Applewood Books, 1998.

65. DAH, vol. 1, pp. 593-595.

66. PH, p. 361.

67. PH, pp. 361-364.

68. Plessy v. Ferguson, 163 U.S. 537

69. DAH, vol. 2, pp. 1-4.

70. DAH, vol. 2, pp. 33-34.

71. DAH, vol. 2, pp 50-52.

72. DAH, vol. 2, pp. 82-84.

73. KD, pp. 295-299.

74. PH, pp. 392-394.

75. DAH, vol. 2.

76. DAH, vol. 2, pp. 239-242.

77. KD, 213-215.

78. Minersville District v. Gobitis, 310 U.S. 586

79. DAH, vol. 2, pp. 451-452.

80. Roosevelt, Franklin D. *The Public Papers of F. D. Roosevelt,* Vol. 10, p. 532.

81. DAH, vol. 2, pp. 446-448.

82. West Virginia State Board of Education v. Barnette, 319 U.S. 624

83. KD, pp. 360-361.

84. DAH, vol. 2, pp. 525-528.

85. DAH, vol. 2, pp. 552-553.

86. Smith, Margaret Chase. *Declaration of Conscience.* Edited by William C. Lewis, Jr. New York: Doubleday, 1972.

87. DAH, vol. 2, pp. 652-654.

88. DAH, vol. 2, pp. 654-656.

89. KD, pp. 392-396.

90. PH, pp. 421-429.

91. United States Congress, Public Law 88352

92. DAH, vol. 2, p. 709.

93. New York Times Co. v. United States, 403 U.S. 713

94. KD, pp. 452-456.

Bold-faced numerals indicate Book number.
For example, **3:** 25 *is page 25 of Book 3.*

Huron Indians, **1:** 54, 149, 151

hurricane, **2:** 34

Hurricane Garden Cottage, **7:** 42

Hurston, Zora Neale, **9:** 46, **10:** 163

Hussein, Saddam, **10:** 196

Hussey, Christopher, **5:** 97

Hutchinson, Anne, **2:** 71-73, **5:** 127, 128

Hyde Park, **9:** 89, 92

I Ice Age, **1:** 16-20, 62
Idaho: immigrants in, **7:** 129; and Oregon Territory, **5:** 13, 48; statehood, **8:** 78; women, **7:** 131

igluviga (igloos), **1:** 27, 28

Illinois, **1:** 152, **6:** 38-42; as free state, **4:** 155; and Mormons, **5:** 44; Native Americans of, **4:** 129, 132; prairie, **7:** 74; roads, **4:** 112; statehood, **4:** 162; and women's rights, **7:** 137; and workers, **8:** 73, 96, 116

Illinois Indians, **1:** 42, 152

I Love Lucy, **10:** 55, 137-38

immigrants, **5:** 29, 31, 108, 112, **7:** 13, 111-18, **8:** 9-10, 43, 46-49, 86, **10:** 198-200, 202; attitudes toward, **5:** 73, **7:** 45, 119-29, 179, **8:** 83, 84, 85, 139, **9:** 36, 118-19; in cities, **4:** 35, 154, **8:** 168; education of, **8:** 70, 71, 141; as factory workers, **4:** 153; and gold rush, **5:** 72; homesteaders, **7:** 69-70; housing of, **8:** 67; and Native Americans, **4:** 126-27; and slaves, **5:** 177; and reformers, **8:** 170, 172; and unions, **8:** 93, 96, 119-20; during war, **9:** 115; work of, **7:** 51, 58, 60, 119, **8:** 10, 83, 90, 103. *See also specific groups*

impeachment, **7:** 30, 31, 32-35, **10:** 178

imperialism, **8:** 149, 155, **9:** 168

Inca empire, **1:** 113-15, 117

indentured servants, **2:** 38, 40-41, 53, 56, 96, 116, 130-31, **3:** 13, 42, 121, 152, **4:** 11, **5:** 142, **6:** 12, 50, 51. *See also* apprentices

Independence, Missouri, **5:** 26, 32, 38, **10:** 16

Independence Hall, **3:** 16, 85, 103, 130 167

India, **1:** 24, 48, 71, **5:** 29; immigrants from, **7:** 121

Indiana, **6:** 35, 36; as free state, **4:** 155, 159; immigrants in, **7:** 129; settlers in, **5:** 112-15; statehood, **4:** 162; territory, **4:** 70, 72; and women's rights, **5:** 132

Indian Queen Tavern, **3:** 163-64

Indian Removal Act, **4:** 127-28, 134

Indians, **1:** 103-15, 131-37, 139, 142-45, 149-53, 157-62; diet of, **1:** 84; languages, **4:** 63; mound building, **1:** 49-53, 100; of Northwest, **1:** 35-39; of Plains, **1:** 44-48; of Southwest, **1:** 31-34. *See also* Native Americans *and names of tribes*

Indies, **1:** 71, 79

indigo, **2:** 133, 135, **3:** 42, 43, 45, **4:** 104

industrial revolution: in America, **4:** 104-109, **5:** 10, **7:** 77, **8:** 88, 89; in England, **4:** 103-109; in Scotland, **8:** 13

Industrial Workers of the World (Wobblies), **8:** 116-21

industry, **5:** 9, 108, 138-41, **6:** 73, **7:** 45, 47, 147. *See also* factories

influenza, **9:** 21-23

Information Age, **10:** 204

Inquisition, Spanish, **1:** 101, 139

integration, racial, **7:** 37, **10:** 73, 83. *See also* segregation

internment camps, **9:** 115, 144-48

Intrepid (ship), **4:** 88

Inuit, **1:** 26-30

inventions, **4:** 107, 108, 117-23, **5:** 81-84, 107, 161, **6:** 82-83, 94, **7:** 41, 52, 73, 74, 76, 79, 97, 98, 100, 106, 108, 111, 122, 147-50, 155-59, **8:** 10, 35, 39, 42, 90, 133, 137, 174-75, 177-82, 192. *See also* technology

Iowa: and Centennial Exposition, **7:** 148; Civil War, **6:** 80; frontier life in, **5:** 35-36; immigrants in, **7:** 129; and Louisiana Purchase, **5:** 13; as Plains state, **7:** 68; statehood, **4:** 164, 165

Iowa City, Iowa, **5:** 47

Iowa Indians, **1:** 44

Iran, **10:** 181

Iraq, **10:** 196, 197

Ireland, **4:** 114, **5:** 29, 82; immigrants from, **4:** 126-27, **5:** 29, 72, 115, **7:** 25, 60, 113, 115, 117; and potato famine, **7:** 113, 115

iron, **4:** 104, **5:** 138-41, **6:** 59, 103

Iron Age, **1:** 15

Iron Curtain, **10:** 27-29, 188

"iron horse." *See* railroads

Iroquois Indians, **1:** 57, 58-61, 100, 149, 151, **2:** 14, **3:** 23, 28, 29, 31, 37, 55, 108, **4:** 64-67, **11:** 96-97

Irving, Washington, **5:** 153-54

Isabella, queen of Spain, **1:** 76, 81, 84, 88, 101, 133, 133-39

Islam. *See* Muslim religion

Isle of Man, immigrants from, **5:** 29

isolationism, **9:** 20, 122-24, 129

Israel: and Egypt, **10:** 181; history, **10:** 34-35; and PLO peace accord, **10:** 215

Italy, **1:** 142, **9:** 86, 110; immigrants from, **7:** 115, 116, 118; in World War I, **9:** 14, 18; in World War II, **9:** 130, 156-57, 158

Ives, Charles, **9:** 60, 61

ivory, **5:** 96, 101. *See also* whaling

Iwo Jima, **9:** 166

IWW. *See* Industrial Workers of the World

Iztapalapa, **1:** 112

as Plains state, **7:** 68; statehood, **4:** 167

Minnesota Indians, **7:** 84

mint, U.S., **8:** 76

minutemen, **3:** 73, 74, 85

missionaries: American, **4:** 64, 66-67, 126; French, **1:** 150, 152; in Hawaii, **8:** 156, 159; Spanish, **1:** 131-32, **2:** 88-91, **3:** 35, 114-15, 138-39, **4:** 161, **5:** 50, 51, 58, 60

Mississippi: blacks in, **7:** 171; and civil rights, **10:** 103; Civil War, **6:** 92, 97, 118; and Great Migration, **10:** 144, 145, 146; immigrants in, **7:** 129; Reconstruction, **7:** 25, 39, 40-43, 46, 169; secession of, **6:** 59; and slaves, **4:** 155, **6:** 51; statehood, **4:** 162

Mississippi River, **1:** 42, 49, 130, 152, 153, **4:** 118, 160, **5:** 32-34, 55; bridge, **8:** 39; Civil War, **6:** 64, 97, 118; flood, **8:** 42; and Mark Twain, **7:** 105, 107

Missouri: as border state, **6:** 60, 61, **10:** 16; Civil War, **6:** 92, 105; and Louisiana Purchase, **5:** 13; and Mormons, **5:** 44; as Plains state, **7:** 68; railroads in, **5:** 86; and slavery, **4:** 154-55, **5:** 57, 62, 175, 181; statehood, **4:** 164, **5:** 21; and Mark Twain, **7:** 105-106, 108, 109

Missouri Compromise, **4:** 91, 154-55, 164, **5:** 62, 175, 176, 181

Missouri Indians, **1:** 44

Missouri River, **1:** 42; exploration of, **4:** 59, 62, 63, **5:** 14, 55; and pioneers, **5:** 32, 33; and railroad, **7:** 65

Mitchell, Jackie, **9:** 53

Mitchell, William "Billy," **9:** 123, 135

Miyatake, Toyo, **9:** 148

Moby-Dick (Melville), **5:** 153

Moctezuma (Montezuma), **1:** 103-107, 131

Model A Ford, **9:** 43, 99

Model T Ford, **8:** 175, 176, **9:** 193

Modigliani, Amadeo, **9:** 190

Mohawk Indians, **1:** 58, **2:** 14, **3:** 25-27, 108, **4:** 64

Mohican Indians, **2:** 86

Moluccas. *See* Spice Islands

monarchy, **3:** 59, 87, **4:** 11, 18-19, 24, 25

money: colonial, **2:** 92, 112-13, 114, 138, 155, **4:** 28; Confederate, **6:** 63, 133; English, **3:** 17; Spanish, **2:** 138, **5:** 22; U.S., **4:** 9, 41, **5:** 9-11, 49, 56, **6:** 63. *See also* economy

Mongolia, **1:** 14

Monitor (ship), **6:** 94, 96, 97

monkey trial. *See* Scopes trial

monopolies, **8:** 21, 29, 30-34, 54, 141

Monroe, Elizabeth, **4:** 92

Monroe, James, **2:** 117, **4:** 55, 90-92, 99, 112, 116, 161, **5:** 14, **11:** 102-104

Monroe, Marilyn, **10:** 49, 50

Monroe Doctrine, **4:** 92, 161, **11:** 102-104

Montague, Samuel, **7:** 59

Montana: gold in, **5:** 76; and Louisiana Purchase, **5:** 13; lynchings, **7:** 171; and Native Americans, **7:** 82, 92; natural features of, **8:** 136; and Oregon Territory, **5:** 48; pioneers, **5:** 38; statehood, **8:** 78; women, **7:** 131

Montcalm, Louis, **3:** 32, 39

Montes, Pedro, **5:** 167, 168

Monte Verde, Chile, **1:** 19

Montgomery, Alabama, **10:** 77-82, 124-27

Montgomery, Benjamin, **7:** 41, 42

Montgomery, Bernard, **9:** 161

Montgomery, Isaiah, **7:** 42, 169

Montgomery, Mary Lewis, **7:** 42

Montgomery, Mary Virginia, **7:** 40, 41-43

Montgomery Ward's, **8:** 87

Monticello, **3:** 120, 155, **4:** 95, 97, 98, **9:** 12

Montpellier, **4:** 95

Montreal, Canada, **3:** 32, 33, 78

Mooney, William, **7:** 97

Moran, Thomas, **7:** 71

More, Sir Thomas, **1:** 156, 157

Moreno, Graciela, **10:** 150

Morey, Katherine, **9:** 29

Morgan, J. P., **7:** 158, 159, **8:** 18, 27-29, 75

Mormons, **5:** 43-47

Morocco, **4:** 86-88; immigrants from, **5:** 29

Morrill Act, **7:** 79

Morris, Esther, **7:** 130

Morris, Gouverneur, **3:** 13, 169-70, 178, **4:** 37, **9:** 27

Morris, Robert, **3:** 118, 119-20, 168, 169

Morrison, Toni, **10:** 163, 208

Morse, Jedidiah, **4:** 127

Morse, Samuel F. B., **5:** 14, 81-84, 106, 107, 164

mortgages, **8:** 62, 68

Morton, Kathryn Harris, **10:** 73

Moses, Franklin J., Jr., **7:** 37-38

mosquitoes, **7:** 167

Moss, Thomas, **7:** 170, 172

motels, **10:** 57

Mothershed, Thelma, **10:** 84

motion pictures, **9:** 41, 46, 62

Mott, Lucretia, **5:** 130, 131, 134

Moultrie, William, **3:** 95, 96

mound builders, **1:** 49-53, 100

mounds, **1:** 49-53

Mount, William Sidney, **5:** 164

mountain men, **5:** 15-20, 21, 32, 42, 53, 54

Mount Holyoke College, **5:** 122, 123, **7:** 134

Mount Rushmore, **9:** 43

Mount Vernon, **3:** 19, **4:** 13, 14, 15, 22, 38-39

muckrakers, **8:** 113, 125-31, **10:** 206

Mudd, Samuel, **7:** 167

Muir, John, **8:** 132-34, 140, 148-49

mulattoes, **1:** 117

Mulligan Guards' Plays, **7:** 104

Murrow, Edward R., **10:** 46-47, 48

Steven Mintz is John and Rebecca Moores University Scholar and Professor of History at the University of Houston. He is the coauthor of *Boisterous Sea of Liberty: A Documentary History of America from Discovery to the Civil War,* and has published works on slavery, American reform movements, and the history of the American family.